# RASTAFARI
### AND
# REGGAE

# RASTAFARI
## AND
# REGGAE

## A Dictionary and Sourcebook

### Rebekah Michele Mulvaney

*Bibliography by Carlos I.H. Nelson*
*Illustrations by Barbara Boyle*

**G P**

**GREENWOOD PRESS**
Westport, Connecticut • London

**Library of Congress Cataloging-in-Publication Data**

Mulvaney, Rebekah Michele.
   Rastafari and reggae  :  a dictionary and sourcebook  /  Rebekah
Michele Mulvaney ; bibliography by Carlos I.H. Nelson  ;
illustrations by Barbara Boyle.
     p.    cm.
   Discography: p.
   Videography: p.
   Includes bibliographical references and index.
   ISBN 0-313-26071-0 (lib. bdg.  :  alk. paper)
    1. Ras Tafari movement—Dictionaries.  2. Reggae music—
Dictionaries.  3. Ras Tafari movement—Bibliography.  4. Reggae
music—Bibliography.  5. Reggae music—Discography.  I. Nelson,
Carlos I. H.  II. Title.
BL2532.R37M84   1990
299'.67—dc20       90-3591

British Library Cataloguing in Publication Data is available.

Library of Congress Catalog Card Number: 90-3591
ISBN: 0-313-26071-0

First published in 1990

Greenwood Press, 88 Post Road West, Westport, CT  06881
An imprint of Greenwood Publishing Group, Inc.

Printed in the United States of America

The paper used in this book complies with the
Permanent Paper Standard issued by the National
Information Standards Organization (Z39.48-1984).

10 9 8 7 6 5

To those Rastas and reggae musicians who persist in confronting African Jamaicans with their African heritage.

# Contents

# Preface

Publication of this reference book coincides with the sixtieth anniversary of Rastafari and over twenty years of reggae music. This reference work traces relationships between Rastafari and reggae music, two intertwined aspects of Jamaican culture which confront the historically situated position of African Jamaicans as members of the larger African diaspora. Rastafari and reggae music are important voices in the ongoing dialogue concerning Jamaica's search for a national identity. Indeed, they have functioned as forms of resistance against neocolonial oppression and continued widespread economic disadvantage in Jamaica. Similarly, they reveal much of Jamaica's cultural and psychological history, they affirm the African Jamaican heritage of resistance to oppression, and they are important illustrations of the various freedom struggles occurring among African peoples around the world. Internationally, reggae music and its Rastafarian messages have had a significant impact on both music and culture. In Israel, musicians sing Hebrew lyrics to reggae rhythms; the Hava Supai Indians of the Western United States celebrate Bob Marley as a prophet, if not a god. "White Rastas" in the Midwestern United States grow dreadlocks, while Alpha Blondy of the Ivory Coast sings praises to Jah. At the same time, reggae musicians have been at the vanguard of international artistic expression against increasing global militarism and the Apartheid regime in South Africa. And, many internationally known musicians have been influenced significantly by reggae music. Finally, and perhaps inevitably, the advertising world has cashed in on the international appeal of reggae music, adopting hypnotic reggae rhythms to sell the most mundane, if not offensive, products and services.

Yet, despite the global influence of Rastafari and reggae and the ever increasing number of materials on these subjects, little systematic documentation of works in these related areas has been published to date. While many brief bibliographies, dictionaries, and discographies have been published as independent documents or as ancillary material within larger documents, no cohesive reference work addressing both areas has been available to researchers. This book aspires to narrow that gap by offering a relatively comprehensive dictionary of terms, people, places, and concepts relevant to Rastafari, reggae music, and their related histories; annotated documentation of representative reggae music, films, and videos; an annotated bibliography of written sources on these subjects; and appendices which list relevant periodicals as well as reggae artists and bands. Although the primary purpose of the work is to furnish a simple reference guide, annotations are offered to illustrate major trends and issues in these areas. From these pages the reader can trace various perspectives on Rastafari (as a true liberation movement or as an idealistic subculture wrought with contradictions); become familiar with some of the major beliefs and practices of Rastafari; note major historical developments in Jamaican music; appreciate political, religious, cultural, and economic historical factors which have influenced the development of Rastafari and reggae; catalog lyrical themes and interpretations of Rastafari and reggae; understand the role of soundsystems and recording producers in Jamaican and reggae music; observe the various subgenres and offshoots of reggae music; appreciate the tradition of harmony vocals in Jamaican music; trace the relationships among an array of musical idioms and genres which influence reggae music (traditional African and African Jamaican music, ska, rock steady, jazz, rhythm and blues, soul, rock, and Latin American music); respect the role a relatively small number of proficient musicians have played in the history and development of reggae music; sketch relationships among Rastafari, reggae music, and Jamaican politics; and so on. In each of the book's entries and/or within the range of entries chosen, historical and cultural context as well as straightforward description is considered. Yet, the very process of documenting these materials distorts the nature of these subject matters: the printed word tends to characterize these dynamic cultural processes as static phenomena. At this writing, new trends in reggae music and changes in the character of Rastafari continue to occur. Hence, materials included within the book are necessarily time bound and are inadequate in addressing future developments in Rastafari and reggae. Therefore, this book should function to initiate a dialogue on the continued need for and problems inherent in documenting materials on Rastafari and reggae music.

The dictionary is organized alphabetically and functions as the focal point for most cross referencing for the entire book. Dictionary entries were selected for their direct relationship to Rastafari and reggae and/or for their historical value in offering a broader context from which to better understand these related subject matters.

The discography is organized alphabetically by musician/band name. Various styles of reggae music are discussed in annotations (Nyabinghi or Rasta music, roots reggae, rockers, deejay music, dancehall music, dub music, lovers rock, dub poetry, and international reggae), but entries are not arranged according to style or subgenre. The discography includes two hundred entries, primarily long playing record albums accessible in both Jamaica and the United States through quality record stores and catalogs. Discography entries were selected to represent a cross section of reggae music from around 1968 to 1990. Generally, choices were grounded in the premise that reggae music is a form of resistance music (in lyrics, rhythmic idioms, and dance style) conceived out of the struggles of African Jamaicans and best represented by those compositions which offer original musicianship and cultural and political critiques and alternatives for Jamaica and/or the world. The discography, then, focuses on what might be called the "golden years" of reggae music: the legacy of the Alpha Boys' Band musicians; The Skatalites; Count Ossie and other Nyabinghi drummers; The Wailers and other Trench Town musicians of the 1960s; international ambassadors of reggae like Bob Marley, Jimmy Cliff, and Toots Hibbert; and the many legendary Jamaican harmony trios as well as their various offshoots. To offer a rounded historical context, the collection includes samples of reggae's immediate precursors, ska and rock steady, as well as illustrations of reggae's international appeal with samples from around the globe. Although entries were selected primarily for their representative characteristics, works that are classic, unique, particularly accessible, or illustrate development, change, or progression in a musician, band, or genre's style are also included. The discography does not focus on rock or punk music influenced tangentially by reggae. And, while the collection includes entries by important deejay artists, it does not focus on the recent trend toward highly formulaic, imitative deejay/dancehall music.

The videography is organized alphabetically by title and includes a small, representative sample of documentary, concert, and narrative fiction videocassettes (and a few films) which address aspects of Rastafari and/or reggae music. Short, promotional music videos are not included.

Facts, about Jamaica, as Timothy White noted in the introduction to his biography of Bob Marley, are illusive, particularly when researching Jamaican music. For any errors in the above mentioned sections of the book, the author accepts full responsibility. Suggestions and corrections are welcome.

To compile information and prepare the manuscript for a reference book of this nature requires the expert assistance of a variety of people.

In reference to the dictionary, discography, and videography, I especially would like to acknowledge the following people: Barbara Boyle for her fine illustrations and her invaluable assistance in helping me round out the discography and videography collections, Canute Campbell and Terry "Truthawk" Hale for their advice as reggae musicians, Dr. Mary Piccirillo for her technical knowledge of music, Abdul Wali for his suggestions about the videography early on, the people at Rankin Records in North Miami and Lauderdale Lakes, Florida, for helping me finalize selections in the discography, the people at Video Cove in Lauderhill, Florida, for their assistance in helping me complete the videography collection, Alan Young for his kindness in accompanying me on various record and video locating/buying trips, my family for their moral support, and the many people both inside and outside Jamaica who, through the years, have been instrumental in my education about Jamaican culture and history. I also wish to thank Elaine Stern, administrative secretary in the Department of Communication at Florida Atlantic University, and Sue Williams, secretary in the Reference Department of the Wimberly Library at Florida Atlantic University, for their gracious assistance with basic computer programming, formating, and printing questions. I especially wish to thank Gordon Swan, supervisor of Computer User Services at Florida Atlantic University, who kindly offered his assistance in the final stages of preparing the manuscript. Gordon generated the computer graphics from the artist's original drawings, composed the camera ready layout for the book manuscript, and provided indispensable computer expertise.

**Rebekah Michele Mulvaney**

The impact of the Rastafarian movement and reggae music continues to reverberate throughout the world. No facet of Jamaican life in particular has escaped the impact of the Rastafarian influences and reggae vibrations. Both of these phenomena have given powerful lessons with their African-centric perspectives which have spread in a variety of ways within the Jamaican society.

A bibliography is one of the best means of gaining an indepth view of a particular subject area. It can indicate what work has been completed, as well as what additional work needs to be done. The need for a bibliography of Rastafari and reggae reference and research materials is both genuine and immediate because more scholars throughout the world are continuing the teaching of the Rastafari movement and reggae music. This source is intended partially to fulfill the preceding need. While this bibliography is not complete, it seeks to provide a thorough selection of articles (in journals/magazines), creative works, dissertations, books, interviews, parts of books, reviews, and theses written by and about Rastafarians and reggae musicians. It covers the past importance and present significance, as well as future legacies of the Rastafarian movement and reggae music.

The scheme utilized for the bibliographic section is to arrange the main entries (author or title) in one alphabetical sequence (A-Z). In an endeavour to accelerate quick means for the researcher, several items by the same author are organized by an alphabetical title order, with the review essays coming at the end. Given that the users of this type of bibliography often are in search of works by a particular author, I believe that the format accords more closely with actual research needs.

For any errors in this section of the book, the compiler accepts full responsibility.

Any effort of this nature includes the assistance of many persons.

In reference to the bibliography, the compiler would especially like to acknowledge a few who gave invaluable service: Dahrl Moore, Interlibrary Loan librarian, and her coworkers in the Reference Department, Wimberly Library, Florida Atlantic University, who located most of the materials used in the bibliography; Sue Williams, secretary in the previously named department of the library, who with such patience and graciousness prepared the manuscript of the bibliography by placing it on disk; Eulah Lee Singh at the West Indian Collection, University of West Indies Library, (Mona) Kingston, Jamaica, who rendered invaluable assistance; Stephney Ferguson, the director of the National Library of Jamaica (West India Reference Collection), and other staff members who identified a number of relevant items.

**Carlos I. H. Nelson**

# Codes, Abbreviations, and Symbols

CROSS REFERENCE CODES

B000            B, followed by a three digit
                number is a bibliography entry number.

D000            D, followed by a three digit number is a discography entry
                number.

V00             V, followed by a two digit number is a videography entry
                number.

B000:00         A number or numbers following a colon in a bibliography
                entry number refer to a page number or numbers of that
                written work.

*               Asterisks are located within the text of dictionary entries
                only and indicate that the word or phrase following it
                has a separate entry of its own within the dictionary.

ABBREVIATIONS AND SYMBOLS

Comp.           Compiler

D.MIN.          Doctor of the Ministry

Dip.DS.         Diploma in Developmental Studies

Diss.           Dissertation

| | |
|---|---|
| ED.D. | Doctor of Education |
| ed. | editor |
| et.al. | and other(s) |
| M.A. | Master of Arts |
| M.Phil. | Master of Philosophy |
| M.Sc. | Master of Science |
| Ph.D. | Doctor of Philosophy |
| n.d. | No date of publication |
| n.n. | No number |
| n.p. | No paging |
| S.I. | City and country of publisher was not given |
| s.n. | Publisher was not stated |
| [ ] | Includes information provided by the bibliographer |
| ( ) | Incorporates language supplied by the bibliographer to explain or identify, the word it follows |
| ? | Could be the possible year of publication |
| + | There are additional pages |

# Dictionary

## A

**Abacush.** London based band which combines jazz, African, and reggae musical elements.

**Abeng.** 1. The *Maroon horn, made of cow's horn and used by the Maroons to send messages up and down the hills of Jamaica. Derived from the *Ashanti horn, <u>abertia</u>. 2. A New York based reggae band.

**Abyssinians.** An important *roots reggae harmony trio founded in 1969 and best known for their original song "Satta Massagana." The Abyssinians is composed of Bernard *Collins, Donald *Manning, and Linford *Manning. (D001;V26) See *Satta Massagana.

**Abuna.** The head or patriarch of the *Ethiopian Orthodox Church.

**Accompong.** 1. Supreme deity (Nyame or *Nyankopong) of the ancient *Akan-Ashanti people. Accompong appears in Jamaican *Myalism. 2. A brother of the famous *Maroon warrior *Cudjoe. Accompong was captain under Cudjoe's command. 3. A Maroon village in the northern part of the parish of St. Elizabeth, Jamaica, at the southwestern edge of the Cockpit country.

**Accompong Nanny.** A *Maroon warrior and leader; thought to be *Cudjoe's wife or sister. Sometimes called Nanny the Maroon, she is one of Jamaica's national heroes.

**Ace, Charlie.** Veteran operator of a mobile record shop in downtown Kingston.

**Aces.** Desmond *Dekker's band.

**Adams, Glen.**  Keyboardist and singer for The *Heptones, The *Hippy Boys, and The *Upsetters.

**Adebambo, Jean.**  British *lovers rock vocalist.

**Africa For The Africans.**  A slogan of the *Garvey movement.

**African Methodist Episcopal Church.**  Originally established in Philadelphia in the nineteenth century, this church was founded in Kingston in the 1930s and was associated with the *Garvey movement.

**African Reformed Church.**  Church founded by early Rasta leader Claudius *Henry.

**Afrikan Museum.**  Gregory *Isaacs' recording label and record store located on *Chancery Lane in downtown Kingston.

**Afua.**  *Dub poet. (D183)

**Aitken, Laurel.**  Early Jamaican pop singer who covered North American rhythm and blues hits.

**Aitkens, Bobby.**  Reggae guitarist.

**Akan-Ashanti.**  West African people of Ghana who speak Akan and from which the *Maroon name *Accompong and the Anansesem or *Anancy spider stories are derived.

**Akette.**  (Akete)  An African drum with a high pitch sometimes used in Rasta and reggae music.  Also called the *repeater.

**Alcapone, Dennis.**  See *Smith, Dennis.

**Alimantado, Doctor.**  See *Thompson, Winston James.

**Allen, Lillian.**  Jamaican born Canadian *dub poet.

**Alligator Records.**  Chicago based record company owned by Bruce *Iglauer which specializes in blues and reggae.

**Alpha Blondy.**  See *Blondy, Alpha.

**Alpha Boys Band.**  See *Alpha Boys Catholic School.

**Alpha Boys Catholic School.** (Alpha Boys Band) Located in West Kingston, this Catholic School for wayward boys and its band has trained many of Jamaica's finest musicians including Rico *Rodriquez, Don *Drummond, and Leroy "Horsemouth" *Wallace.

**Alphonso, Noel.** Drummer with *Jah Malla and son of Roland *Alphonso.

**Alphonso, Roland.** Legendary Jamaican saxophonist and member of The *Skatalites. (D174)

**Althea & Donna.** Jamaican *deejay duo. (V14)

**Alvaranga, Filmore.** One of the *Three Wise Men.

**Amazulu.** British female harmony trio. (D004)

**Ambessa, Moa.** British *blues dance sound engineer.

**Amerindians.** Groups or tribes who migrated from North and South America into the Caribbean and Central America. The *Arawaks were Amerindians.

**Amharic.** A language of Ethiopia which some Jamaican Rastas have learned and teach to their children in an effort to reassert their African identity and heritage.

**Anancy.** The spider or trickster. A dominant character in Jamaican folk stories, Anancy originated in *Akan-Ashanti tales called the <u>Anansesem</u> or spider stories. The small but crafty Anancy traditionally has played a role in the psyche of African Jamaicans. (B119:214-236) (See enlarged illustration, p. 94)

**Anansesem.** See *Anancy.

**Anderson, Al.** African American blues rock guitarist. Originally a bassist, Anderson joined *Bob Marley and The Wailers in 1974 as lead guitarist.

**Anderson, Gladstone "Gladdy."** Reggae keyboardist who has worked with The *Majestics.

**Anderson, Rita.** See *Marley, Rita.

**Andy, Bob.** Veteran Jamaican singer who worked with The *Paragons in the 1960s, recorded with Marcia *Griffiths, and now does solo work. Popular and well known for his poignant *rock steady songs and insightful lyrics. (D005-006;V17)

**Andy, Horace.** See *Hinds, Horace.

**Angel Men.** A name used early on for the *Myal people of Jamaica.

**Antiphony.** A traditional African musical technique used in reggae music in which a lead musical phrase is repeated by an instrumental or vocal chorus.

**Aquarius Studios.** Jamaican studio owned by Herman *Chinloy.

**Arawak.** The *Amerindian tribe indigenous to Jamaica prior to Christopher *Columbus' arrival in 1494. The Spanish had annihilated the entire Arawak population by the time the British invaded Jamaica in 1655. See B035.

**Armond, Wayne.** Vocalist and guitarist with *Chalice.

**Ashanti.** See *Akan-Ashanti.

**Ashanti Records.** British reggae record company formed by Junior *Lincoln in the 1970s.

**Asher, Bongo.** Percussionist with The *Twinkle Brothers.

**Asher, Climax.** Jamaican trumpet, trombone, and saxophone player.

**Aswad.** Internationally successful British reggae band formed in Notting Hill, West London (1975). Original members included George *Oban (bass), Brinsley *Forde (lead vocals, guitar), and Angus "Drummie Zeb" *Gaye (vocals, drums). Oban has been replaced by bassist Tony *Gad. (D008-010;V01-02,V12,V15,V27)

**Atomic, Sir George.** Jamaican record producer.

**Atra Records.** Shortlived British reggae record company formed by Brent *Clarke in the 1970s.

**Austin, Peter.** (Peter Olson) Member of the original *Clarendonians.

**Awareness Art Ensemble.** United States based reggae band.

# B

**Babylon.** 1. In Jamaica, a common name for the police. 2. In Rastafari, a name which refers to any evil force, any institution or system of thought which is anti-progressive, investing in the oppression and division of people throughout the world. 3. A Rasta concept derived from both the Old and New Testaments. It is especially associated with the Book of Revelation and to the decadence of ancient Babylonia. In contemporary times Rasta sees Western powers (especially England, the United States, and Western influenced Jamaican society) as current manifestations of ancient *Rome and Babylon. See B154, B382.

**Back O' Wall.** A shanty town in Kingston in which many Rastas resettled after the destruction of *Pinnacle in 1954. Also the site of the first islandwide Rasta *grounation, 1958. Back O' Wall was bulldozed by police on July 12, 1966, destroying important Rasta camps, leaving hundreds of people homeless, and incurring public criticism against the government.

**Back-To-Africa Movement.** The popular name for Marcus *Garvey's efforts in translating the concepts of *Ethiopianism into social action first in Jamaica and later worldwide. The movement, founded in 1914, focused to regain black dignity by emphasizing the concept of a black god in religion and by emphasizing individual initiative in economic and other secular matters. See *Universal Negro Improvement Association (UNIA). See also B294.

**Backra Massa.** A name used by African Jamaicans to refer to white planters, slave owners, and supervisors. The phrase is derived from "back-cracking master."

**Bagga, Earl.** Reggae bassist.

**Baker, Moses.** Worked with George *Liele in the 1700s in Jamaica to establish an African infused version of the North American Baptist church.

**Bald Head.** 1. A Rasta without *dreadlocks. 2. Those who cut their hair or are clean shaven. 3. A derogatory term used by Rastas to refer to superficial or "unnatural" people. Forsythe notes that bald head is a nickname used for the baboon monkey of China and for the John Crow (a scavenger bird) of Jamaica. Forsythe argues that bald head is a Rasta repudiation of the egotistical Jamaican folk lore character *Anancy, described in story as a "little bald-headed man." (B119:94)

**Baley, Ras Elroy.** Bassist and percussionist with *Black Slate.

**Bamboo Records.** A small but competitive British record company started by Junior *Lincoln and Clement *Dodd in 1969.

**Bamboo Scraper.** A percussive instrument used in *Burru music.

**Bandulu.** Jamaican name for a huckster or criminal.

**Banks, Annicia.** A member of *Light of Love.

**Banton, Pato.** Popular British based *deejay artist of the late 1980s. (D011)

**Baptist Free Church.** A *Native Baptist church established by Alexander *Bedward in Jamaica in 1895.

**Barrett, Aston "Family Man."** Bassist for The *Wailers. Barrett originally teamed up with his brother Carlton *Barrett to form the band called The *Hippy Boys. The Barrett brothers created one of the most famous rhythm sections in reggae history.

**Barrett, Carlton "Carlie."** Drummer for The *Wailers. Early on he formed The *Hippy Boys with his brother, Aston *Barrett, and did session work with his brother under the names *Soul Mates and *Rhythm Force. Carlton Barrett was murdered in 1987. A legendary reggae musician who created the classic *one drop reggae drumming style.

**Barrett, Ephraim "Count Shelley."** London *soundsystem operator in the 1970s.

**Barrett, Howard.** Vocalist with The *Paragons.

**Bass Drum.** Traditional African drum used in *Burru drumming and *Kumina. One of three drums used in Rasta or *Nyabinghi drumming.

**Batista, Martin.** Keyboardist for the reorganized *Wailers (late 1980s).

**Beat and Commercial Company.** (B&C) Established by Lee *Goptal in England primarily for record distribution.

**Beat.** See *English Beat.

**Beckford, Ewart "U-Roy."** Legendary and foundational Jamaican *deejay artist. He has worked with producers Dickie *Wong, Sir George *Atomic, and later with King *Tubby. (D171;V14,V26)

**Beckford, Theophilius.** Reggae session musician and keyboardist.

**Bedward, Alexander.** A *Native Baptist leader of Jamaica in the late 1800s who established the *Baptist Free Church, and who started a millenarian movement which predicted holocaust for whites and redemption for blacks. Bedward asserted that he was Jesus Christ. He was hospitalized in the Bellevue Mental Asylum in Kingston until his death in 1930. See B260.

**Bedwardism.** Name for the millenarial belief system established by Alexander *Bedward and practiced by his followers. See B260.

**Bedwardite.** Name for the followers of the millenarian leader, Alexander *Bedward.

**Benjarano, Raphael.** Keyboardist with *Ipso Facto.

**Bennett, Hedley "Deadly Headly."** Veteran Jamaican saxophonist.

**Bennett, Lorna.** Jamaican singer known primarily for the hit single, "Breakfast in Bed."

**Bennett, Louise "Miss Lou."** A beloved national treasure, Louise Bennett is a storyteller, poet, and singer whose work focuses on Jamaican folk culture. Writing in Jamaican *patois since the 1940s, Bennett has helped legitimize folk art forms in Jamaican society and has paved the way for acceptance of the *dub poets in the late 1970s. (D012,D183)

**Beverley's Records.** Leslie *Kong's record label, particularly influential to Jamaican music in the late 1960s to early 1970s.

**Bible.** Although the Bible is one of the main texts used in Rasta philosophy and religion, it is not accepted uncritically. Rastas realize the Bible's messages have been distorted by colonial powers for various political and economic purposes. For Rastas, the Bible is not a source for rigid doctrine, but a text which, when read critically, reveals the history of Africa and her ancient civilizations. Similarly, Rastas study the Bible to put its messages to use in interpreting and evaluating contemporary situations and personal experiences. Rastas study both the Old and New Testaments and originally were introduced to the King James version of the Bible. See B036, B154, B261.

**Big Three.** Refers to the three main recording studios in Jamaica during the development and growth of reggae music in Kingston: *Federal, *Dynamic, and *Studio One.

**Big Youth.** See *Buchannan, Manley.

**Biggs, Barry.** Jamaican vocalist, producer, and engineer.

**Black Ark Studios.**  Recording studios of Jamaican engineer and producer, Lee *Perry.

**Black Consciousness Movement.**  Similar to the Black Power movement in the United States and later in South Africa.  In Jamaica, Black Consciousness refers to the movement originated by Marcus *Garvey, influenced by writers such as Walter *Rodney, and further defined and developed by Rastafari.  See B180, B273.

**Black Harmony.**  British *lovers rock harmony group.

**Black Kush.**  Roots reggae band of the 1980s.

**Black Man.**  Monthly magazine sponsored by Marcus *Garvey.

**Black, Pablo.**  (Pablov Black)  Jamaican reggae keyboardist.

**Black Roots.**  British reggae band.

**Black Shot.**  A special fighting force created by Jamaican planters, composed of African Jamaican slaves, and used to locate and destroy *Maroon settlements.

**Black Slate.**  British reggae band formed in 1974.  Originally a back up band, Black Slate later recorded its own albums.  Black Slate is composed of Keith *Drummond (vocals, percussion), Chris *Hansen (lead guitar), Desmond *Mahoney (drums), Cledwyn *Rogers (rhythm guitar), Anthony *Brightly (keyboards), and Ras Elroy *Baley (bass, percussion). (D016)

**Black Star Line.**  Black owned shipping line (early 1920s) established by Marcus *Garvey for the purpose of offering black Africans of the diaspora economic independence and freedom of movement--two elements necessary for self confidence, self reliance, and *repatriation to Africa. (B357:101)

**Black Swan Records.**  British record company formed by Chris *Blackwell.

**Black Uhuru.**  An internationally successful reggae band originally formed in 1974 by founding members Derek "Duckie" *Simpson, Don *Carlos, and Rudolph "Garth" *Dennis.  Soon after the band's inception, Carlos and Dennis left and were replaced by Michael *Rose and Errol *Nelson.  In 1978, Puma *Jones replaced Nelson, creating the most memorable vocal trio of Black Uhuru's long history.  In the mid 1980s Rose ended his leadership of the band to do solo work, and Junior *Reid replaced him.  By 1990, Uhuru came full circle, once again consisting of the three original members.  Throughout its history, *Sly and Robbie have played a special role as Uhuru's rhythmic foundation. Grammy winner, 1985, for Best Reggae Recording, <u>Anthem</u>. (D017-020,D179;V11,V15,V24,V27)

**Blackett, Jack "Blackie."** Member of *Blue Riddim Band.

**Blackstones.** British reggae vocal trio of the 1970s.

**Blackwell, Chris.** Born and later educated in England, but raised in Jamaica, Blackwell is the founder of *Island Records and of *Black Swan Records. He is also part owner of *Trojan Records. Blackwell produced <u>Catch a Fire</u>, the first internationally released reggae album and the album which launched Bob *Marley's international career.

**Blake, Eaton.** Bassist with *Matumbi.

**Blake, Paul.** See *Paul Blake and Bloodfire Posse.

**Blanks.** The name given to records whose labels were scratched off by fiercely competitive Jamaican *soundsystem operators. (B163:66)

**Bleach, bleaching.** 1. In Jamaica, this term refers to staying up all night, possibly for several consecutive nights. 2. According to Owens, in traditional Rasta thought the color white is seen as a bleaching out of black (from which all colors are derived). (B247:61-62)

**Blondy, Alpha.** A reggae artist from the Ivory Coast. Alpha Blondy (which means "First Prophet" or "First Bandit") emerged as a new international reggae star in the late 1980s. Working with The *Wailers as well as with his own *Solar System band, Blondy offers an exciting African interpretation of classic *roots *rockers reggae and resistance oriented messages. Several critics have been tempted to compare Blondy with the legendary Bob *Marley. (D002-003,D178)

**Blood Clot.** (Bloodclaat) A curse word used by both Rastas and mainstream Jamaican society. While most writers agree that the term refers to menstruation, Timothy White suggests that it also refers to cloth used by slaves to wipe off blood after beatings by plantation overseers. (B357:26)

**Blood Treaty.** The name given to The *Treaty of 1738 between the *Maroons and the British in Jamaica.

**Blue Beat.** British name for *ska, derived from *Melodisc Records' Bluebeat label.

**Blue Riddim Band.** Active in the early to mid 1980s (until Bob *Zohn's death), Blue Riddim Band was an all white, United States reggae band based in Chicago and Kansas City. Successful in Jamaica, Blue Riddim offers exceptionally fine classic style *ska and *Studio One style reggae influenced by traditional Midwestern jazz and rhythm and blues. Blue Riddim was composed of Bob *Zohn (lead vocals, guitar, bass, drums), Howard *Yukon (guitar, percussion, drums), Andy "Drew" *Myers (bass, trombone, vocals), Patrick "Betty" *Pearce (keyboards, percussion, bass, vocals), Jack "Blackie" *Blackett (sax, percussion), Steve "Duck" *McLane (drums, bass, percussion, vocals), and Scott "Karky" *Korchak (vocals, trumpet, guitar). (D021-022;V02)

**Blue Tonality.** An African derived musical technique used in Jamaican music in which the third, fifth, and seventh notes of the scale are flattened into quarter tones. (B092:26)

**Blues Dance.** (Blues Party) Makeshift nightclubs and reggae *soundsystem dances held by Jamaicans in England.

**Bob Marley Performing Arts Centre.** A compound designed for musical events located on the outskirts of Montego Bay.

**Bob Marley and The Wailers.** The most famous and legendary band in reggae history to date. Originally The Wailers, or The *Wailing Souls, the band began using the Bob *Marley attribute in the mid to late 1960s as Marley's dominance in the original Marley-Wailer-Tosh trio gradually increased and was encouraged by several producers. (B089:53) The Wailers included, at one time or another, the following personnel: Bob Marley (lead vocals, guitar), Bunny *Wailer (vocals, percussion), Peter *Tosh (vocals, guitar, keyboards), Junior *Braithwaite (vocals), Beverly *Kelso (vocals), Cherry *Smith (vocals), The *I-Threes (vocals), Aston "Family Man" *Barrett (bass), Carlton *Barrett (drums), Earl "Wire" *Lindo (keyboards), Tyrone *Downie (keyboards), Junior *Marvin (lead guitar), Al *Anderson (lead guitar), Alvin "Seeco" *Patterson (percussion), Earl "Chinna" *Smith (guitar), and *Zap Pow (horns). (B359:82-83) The classic Wailers vocal trio formed in the early to mid 1960s under the tutelage of Joe *Higgs and producers Clement *Dodd, Leslie *Kong, Lee *Perry, Danny *Simms and Johnny *Nash, and later Chris *Blackwell. The Wailers enjoyed international recognition with the release of the legendary Catch A Fire album in 1972-1973. Between 1974 and 1975, The Wailers experienced significant personnel changes among which was the loss of Tosh and Wailer who both moved on to solo work. From 1973 until Bob Marley's death in 1981, Bob Marley and The Wailers released a series of internationally acclaimed albums and conducted several significant world tours and performances. See also Bob *Marley, The *Wailing Wailers, The *Wailing Rude Boys, The *Wailers, and The *Teenagers. (D023-029,D194;V05-08,V11-12,V14-15,V23) See B081.

**Bobb, Eustace.** Percussionist with *Identity.

**Bobb, Terry.** Drummer with *Identity.

**Bobbin.** The refrain in African derived Jamaican work songs. (B078:21)

**Body Snatchers.** A British *two-tone band.

**Bogle, Paul.** African Jamaican landowner and deacon of the Baptist church. Bogle was a main figure in the *Morant Bay Rebellion. Now a national hero of Jamaica, Bogle was captured by *Maroon mercenaries subsequent to the rebellion and hung by British officials. (B014:58,B078:27)

**Bomma.** The leader in African derived Jamaican work songs, or *jamma songs. (B078:21)

**Bongo Man.** 1. Another name for a Rasta or *Nyabinghi drummer. 2. A nickname for a Rasta man.

**Booker, Cedella.** (Mother Booker, Ciddy, formerly Cedella Marley) A gospel influenced reggae singer and Bob *Marley's mother. See V17.

**Boom Shaka.** A California based reggae band.

**Boothe, Ken.** (Ken Booth) Popular Jamaican singer of the *rock steady and early reggae periods. (D030)

**Bovell, Dennis.** Co-founder (1972) and former leader of the British reggae band, *Matumbi. Bovell worked for *Dip Records, engineered for *Gooseberry Studios, and often served as session musician for and producer of local talent in England. Bovell later left Matumbi to pursue a solo career. (B078:168,B092:158)

**Bowen, Winston "BoPe."** (Bo Peep) Reggae guitarist.

**Bradshaw, Anthony.** Guitarist with The *Burning Band.

**Bradshaw, Devon.** Guitarist with The *Burning Band.

**Braithwaite, Junior.** A singer who worked with The *Teenagers under the direction of Joe *Higgs in *Trench Town at the time that Bob *Marley moved to that community. Braithwaite continued to play with The Teenagers and The *Wailers until 1966. He returned as an original Wailers vocalist on Bunny *Wailer's 1985 Original Wailers production. (D129)

**Brams.** Rural dances in Jamaica which featured *mento. (B359:9)

**Bredren.** (Brethren) A biblical term used by Rastas to refer to one or more of their fellow Rastas.

**Breeze, Sister.** Jamaican *dub poet. (D183-184)

**Brevett, Tony.** Lead and harmony vocalist with The *Melodians.

**Brevette, Lloyd.** Bassist with The *Skatalites.

**Brigadier Jerry.** See *Jerry, Brigadier.

**Bright, Stanley.** Percussionist and engineer with *Channel One Studios.

**Brightly, Anthony.** Keyboardist with *Black Slate.

**Brimstone.** British reggae band formed by Sam *Jones and Gus *Phillips.

**Brimstone and Fire.** Jamaican *deejay team. (D182)

**Broggs, Peter.** Popular Jamaican *roots reggae vocalist. (D032,D178)

**Brooks, Baba.** Musical artist of the early *ska period who was influenced significantly by *mento.

**Brooks, Cedric 'I'M.'** Saxophonist and session musician. Leader of the Rasta band, *Light of Saba. Brooks and his musicians were important members of *Count Ossie and The Mystic Revelation of Rastafari, and Brooks served as a teacher at the *Count Ossie Community and Cultural Centre. See B040.

**Brother Issie Boat's Rasta Camp.** An early Rasta settlement located in the *Wareika Hills. Musicians from the camp worked with *Count Ossie in the early 1960s.

**Brown, Al.** Jamaican vocalist and founding member of *Skin, Flesh, and Bone.

**Brown, Barry.** Jamaican solo singer.

**Brown, Dennis.** Veteran and highly popular Jamaican singer sometimes called the "King of *Lovers Rock." Brown began his musical career as a youngster singing with The Falcons. His solo work was first produced by Clement *Dodd. Brown has produced some of his own albums and today remains a quite prolific and popular musical artist. (D033-D036,D179;V04,V12,V14,V24,V27)

**Brown, Errol.**  Jamaican recording engineer.

**Brown, Hux.**  Studio musician and lead guitarist.

**Brown, Overton "Scientist."**  Brown is one of the finest *dub engineers in Jamaica and is a protege of King *Tubby.

**Brown, Sam.**  Well known Rasta leader and spokesperson.  Brown was the first Rasta to run for political office in Jamaica.  In 1964 he ran as a candidate of the independent Black Man's Party in a West Kingston election under his famous *Twenty-One Points platform.  (B014:147-150)  See also B042-043.

**Brown, Selwyn "Bumbo."**  Keyboardist for *Steel Pulse.

**Brummer, Wade "Trinity."**  Popular Jamaican *deejay since the 1970s whose mentor was *Dillinger. (D164)

**Bryan, Glenville.**  *Dub poet. (D184)

**Bryan, Ras "Dougie."**  Guitarist with The *Oneness Band.

**Bubbo Dread.**  Name given to *dreadlocked Rastas within the *Ethiopian African International Congress.

**Buchannan, Manley "Big Youth."**  (Jah Youth)  One of the few consistently successful *deejay artists in Jamaica who works solely within the realm of conscious deejay music, writing about metaphysical, social, and political issues from the perspective of Rastafari.  Big Youth began in the style of his predecessor, *U-Roy, but developed his own unique and progressive deejay style which has been successful since the 1970s. (D013-015;V02,V03,V25)  See B078:121-123, B208.

**Bulgrin, Lascelles "Whiss."**  Vocalist with *Israel Vibration.

**Bullocks, Lester "Dillinger."**  A popular Jamaican *deejay artist of the 1970s influenced by *U-Roy and Dennis *Alcapone.

**Bumba Clot.**  A curse word used by both Rastas and mainstream Jamaican society.  See *Blood Clot.

**Bunny, Bingy.**  See *Lamont, Eric.

**Burchell, Reverend Thomas.**  Jamaican Baptist preacher of the 1800s and mentor of Sam *Sharpe.

**Burning Band.**  *Burning Spear's backing band, composed of Anthony and Devon *Bradshaw (bass, rhythm, and lead guitars), Nelson *Miller (drums), Alvin *Haughton (percussion), and others.

**Burning Spear.**  1.  Another name for Winston *Rodney.  2.  An internationally known *roots reggae band founded in 1968 by lead singer Winston *Rodney and harmony singers Rupert *Hines and Delroy *Wilmington, who both later left the band.  Rodney is now backed by The *Burning Band. (D037-042,D181;V02,V11,V15,V23)

**Burru.**  (Buru) African derived drumming played by African Jamaicans in the parish of Clarendon in the 1930s and later in West Kingston.  When the destruction of *Pinnacle forced many Rastas into Kingston, the Rastas learned Burru drumming, incorporating the *akette or *repeater, the *fundeh, and the bass drum in the rhythmic pattern of their own Rasta or *Nyabinghi music. Clarke believes Burru refers to a dance from Ghana.  White believes Burru is derived from the three member Ashanti drum family of <u>atumpan</u>, <u>apentemma</u>, and <u>petia</u>. (B078:52-53,B357:135)

**Bertt, Christopher "Sky Juice."**  Veteran reggae percussionist.

**Bush.**  1.  The thickly foliated forests in Jamaica's hills and mountains.  2. Traditional Jamaican medicinal or recreational herbal concoctions including those made with *herb or *ganja.  Hence, "Bush Doctor," "Bush Medicine," "Bush Tea," etc.

**Bushay, Clement.**  British record producer.

**Bustamante, Sir Alexander.**  A primary figure in the Jamaican Trade Union Movement and an early leader of the *Jamaican Labor Party (JLP).

**Buster, Prince.**  See *Campbell, Cecil.

**Byles, Junior.**  Jamaican *roots reggae singer. (D043,D181)

**Byron, Cheryl.**  Female *dub poet. (D183)

# C

**Cables.**  Late 1960s Jamaican band formed by Keble *Drummond, Bobby *Dockerty, and Vincent *Stoddard.  Stoddard was later replaced by Elbert *Steward.

**Call-and-Response.** (Call-and-Answer, Call-and-Refrain)  An African musical technique used in reggae music in which a conversation between solo and chorus instruments or vocals occurs.

**Callie.** (Collie, Kali)  One of many Rasta names for *herb or *ganja.

**Campbell, Al.**  Popular soul and *dancehall style Jamaican singer. (D044)

**Campbell, Cecil "Prince Buster."**  Early on a singer and dancer, Campbell later worked for *Coxsone's *soundsystem and then for his own system, "Voice of the People."  Campbell is a well known Jamaican producer and legendary rhythm and blues, *ska, and *deejay artist. (V27)

**Campbell, Claver.**  Bassist with *House of Assembly.

**Campbell, Cornell.**  Popular Jamaican vocalist.

**Campbell, Mark.**  Guitarist with *House of Assembly.

**Campbell, Michael "Mikey Dread."**  Creative Jamaican *deejay and producer.

**Campbell, "Ska."**  A baritone saxophonist who occasionally recorded with The *Wailers.

**Capital Letters.**  One of many British Jamaican reggae bands which emerged for a short time in the mid 1970s.

**Carlos, Don.**  A well known *roots singer and a founding member of *Black Uhuru.  Carlos currently works as a solo artist. (D045)

**Carlton and The Shoes.**  A *Studio One band composed of leader Carlton *Manning, Carl *Patterson, and Lloyd *Parkes.

**Carol, Sister.**  Jamaican *deejay artist. (V17)

**Carrington, Vernon "Prophet Gad."**  (Gad The Prophet)  Founder of the *Twelve Tribes of Israel and a leader of the 1970s Peace Movement in Jamaica.

**Cassandra.**  British *lovers rock artist.

**Castle Kelly.**  A legendary hilltop Rasta settlement in Jamaica.

**Catta-Stick.**  See *Katta.

**Cayman Music.** Danny *Simms' recording company to which *Bob Marley and The Wailers were contracted from 1968 to 1972.

**Chalice.** 1.  A ritual water pipe used in Rasta *reasoning sessions and *grounations.   The chalice generally consists of a hollowed-out coconut filled with water and fitted with a large conical hardwood bowl or *cutchie which holds the *herb.  Two holes are made on either side of the cutchie, one to hold a mouthpiece, the other to control air intake.  Rastas believe ritual chalice smoking purges body and mind of impurities, thereby facilitating meditation.  See B374, B378, B379.  See also *chillum.  2.  One of the few self-contained reggae bands in Jamaica known for its energetic live performances.   Chalice is composed of Robi *Peart (lead vocals, guitar, percussion), Wayne *Armond (vocals, guitar), Ervin "Allah" *Lloyd (vocals, keyboards, percussion), Desmond *Jones (drums, percussion), Keith Earl *Francis (bass), and Mickey *Wallace (bass, percussion). (D047;V02-04)

**Chambers, James "Jimmy Cliff."** Internationally known pop reggae singer. 1986 winner of the Grammy for Best Reggae Recording.  Cliff began singing *ska in Kingston as a young teenager in the early 1960s.  By the end of the 1960s, Cliff had created international hit songs and later starred in the film The Harder They Come.  Cliff continues to work in films, to release internationally successful albums, and to function as something of a public relations image for Jamaica. (D051-054,D175;V09,V22,V26)

**Chancery Lane.**  (Chancy Lane)  A famous downtown Kingston alleyway located off the Parade.  Chancery Lane is a traditional hangout for musicians, and it houses Gregory *Isaacs' record store.

**Channel One Studios.**  Popular Jamaican recording studio with fine sound quality for classic *dancehall music.   Owned by the *Hookim brothers. (B092:128)

**Chaplin, Charlie.**  Popular and respected Jamaican *deejay. (V04)

**Charlemagne, Deighton.**  Lead vocalist with *Identity.

**Charmers, Lloyd.**  Jamaican vocalist turned record producer who has worked with Ken *Boothe, *Ras Michael, and others.

**Chat Fockery.**  A *patois phrase which means "talking nonsense."

**Chillum.** A pipe traditionally made from a cow's horn and used by Rastas to smoke *herb or *ganja. A ritual pipe used in Rasta *reasoning sessions and *grounations. See also *chalice.

**Chin, Junior "Chico."** Veteran trumpet player and member of *Ras Brass.

**Chin, Tony.** Reggae guitarist who has worked with The *Soul Syndicate, The *Revolutionaries, and others.

**Chinloy, Herman.** Owner of *Aquarius Studios.

**Cho.** A *patois exclamation, usually used to express disagreement, dissatisfaction, or disbelief.

**Chung, Geoffrey.** One of the finest sound engineers in Jamaica, Chung is associated primarily with *Dynamic Sounds.

**Chung, Michael "Mikey."** Veteran Jamaican drummer, keyboardist, guitarist, and bassist. Worked with *Now Generation. Chung was guitarist for Peter *Tosh and *Word, Sound, and Power.

**Church.** For Rastas, the human body and particularly the human heart are the locus of spiritual and religious activity. Hence, Rastas see no need for construction of a physical structure within which to house such activities. (B247:128) See B154.

**Churchical.** An adjective used by Rastas to refer to affairs of the church or theocratic affairs (for example, "churchical chants").

**Cimarron.** Spanish word meaning "wild and untamed" from which *Maroon was most likely derived. (B089:3,B223:10)

**Cimmarons.** A British reggae group of the 1970s.

**Clapton, Eric.** Rock star whose successful rock version of *Marley's "I Shot the Sheriff" in 1974 helped to legitimize Marley's name in rock circles, but at that time Clapton's recording received far more media coverage and airplay in Jamaica than did Marley's productions. (B089:135)

**Clarendonians.** Popular vocal duo of the *rude boy era comprised of Ernest *Wilson and Peter *Austin. Later, a very young Freddie *McGregor joined the group. (D049)

**Clarke, Brent.** Founder of *Atra Records. A promoter from Trinidad who worked for Johnny *Nash and The *Wailers while they were in London in 1972. Clarke negotiated The Wailers contract with *Island Records, but The Wailers did not sign him on as their manager. (B078:105-106)

**Clarke, Danny "Fire One."** Harmony vocalist for The *Meditations.

**Clarke, Bunny "Rugs."** Lead vocalist and rhythm guitarist for *Third World.

**Clash.** British punk band which maintains an allegiance to reggae both in musical style and in political resistance.

**Clayton, Samuel.** A member of the *Mission to Africa, Clayton presents Rasta *reasonings for recordings and live performances. He performed on the classic Grounation album. (D127)

**Cliff, Jimmy.** See *Chambers, James.

**Coach House Studios.** British studio owned by pop reggae artist Eddy *Grant.

**Coco Tea.** Popular Jamaican vocalist (1980s). (V04)

**Coffie, Carlton.** Current lead singer for *Inner Circle.

**Cofi.** (Cuffee, Koffie) Captain under and relative of *Cudjoe.

**Cole, Alan "Skill."** Jamaican soccer player and close friend to Bob *Marley.

**Cole, Stranger.** Popular veteran Jamaican artist of the *ska and *rock steady eras.

**Collie.** (Callie, Kali) One of many Rasta names for *herb or *ganja.

**Collins, Ansell.** Keyboardist who infused reggae with jazz and funk riffs. A well known session musician and member of The *Revolutionaries.

**Collins, Dave.** Reggae musician who worked with *Trojan Records in the 1970s.

**Colonial Church Union.** One of many white groups reacting against *Native Baptist leader *Samuel Sharpe and the slave rebellion named after him.

**Columbus, Christopher.** Purported "discoverer" of Jamaica (1494), Columbus is criticized by Rastas for the annihilation of the *Arawak Indians and for the role he played in the initial colonization of Jamaica. To Rastas, he is a symbol of European imperialism and oppression.

**Concrete Jungle.** 1. Originally a phrase coined to describe the physical environment of West Kingston after the government constructed high rise apartment buildings in the area. 2. A phrase referring generally to urban areas or ghettos.

**Congo Ashanti Roy.** See *Johnson, Roydel.

**Congos.** Originally a harmony trio formed in 1975 and dissolved in 1984. Composed of RoyDel *Johnson, Cedric *Myton, and Watty *Burnett. (D046)

**Conquoring Lion of The Tribe of Judah.** See *Lion of The Tribe of Judah.

**Convince.** A religious practice related to *Myal which employs rhythmic handclapping in it cermonies. (B092:30)

**Cool Ruler.** See *Isaacs, Gregory.

**Cool Runnings.** A Rasta expression used to indicate that "all is well." The phrase also is used as a greeting.

**Cooper, Michael "Ibo."** Keyboardist and founding member (with Stephen *Coore) of *Third World. Prior to forming Third World, Cooper and Coore worked with *Inner Circle.

**Coore, Stephen "Cat."** Lead guitarist and founding member (with Michael *Cooper) of *Third World. Prior to forming Third World, Coore and Cooper worked with *Inner Circle.

**Coperring, Greg.** Bassist with *Identity.

**Coptic.** (Coptic Church, Ethiopian Coptic Church) "Coptic" means "Egypt" in Arabic. Coptic and Ethiopian churches split from Western Christianity at the Chalcedon Council in 451 A.D. Unlike Western Christianity, which views Jesus as both human and divine, the Coptic and Ethiopian churches believe Jesus is purely divine. Early on some Rastas were interested in the Coptic tradition and urged the church's establishment in Jamaica (1969). (B014:201-203)

**Coptic Theocratic Temple.** Located in *Back O' Wall, Kingston, this was the site of the first islandwide Rasta *grounation (*Nyabinghi) in 1958.

**Coral Gardens Incident.** At Coral Gardens (outside Montego Bay) in 1963 a gang of alleged Rastas attacked a gas station, hotel, and mobile police unit, killing several people.  Due to allegations linking the crimes to Rastas, a period of brutality against Rastas ensued.  (B062:31,B247:244)

**Coromantees.**  (Coromantins, Koromantyns)  Name given to African Jamaican slaves of Ashanti and Fanti background who were transported from the Gold Coast town Koromantyn, located in present day Ghana.  The free *Maroons of Jamaica are thought to have been Coromantees.  (B014:31,B223:16)

**Coronation Market Incident.**  Fighting and vegetable throwing at a Kingston market on May 7, 1959, between a Rasta gatekeeper and a policeman.  The incident is significant because the people sided with the Rasta, and because the police reacted by raiding *Back O' Wall.

**Corrigan, Kevin.**  Guitarist with Identity.

**Cotchie.**  See *Cutchie.

**Count Machouki.**  See *Machouki, Count.

**Count Ossie.**  See *Williams, Oswald.

**Count Ossie Community and Cultural Centre.**  A center for Rasta activities founded by *Count Ossie and others in 1974.

**Count Ossie and The Mystic Revelation of Rastafari.**  Rasta band formed in the late 1960s. It was the first to record traditional *Nyabinghi drumming and chanting accompanied by *Alpha Boys School style jazz horns.  The band consisted of *Count Ossie and his drummers as well as Cedric *Brooks and his group of horn players, guitarists, and trap drummers.  The band recorded the classic three album set, Grounation. (D127;B078:54)

**Count Shelley.**  See *Barrett, Ephraim.

**Country.**  In *Kumina, "country" is an African dialect known only to the spirits and their mediums.  It is used in some ritual Kumina songs. (B223:61)

**Countryman.**  A Rasta fisherman who starred in the film Countryman. (V12)

**Cowan, Tommy.**  Originally a singer with The Jamaicans (a *rock steady group), Cowan has become successful in the music industry as a businessman. (B078:75)

**Cox, Sandy.**  Founder of the *National Club in Jamaica (1900).

**Coxone, Lloydie.**  British *blues dance sound engineer.

**Coxsone.** See *Dodd, Clement.

**Craig, Albert "Apple."** Vocalist with *Israel Vibration.

**Craigland, Ansel "Scandal."** Lead vocalist with The *Meditations.

**Creary, Basil "Benbow."** Drummer with The *High Times Players.

**Creator, Lord.** See *Patrick, Kentrick.

**Creole.** 1. Briefly put, a word describing the combination of European and African traditions in Jamaican society. 2. Another name for Jamaican speech or *patois. (B119:213,B247:55)

**Creolization.** The process of combining African and European traditions. See *Creole.

**Cromwell, Oliver.** Cromwell's plan to win the Caribbean from Spain for England led to the British attack on Jamaica in 1655.

**Cross, Sandra.** British reggae vocalist.

**Crossroads.** A major intersection and mass transit stop in North Kingston; it also reflects a crossroads between wealthier and poorer sections of the city.

**Crucial.** Used to describe something serious, heavy, or *dread (eg. music, politics, economics, society, environment, philosophy, etc).

**Cudjoe.** Member of an important *Maroon family whose members were all fighters in Africa as well as in the struggle against the British planters in Jamaica. Cudjoe became leader of the fighting Maroons in the late 1600s and effectively thwarted British advances until persistent aggressions by bounty hunters and government expeditions in the 1700s led to the signing of a peace treaty with England in 1738. See *Treaty of 1738. (B014:30-33)

**Culture.** 1. (Kulcha) Used by Rastas to refer to respect for, pride in, and preservation of traditional African and African Jamaican culture. 2. Successful Jamaican *roots reggae harmony group formed in the mid 1970s and comprised of Joseph *Hill (lead vocals), and Albert *Walker and Kenneth *Paley (harmony vocals). (D056-057)

**Culture, Bobby.** Jamaican *deejay artist. (D182)

**Culture Corner.** The name of a Jamaican radio show developed by engineer Errol Thompson which incorporated sound effects with quotes from biblical scriptures and other sources.

**Cumina.** See *Kumina.

**Cup.** Another name for a *chalice.

**Cush. Cushite.** (Kush, Kushite) Important to Rastafari as a people mentioned in the Bible who were either from black Africa or were Arabian people of African descent. Barrett notes that Cush is a Hebrew word meaning "black." (B014:71) Clarke associates Cush with Nubia. (B078:37)

**Cutchie.** (Cotchie, Kotchie) A cylindrical hollow object often carved from wood and generally used as the bowl for the *chillum or *chalice water pipes used by Rastas. Sometimes used alone with a piece of cloth for a mouthpiece filter.

# D

**DaCosta, Glen.** Tenor saxophonist and member of *Zap Pow.

**DaCosta, Tony.** *Skatalite vocalist, formerly a singer for The *Deccas, The *Rivals, and The *Sheiks.

**Daley, Richard "Bassie."** Bassist with *Third World.

**Dallol.** Ethiopian reggae band. Backing band for *Ziggy Marley and The Melody Makers. (D178;V28)

**Dambala.** British reggae band of the 1970s.

**Dancehall Music.** Used to describe *soundsystem dance music in Jamaica. Refers to *deejay style dance music which emphasizes a heavy bass line and conventional, yet lilting rhythms.

**Davis, Carlene.** Popular Jamaican vocalist. (D179;V24)

**Davis, Carlton "Santa."** Successful and well known reggae drummer and session musician.

**Davis, Ronnie.** Harmony vocalist with The *Itals.

**Davis, Vernal.** One of several spokespersons of the early Rasta movement of the 1930s.

**Dawta.** (Daughter) Rasta word for a girl, woman, or female companion.

**DAWTAS.** See *Dawtas United Working Toward Africa.

**Dawtas United Working Toward Africa (DAWTAS).** Formed in 1980, DAWTAS is a Rasta women's organization whose work focuses on education and social services. (B282:20)

**De Bolas, Juan.** See *Lubolo, Juan.

**Deccas.** Jamaican harmony trio (circa 1950s-1960s) composed of Vivian *Smith, Tony *DaCosta, and Jimmy *Haughton.

**Deejay.** The deejay in Jamaica has played an active role in musical expression since the rhythm and blues era. Sound assistants scatted into the microphone while playing records, thus taking early steps toward the development of Jamaican *deejay music. Deejays, acting upon rather than reacting to the discs which crossed their turntables, blurred distinctions between audience and musician, creating a folk form clearly reflective of traditional African perspectives of music. (B078:118)

**Deejay Music.** A variation of reggae music which finds its inspiration in the storytelling traditions of African Jamaican culture. *Deejay, *toasting, or *dancehall music is highly vocal in character and highly formulaic in its choice of melodies and rhythmic conventions. Developed from the use of deejay talk-overs at *soundsystems dances, deejay music juxtaposes nonsensical phrases and nursery rhymes with social commentary. (B092:111) A division exists within deejay music between artists who focus on nonsense and sex (slack lyrics) and those who focus on social and political commentary (conscious lyrics).

**Dekker, Desmond.** Vocalist, *Marley contemporary, and leader of The *Aces. Dekker helped introduce Jamaican music to both England and the United States. With producer Leslie *Kong, Dekker released "Israelites," an international hit (1968-1969). (D058,D175)

**Delgado, Junior.** A Jamaican vocalist.

**Denham Town.** A West Kingston ghetto.

**Dennis, Rudolph "Garth."** A founding member of *Black Uhuru. Harmony vocalist with The *Wailing Souls.

**Dibango, Manu.** Vocalist, saxophonist, and pianist from the Cameroon. (D059)

**Digging Songs.** Work songs of African Jamaican slaves sung in the "African antiphonal style." (B092:27)

**Dillinger.** See *Bullocks, Lester.

**Dinkie-Minnie.** An African Jamaican ritual dance form created by slaves as a therapy for the bereaved. Louise *Bennett traces reggae back to this tradition. (B163:43)

**Dip Records.** British reggae record company established in the early 1970s.

**Divine Theocracy Order of Nyabinghi.** One of many Rasta organizations.

**Divine Theocratic Government of Rastafari Selassie I.** One of many Rasta organizations in Jamaica. The group plans the annual Rasta *grounation and conducted a series of conferences with Prime Minister Michael *Manley in the late 1970s.

**Dizzy, Ras.** Rasta poet. (B096-105)

**Dobson, Dobbie.** Ballad singer, founder of The *Deccas, former singer for The *Sheiks, and producer for The *Meditations.

**Dockerty, Bobby.** Member of The *Cables.

**Doctor Bird Records.** British record label owned by Graham *Goodhal.

**Doctor Dread.** See *Himmelfarb, Gary.

**Dodd, Clement "Sir Coxsone Dodd."** Legendary Jamaican record producer; owner of *Studio One and the *Coxsone/Downbeat labels. Dodd has recorded classic and popular reggae since the 1950s and was the first to introduce Jamaica to two-track recording and *dub music to the LP format. An immensely important figure in the development and promotion of reggae music.

**Domingo, W.A.** Contemporary to and opponent of Marcus *Garvey.

**Donaldson, Bunny.** Drummer for *Matumbi.

**Donaldson, Eric.** Early and popular Jamaican vocalist.

**Donovan.** Popular Jamaican *dancehall style vocalist (late 1980s). (D060)

**Douglas, Cleon.** Leader and lead vocalist for the New York based reggae band, *Jah Malla.

**Douglas, Errol.** Lead vocalist with *Foundation.

**Douglas, Val.** Reggae bassist.

**Dowe, Brent.** Lead and harmony vocalist for The *Melodians.

**Downbeat.** Jamaican recording label owned by Clement *Dodd.

**Downie, Tyrone.** Early on a keyboardist for The Youth Professionals where he met the *Barrett brothers. Keyboardist for *Bob Marley and The Wailers in the early 1970s.

**Downpress.** (Downpression, Downpressor) A Rasta word substituted for "oppress" and its various forms.

**Dr. Alimantado.** An eccentric *deejay who early on worked for "Tippatone" and other *soundsystems, later recording for Lee *Perry.

**Dragonaires.** Early *ska band headed by Byron *Lee.

**Dread.** 1. A common term used to address individuals who wear *dreadlocks as well as anyone who adheres to Rasta philosophy. 2. A term used by Rastas to describe a serious political, economic, spiritual, cultural, or social situation. 3. A concept connoting the existential position of Jamaica's poor. Owens defines dread as "an experience: it is the awesome, fearful confrontation of a people with a primordial but historically denied racial selfhood." (B247:3)

**Dread, Ranking.** A Jamaican *deejay and protege of Tapper *Zukie.

**Dread Talk.** See *Rasta Talk and *I-Words.

**Dreadlocks.** The natural hair "style" adopted by many African Jamaican Rastas (as well as others) which results from the practice of neither combing nor cutting the hair. Dreadlocks are thought to be inspired by various sources: Old Testament prescriptions; exposure to photographs of African warriors; an attempt to emulate the symbolic lion's mane; and as part of a simple, natural, or *ital lifestyle. Some Rastas claim that psychic or spiritual sensitivity is heightened by wearing dreadlocks. See B077, B170.

**Dream.** See *Walker, Constantine.

**Drum and Bass.** A phrase focal to reggae music as the combined rhythms of the two instruments make up the foundation of all reggae music. The drum and bass track is recorded first in reggae music.

**Drumbago's All-Stars.** Another name for The *Soul Brothers.

**Drummond, Don.** Legendary Jamaican jazz trombonist. Originally a student of *Alpha Boys Catholic School, Drummond was a member of the original *Skatalites and was considered the best trombonist in Jamaica before his tragic death in the late 1960s.

**Drummond, Keble.** Member of The *Cables.

**Drummond, Keith.** Vocalist and percussionist with *Black Slate.

**Dry Harbour.** North coast site of Christopher *Columbus' arrival in Jamaica. Now Discovery Bay, St. Ann's parish.

**Dub Music.** A variation of reggae music which is instrumental in character. It offers a rhythm solo and a variety of mixing techniques to manipulate patterns of sound in a number of innovative ways. Dub music is unique in the degree to which its relies on the engineer for the finished artistic expression. (B078:128,B092:106)

**Dub Poetry.** A relatively new poetic form in Jamaica (late 1970s) which uses the rhythms of Jamaican speech and reggae music as a framework for cutting-edge poetry. Dub poetry is often written in *patois, is sometimes backed by instrumental reggae, and is nearly always political, if not confrontational and revolutionary in its messages. (B092:189)

**Duggan, Hal "Saint."** Keyboardist with *Messenjah.

**Dunbar, Noel "Sly."** (Lowell Dunbar) Internationally known reggae drummer who, with bassist Robbie *Shakespeare compose the most famous and legendary Jamaican reggae rhythm duo. (D061,D145-146)

**Dungle.** A Jamaican word which combines "dung" and "jungle" to describe the worst of Kingston's ghettos. (B014:169)

**Dunkley, Archibald.** A minister and founder of one of the several groups in 1930s Kingston which claimed the divinity of *Selassie and developed early Rastafarian doctrine. Dunkley (as well as other early Rasta leaders) was arrested in a government attempt to stop the growth of the movement.

**Duppy.** (Duppie, Duppe) A Jamaican word derived from the *Ashanti <u>dupe</u>, which refers to a ghost. In Jamaican lore, the duppy is a roving spirit of the dead which may be manipulated by *Obeah to do harm.

**Dylan, Bob.** North American folk rock artist who has adapted aspects of reggae music into his original works.

**Dynamic Sounds.** Well known recording studio, at one time one of the *Big Three studios in Jamaica. The *Wailers and many others have recorded there, and Dynamic is often chosen by British and U.S. artists. (B089:85,B092:129)

# E

**Eastwood, Clint.** Jamaican *deejay artist.

**Echo, General.** Popular, successful *deejay of the 1970s who was killed in a shoot out with police in 1980.

**Edwardite.** Those who were followers of Prince Edward *Emmanuel.

**Edwards, Wilford Jackie.** Popular Jamaican singer who imitated Nat King Cole during the rhythm and blues boom of the 1950s, but with touches of *mento and *ska.

**Eek-A-Mouse.** See *Hylton, Ripton.

**Elect of God.** One of several titles attached to Haile *Selassie's name by Rastas.

**Ellis, Alton.** Jamaican dancer turned singer, Ellis remains a well known artist and originally was associated with the *rock steady era. (D062)

**Ellis, Bobby.** Veteran Jamaican trumpet player.

**Ellis, Hortense.** Jamaican female solo vocalist of the 1960s.

**Ellis, Tomlin.** Dub poet. (D184)

**Emmanuel, Prince Edward.** One of the earliest and oldest leaders of the Rasta movement, Prince Emmanuel was instrumental in convening the first national *Nyabinghi in 1958. He also established the *Ethiopian National Congress.

**English Beat.** (The Beat)  One of several British bands of the 1970s and 1980s who played what is sometimes called *two-tone music.  The Beat offers an eclectic sound fusing jazz, African, Cuban, rock, and reggae music.

**Epiphany Records.**  Small San Francisco based reggae label headed by Warren *Smith.

**Equals, The.**  British pop band of the 1960s whose lead singer was Eddy *Grant.

**Erlington, Paul.**  One of several spokespersons of the early Rasta movement of the 1930s.

**Ethiopia.**  Ethiopia holds a fascination for African Jamaicans in general, and for Rastas in particular as a powerful symbolic image of a free and sovereign Africa.  Rastas often use Ethiopia to refer to the entire African continent.  For Rastafari, Ethiopia is a powerful geographical symbol representing the home or center of African spirituality.  See B113, B369.

**Ethiopian African Congress.**  Another name for the *Ethiopian National Congress.

**Ethiopian Baptist Church.**  Established in Jamaica (1784) by George *Liele. It successfully combined Christianity with traditional African and African Jamaican religious practices.

**Ethiopian African International Congress.**  One of many organizations within the Rasta movement.

**Ethiopian Flag.**  A tri-colored, red-gold-green flag adopted by Rastas.  The colors represent aspects of colonialism and the slave trade in Africa: red representing the blood shed by Africans, gold representing the wealth stolen from Africans, and green representing the land taken by colonialists.  Sometimes a black band is added to the flag, representing the color of the African people.

**Ethiopian National Congress.**  A hierarchically organized, strictly disciplined, and highly religious sect of Rasta formed by Prince Edward *Emmanuel in which Emmanuel is worshipped as a priest, if not a deity.

**Ethiopian Orthodox Church.**  Elements of this African institution's beliefs can be found in Rasta early on.  The *UWI report recommended inviting the church to establish itself in Kingston, and, in 1969, it did. (B014:201-209) See B307.

**Ethiopian Salvation Society.** An organization established by Leonard *Howell in 1940, possibly aided by the *Ethiopian World Federation in New York.

**Ethiopian World Federation (EWF).** First established in New York in 1937 under the direction of Haile *Selassie to garner support for the Ethiopian war against Italian invaders. The purpose of the organization later broadened to work for unity among all African peoples. Branches were established in Jamaica in 1938, but friction between EWF and *dreadlocked Rastas ensued. (B078:45,B247:19,B186)

**Ethiopianism.** Developed out of a Jamaican fascination toward Ethiopia, Ethiopianism is a preoccupation with the people, land, culture, and myths of Ethiopia. This sentiment developed in eighteenth century Jamaica and served as a precursor to Rastafari. For further analysis, see B014: 68-102, B113, B261, B369.

**Ethiopians.** A Jamaican vocal group of the *rock steady era whose *roots style, in part, paved the way for reggae of the 1970s.

**Ethnic-Fight Records.** Independent black reggae label formed in England by Jamaican singer Larry *Lawrence.

**Evans, Tyrone.** Vocalist with The *Paragons.

**Everliving.** Rasta substitution for the word "everlasting," as "last" to Rasta has a negative rather than a positive connotation.

**Ewen, Alvin.** Bassist for *Steel Pulse.

**Eyre, Governor Edward John.** English governor of Jamaica who was an antagonist in the 1865 *Morant Bay Rebellion. Eyre established brutal martial law during the series of rebellions beginning at Morant Bay. Under such rule over one thousand people were killed. Eyre also pushed illegally for a guilty verdict in the trial of George William *Gordon, spokesperson for the rebellion.

# F

**Facey, Barry.** Guitarist with *Misty In Roots.

**Fagan, Glen "Bagga."** Vocalist for *Matumbi.

**Faith, George.** Jamaican vocalist.

**Faith, Horace.** Vocalist who recorded commercial and melodic reggae for *Trojan records in the 1970s.

**Far Eye.** (For I) The Rasta pronunciation of "Fari," the latter half of Haile *Selassie's family name "Tafari." Also the last two syllables of "Rastafari," the movement name taken from Selassie's early title and family name "Ras Tafari." The intentional spelling "Far Eye" emphasizes the breadth of spiritual wisdom and insight in Rastafari as the spelling "For I" emphasizes that Rastafari is a philosophy of and for the people.

**Far I, Prince.** Jamaican *deejay artist known for his gravelly voice and unique *toasting style.

**Farguharson, Charles.** Keyboardist with *Inner Circle early on.

**Fat Man Hi-Fi.** British *blues dance sound engineer.

**Fearson, Clinton.** Vocalist with The *Gladiators.

**Federal Records.** One of three main recording studios in Jamaica in the 1960s. Federal was an outgrowth of Ken *Khouri's *Pioneer Company.

**Feel No Way.** A Rasta and Jamaican phrase meaning "don't take offense, don't worry about it." (B092:69)

**Ferguson, Lloyd "Judge."** Harmony vocalist with The *Mighty Diamonds.

**Fifteen-Sixteen-Seventeen (15-16-17).** British *lovers rock band.

**Fitzroy, Edi.** Popular Jamaican sufferer and *dancehall style vocalist. (D063)

**Fly, Lord.** Popular *mento singer.

**Flyers.** (Flying Cymbal) A drumming technique in reggae associated with drummers Carlton *Davis and Sly *Dunbar. (B092:52,130)

**Flying Fish.** Chicago based record company specializing in jazz, blues, African music, and some reggae.

**Fontana Records.** British recording company of the 1960s.

**For I.** See *Far Eye.

**Ford, Vincent "Tartar."** Close friend of Bob *Marley during the formative days in *Trench Town; writer and co-writer of some of Marley's songs.

**Forde, Brinsley.** Lead vocalist, rhythm and lead guitarist for *Aswad.

**Forward.** An important word in Rasta language which refers to moving forward, or moving positively toward or in the future.

**Foster, Winston "Yellowman."** Jamaican *deejay who reached phenomenal popularity in the 1980s and has become an internationally known deejay artist. (D199;V03-04,V17)

**Foundation.** Slick *rockers harmony trio founded in the late 1980s and composed of Errol *Douglas (lead vocals) and Euston *Thomas and Emillo *Smiley (background vocals). (D064)

**Francis, Keith.** Bassist with *Chalice.

**Fraser, Neil "Mad Professor."** British *dub engineer and producer.

**Frazer, Dean.** Veteran Jamaican saxophonist. Member of *Ras Brass. (V24,V27)

**Freddie Notes and The Rudies.** British band which recorded for *Trojan Records in the 1970s.

**Functional Rasta.** Both Nettleford and Barrett use this phrase to refer to Rastas who operate, in the main, outside of Rasta organized churches and have influenced a significant number of Rastas to secularize. In this group Barrett includes the disaffected and alienated *dreadlocks, youths, unemployables, self-employed, the clean-shaven Rastas integrated into mainstream society, and musical artists who present the Rasta personae to the world. (B014:220-221,B234:94)

**Fundeh.** A drum used in both *Burru and Rasta music. The fundeh plays rhythm in Rasta music.

# G

**Gad, Tony.** See *Robinson, Tony.

**Ganguru.** Another name for Leonard *Howell.

**Ganja.**  Common Jamaican term for marijuana.  Commonly called *herb by Rastas.  See B066, B107, B112, B122, B137, B283-284, B374, B378-379.

**Gardiner, Boris.**  Jamaican vocalist.

**Garrick, Neville.**  Veteran artistic director in the reggae industry.  Record jacket designer for *Tuff Gong Records and lighting director for Bob *Marley.

**Garvey, Marcus Mosiah.**  (1877-1940)  A Jamaican national hero; an internationally known black leader.  Garvey established the *Universal Negro Improvement Association (UNIA) in 1914.  Garvey used sentiments of *Ethiopianism to create a coherent and proud African identity and perspective of religion, and a sense of independence and self sufficiency for African Jamaicans as well as other members of the African diaspora.  In general, Garvey's work paved the way for the development of Rastafari.  And, specifically, undocumented words ostensibly from his 1916 speech in New York, "Look to Africa for the crowning of a Black King, he shall be the Redeemer," were later viewed by Rastas as a prophecy foretelling the 1930 coronation of Haile *Selassie in Ethiopia.  See B053-054, B150, B198, B214-215, B294, B321, B339.

**Garveyism.**  A term used to refer to the beliefs of the *Garvey movement.  See B045, B199.

**Garveyite.**  A follower of Marcus *Garvey's movement.

**Gaye, Angus "Drummer Zeb."**  Drummer for *Aswad.

**Gaylads.**  *Mento influenced popular *rock steady vocal group of the 1960s.

**Gaylettes.**  A female vocal trio in which Judy *Mowatt began her singing career.

**Gaynair, Wilton "Bogey."**  Jamaican jazz musician of the 1950s.

**Geez.**  (Ghez)  Language of books found only in the Ethiopian Bible and used by the *Ethiopian Orthodox Church.

**General Echo.**  See *Echo, General.

**George, Sophia.**  Popular Jamaican vocalist best known for her 1986 hit "Girlie Girlie."

**Gerry, Jah.**  Veteran Jamaican guitarist; member of The *Skatalites.

**Gibb, George.** Worked with George *Liele in the late 1700s to develop the *Native Baptist Church in Jamaica.

**Gibbidom, Basil.** Original lead guitarist for *Steel Pulse.

**Gibbs, Joe.** Legendary veteran Jamaican record producer and owner of *Joe Gibbs Recording Studio.

**Gifford, Marlene "Precious."** A member of Rita Anderson *Marley's first singing group, The *Soulettes.

**Girmawi-Ya-Girmawi.** *Amharic title "Lord of Lords" attributed to Haile *Selassie's name by Rastas.

**Gladiators.** Successful and foundational *roots reggae harmony trio who began their recording career in 1966 and remain popular today. Originally composed of Albert *Griffiths (lead vocals) and Clinton *Fearon and David *Webber (harmony vocals). Webber was later replaced by Dallimore *Sutherland. (D065-066;V26)

**Gong.** A nickname for Bob *Marley.

**Goodhal, Graham.** Owner of *Doctor Bird Records in England.

**Gooseberry Studios.** British studio which records local reggae.

**Goptal, Lee.** East Indian Jamaican accountant in England. Goptal turned to the recording industry and as a record distributor he created *Beat and Commercial Company. In 1968 Chris *Blackwell and Goptal formed *Trojan records, for which Goptal became the chairperson.

**Gordon, George William.** A *Native Baptist minister, legislator, and political spokesperson for the poor and oppressed in Jamaica. Gordon was subsequently hung (1865) for his writings against Governor Edward John *Eyre and for his influence in the *Morant Bay Rebellion.

**Gordon, Joseph "Lord Tanamo."** A *mento and calypso singer who later became a vocalist for The *Skatalites.

**Gordon, Vin.** Well known Jamaican trombonist.

**Gorgon.** Rasta name for someone with massive *dreadlocks.

**Grant, Aston.** Lead guitarist with The *Twinkle Brothers.

**Grant, Don.** Guitarist with The *Majestics.

**Grant, Eddy.** Internationally known pop reggae singer from Barbados. Formerly the lead singer of The *Equals and owner of *Coach House Studios and *Ice Records in England. (B078:170)

**Grant, Norman.** Lead vocalist with The *Twinkle Brothers.

**Grant, Ralston.** Rhythm guitarist with The Twinkle Brothers.

**Great Jubilee.** The name African Jamaicans gave to their celebration of emancipation in 1835.

**Great Religious Revival (Great Revival).** Islandwide religious revival in Jamaica (1860-1861) started by Christian missionaries, but taken over by *Native Baptist and *Myal people. Led to the development of two major African Christian religious groups in Jamaica: *Pukkumina and *Zion Revival. (B163:39)

**Green Bay Massacre.** Violent political purge in 1977 in which the Jamaican army opened fire on a group of *PNP leaders. (B357:299)

**Grey, Owen.** Jamaican ballad singer, popular during the rhythm and blues era of the 1950s.

**Griffiths, Albert.** Lead vocalist with The *Gladiators.

**Griffiths, Marcia.** Famous Jamaican female vocalist. Griffiths began her singing career in the 1960s recording soul music. She has worked as a solo artist and became popular when she recorded Young, Gifted, and Black (Trojan) with Bob Andy. Griffith is known internationally primarily as a member of The *I-Threes. (D067;V24)

**Grounation.** (Groundation) 1. The first nationwide Rasta convention in Jamaica, March 1958. 2. A word used to refer to any Rasta gathering similar to that of the original 1958 grounation and particularly to the annual nationwide grounation or similar gatherings which include Rasta chanting, drumming, dancing, and smoking of *herb. Sometimes called *Nyabinghi.

**Groundings.** The name given to Walter *Rodney's political and educational sessions in Jamaican communities in the 1960s.

**Grove Music Studio.** Ocho Rios recording studio.

**Gumbay.** (Gumbe, Gumba) 1. A square, single-headed drum originally used by the *Maroons. 2. A cult which used drums and is associated with *Myal.

3. Specifically, a dance of the *Myal related cult, or more generally any number of traditional African derived dances in Jamaica.

# H

**Hagens, Nina.** Punk rock artist influenced by reggae music.

**Haile Selassie I.** Royal title taken by *Ras Tafari when he was crowned emperor of Ethiopia in 1930. The title means "Might of the Trinity" or "Power of the Trinity." Rastas pronounce the Roman numeral "I" as a long "i" to correspond with the "i" at the end of "Tafari" and to further stress the significance of the letter *I.

**Hall, Sir Lancelot.** Drummer for *Inner Circle.

**Hammond, Beres.** Popular Jamaican vocalist; works with *Zap Pow. (D068;V10)

**Hansen, Chris.** Lead guitarist with *Black Slate.

**Harley, Lloyd.** Part owner of *Planitone Records.

**Harriot, Derek.** Popular Jamaican vocalist of the 1950s. (D175)

**Harry J's Studio.** Jamaican recording studio owned by Harry *Johnson.

**Harsevoort, Tommy "Blade."** Guitarist with *Ipso Facto.

**Harvey, Bernard "Touter."** Keyboardist with *Inner Circle; occasionally played with The *Wailers.

**Haughton, Alvin.** Percussionist with The *Burning Band.

**Haughton, Jimmy.** Jamaican vocalist and member of The *Deccas.

**Hava Supai.** Native American nation important to reggae and Rastafari due to the discovery of the ritual-like following of Bob *Marley by some members since the early 1970s. (B359:127)

**Haye, George "Buddy."** Harmony vocalist with The *Wailing Souls.

**Heartbeat Records.** Boston based record company headed by Bill *Nowlin which is devoted exclusively to *roots reggae and African music.

**Heartman, Ras Daniel.**  Well known Rasta artist.

**Hell and Fire.**  A *Channel One studio band.

**Henry, Claudius.**  Jamaican minister who organized a failed repatriation movement in 1959-1960.  Self-titled "The Repairer of the Breach," Henry sold hundreds of phony "passports" to be used at his Emancipation Jubilee and purportedly for passage back to Africa on October 5, 1959.  Later he was thought to be planning a military takeover and was imprisoned for six years under breach of treason laws.  See B072.

**Henry, Ronald.**  Took up the armed struggle against the Jamaican government when his father (Claudius *Henry) was imprisoned.  Ronald Henry and others of his group were sentenced to death.

**Henry, Tony.**  Bassist with *Misty In Roots.

**Heptones.**  Important and popular harmony trio originally of the *rock steady era.  Formed by Leroy *Sibbles, Barry *Llewellyn, and Earl *Morgan.  Sibbles was replaced by Naggo *Morris in the late 1970s.  The Heptones are known for their smooth, precise harmonies both in *call-and-response *roots songs and in romantic tunes. (D069-070;D181)

**Herb.**  Common Rasta term for *ganja.  Rastas imbue the use of herb with spiritual significance and oftentimes turn to biblical passages to substantiate their claim that "herb is the healing of the nation" and that herb is the "wisdom weed" (for example, see Genesis 1:11-12).  Used ritually in *reasonings and *grounations.  See B066, B077, B107, B112, B122, B137, B283-284, B374, B378-379.

**Herman, Bongo.**  Jamaican vocalist.

**Hibbert, Frederick "Toots."**  International reggae star, soul reggae vocalist, and leader of The *Maytals.  Still popular and productive today, Hibbert often is accredited with coining the term "reggae" in his 1968 song "Do the Reggay." See *Toots and The Maytals.

**Hibbert, Joseph Nathaniel.**  Early leader of the Rasta movement, Hibbert lived in Costa Rica for twenty years before returning to Jamaica to develop and spread early Rasta doctrine in the 1930s.  Hibbert, along with other early leaders, suffered arrest by apprehensive authorities in Jamaica.

**Hibbert, Ossie.**  Jamaican keyboardist and engineer.

**Higgs, Joe.** Important singer and songwriter originally of the rhythm and blues era in Jamaica. Part of the singing duo *Higgs and Wilson. Best known as singing coach for *Marley, *Wailer, *Tosh, and *Cliff. His songwriting and singing talents continue to play an important role in reggae music. (D071-072;V26)

**Higgs and Wilson.** (Joe Higgs and Roy Wilson) Kingston singing duo formed in 1950 which was popular and widely sought after throughout the 1950s.

**High Note Records.** (Hi Note) Jamaican record label owned by Sonia *Pottinger.

**High Times Players.** Backing band for *Mutabaruka and others. Composed of Christopher *Meredith and Leebert "Gibby" *Morrison (bass), Basil "Benbow" *Creary (drums), Earl "Chinna" *Smith (guitar), Errol "Tarzan" *Nelson (keyboards), and others.

**Hill, Joseph.** Lead singer of *Culture.

**H.I.M.** "His Imperial Majesty." An acronym used by Rastas to refer to Haile Selassie. (B247:123)

**Himmelfarb, Gary "Doctor Dread."** Founder, owner, and operator of *RAS Records.

**Hinds, David.** Lead vocalist and rhythm guitarist for *Steel Pulse.

**Hinds, Horace "Horace Andy."** Jamaican singer of smooth reggae later influenced by Rasta. (D007)

**Hinds, Justin and The Dominoes.** Popular vocal trio primarily of the *ska and *rock steady periods whose lyrics were often religious and political in character. (D181)

**Hinds, Robert.** Minister and early leader of the Rasta movement. Hinds was Leonard *Howell's deputy.

**Hines, Jerry "Jah Jerry."** Guitarist for The *Skatalites.

**Hines, Rupert.** Harmony vocalist with the original *Burning Spear trio.

**Hippy Boys.** Road band formed by Aston and Carlton *Barrett in 1967. Included Alva *Lewis (guitar) and Glen *Adams (keyboards). (D174)

**Hoffman, Stanton.** Keyboardist, key bassist, and vocalist with *Killer Bees.

**Holt, Errol "Flabba."** Legendary reggae bassist and member of The *Roots Radics.

**Holt, John.** Joined the popular *Paragons as a vocalist in 1965. Holt began solo work in 1968 recording both in Jamaica and England. (D073;V04)

**Holy Piby.** According to White, the Holy Piby is a "black" bible compiled by Robert Rogers of Anguilla in the early twentieth century and used as a foundation for Rasta beliefs. (B357:9)

**Holy Thursday Massacre.** 1963 incident in St. James parish among police, Rastas, and other civilians which ended with several people dead.

**Hookim, Ernest.** Engineer for and part owner of *Channel One Studios.

**Hookim, Jojo.** Part owner of *Channel One Studios.

**Hope, Allan "Mutabaruka."** Jamaican poet and *dub poet. In the 1980s, Mutabaruka's personal style and cutting edge *dub poetry has made him an internationally known recording artist, revolutionary spokesperson, and something of an eccentric to the Jamaican people. (D125-126,D184;V02-03,V18;B225)

**House of Assembly.** Successful Philadelphia based reggae band composed of Mark *Campbell (guitar), Claver *Campbell (bass), Louis *Putmon (keyboards, lead vocals), and Norman *Bailey (drums). (D074)

**House of Dreadlocks.** One of many Rasta organizations. See B067.

**Howell, Leonard P.** Originally a West Kingston minister, Howell became a major figure in the early development of Rasta doctrine and the movement. Howell developed a set of principles for the movement early on and was arrested and convicted in 1934 for selling photographs of Haile *Selassie as passports and for his seditious rhetoric. After his release from prison, Howell developed the legendary *Pinnacle Rasta commune in the 1940s and returned to West Kingston after Pinnacle was destroyed in 1954. (B014:85) See B111, B147.

**Hudson, Keith.** Jamaican vocalist and successful record producer. See B078:135,197 for a discussion of Hudson's groundbreaking recordings.

**Hunt, Virginia.** Keyboardist with *Identity.

**Hunte, Vernon.** Keyboardist with *Misty In Roots.

**Hyatt, Karl.** Percussionist with The *Twinkle Brothers.

**Hylton, Ripton "Eek-A-Mouse."** Popular Jamaican *deejay known for his distinctive scat singing. (D179;V02-04)

**Hylton, Sheila.** Popular Jamaican female vocalist of the 1970s-1980s. (D179;V24)

# I

**I.** The most important word and letter in the Rasta vocabulary. The first person pronoun "I" is preferred over the creole choice "me." For example, "I have I shoes" replaces the *creole or *patois "Me have me shoes." Rastas believe "me" connotes subservience or objectification of the human individual whereas "I" is thought to emphasize the subjective and individual character of a person. The extensive use of "I" is also an extension of the Roman numeral "I" at the end of *Selassie's title; Rastas pronounce the "I" in Selassie's name as the first person pronoun "I."

**I and I.** (I n I) Both a singular and plural pronoun in Rasta language. As singular, the speaker chooses I and I to signify the ever presence of *Jah. As plural, the choice of I and I signifies the existence of a spirituality and metaphysically intimate relationship among the speaker, other individuals present or spoken of, and Jah. "The I's" is an alternative form of this usage.

**I Jah Man Levi.** See *Sutherland, Trevor.

**Ice Records.** Eddy *Grant's record label.

**Identity.** Reggae band formed in the 1980s and composed of North Americans and St. Lucians. Includes Deighton *Charlemagne (lead vocals, steel drums), Virginia *Hunt (keyboards, vocals), Kevin *Corrigan (guitar), Greg *Coperring (bass), Terry *Bobb (drums), and Eustace *Bobb (percussion, vocals). (D075)

**Idler's Rest.** Legendary musicians' hangout on *Chancery Lane in Kingston.

**Iglauer, Bruce.** Owner of *Alligator Records.

**Iley.** A Rasta word for *herb or *ganja.

**I-Man.** *Rasta Man.

**Immortals.** Jamaican vocal group.

**Inner Circle.**  Popular session band and concert band formed in 1968 by Jacob *Miller (vocals), Ian *Lewis (bass), and Roger *Lewis (guitar).  Personnel also included Bernard "Touter" *Harvey (keyboards), Calvin "Rasheed" *McKenzie (drums), Charles *Farguharson (keyboards), David "Black Spy" *Jahson (percussion), and Joe "Gitzy" *Ortiz (lead guitar).  The group was dormant after Miller's death until they re-formed in the late 1980s with Carlton *Coffie (lead vocals), Michael *Sterling (lead guitar), Bernard Harvey (keyboards), and Lancelot *Hall (drums). (D077-078,D181;V14,V26)

**International Herb.**  Rasta phrase referring to marijuana or *ganja.  The phrase illustrates the belief that the ritual, communal use of herb enables divergent peoples to come together peacefully.

**Ipso Facto.**  Successful and award winning Minneapolis based reggae band composed of sibblings Wain *McFarlane (lead vocals), Juju *McFarlane (bass, vocals), *Julitta *McFarlane (drums, vocals), and Greg *McFarlane (drums) as well as Tommy "Blade" *Harsevoort (guitar), Craig *Markham (saxophone), *Markiss (guitar), Orvin *Thompson and Raphael *Benjarano (keyboards), and Tony *Paul (percussion). (D079)

**Iration.**  Rasta word for creation; the highest form of *Jah's creation. (B357:26)

**Irie.**  1.  Rasta word referring to a spiritually high state of mind or being.  2.  Feeling exceptionally good.  3.  A common Rasta greeting.

**Irie, Tippa.**  British *deejay artist.

**I-Roy.**  See *Reid, Roy.

**Isaacs, David.**  Harmony vocalist for The *Itals.

**Isaacs, Gregory "Cool Ruler."**  Internationally known Jamaican *lovers rock singer with a signature smoothness to his voice and a habit of getting in trouble with the police--a habit which has made him something of a folk hero in Jamaica.  Owner of the *Afrikan Museum. (D081-084,D176,D179,D181;V04-05,V17,V24,V25)

**Ises.**  1.  Rasta word meaning "praises."  2.  A Rasta greeting.

**I-Shence.**  Rasta word for *herb or *ganja.

**Island House.**  An old Kingston home bought by Chris *Blackwell in the early 1970s and later given to Bob *Marley.  As Marley's home, 56 Hope Road or Island House became a central meeting place for musicians and friends.  Island House is now a museum commemorating the life and works of Bob Marley.

**Island Records.** An international record company owned by Chris *Blackwell. Originally a rock and roll company. Production, recording, and promotion of reggae music by Island in the 1970s played a significant role in bringing reggae to the international pop music audience. Most noteably, Island signed Bob *Marley and released his first internationally known album, Catch a Fire.

**Israel Vibration.** A Jamaican harmony group formed in the 1970s and influenced heavily by Rasta themes and concerns. Composed of Cecil *Spence, Albert *Craig, and Lascelles *Bulgrin. (D085)

**Israelites.** 1. A name used by Rastas to claim association with the ancient black Israelites. (B120:76-78) 2. A song by Desmond *Dekker which introduced Jamaican music to many people outside the island. (D058)

**Ital.** A Rasta word for "total" or "vital." Ital refers to purity, natural living, organic whole food, etc. Although predominant usage is to the Rasta diet, application of the term can be broad. For example, "I walk ital today" may mean the speaker is going barefooted. See B002-003, B109, B133, B190, B207.

**Itals.** Important and successful *roots harmony trio composed of Alvin Keith *Porter (lead vocals) and Ronnie *Davis and David *Isaacs (harmony vocals). (D086-088)

**Ites.** 1. A Rasta word for "heights," analogous in meaning to a spiritual meditation or high. 2. A common Rasta greeting. 3. The color red.

**Ites, Green, and Gold.** The colors of the Rasta or *Ethiopian flag. In this context, *ites means red.

**I-Threes.** Female harmony trio with *Bob Marley and The Wailers. Formed in 1975, the trio is composed of Marcia *Griffiths, Rita *Marley, and Judy *Mowatt. More recently The I-Threes have recorded as an independent vocal trio. (D089,D179;V14,V22,V24)

**I-Words.** The virtually limitless number of words to which Rastas attach "I." For example, "iration" for "creation," "iver" for "forever," etc. See B002-003, B082, B258-259, B313, B338.

**Iya.** Rasta word meaning "I live."

**Iyanola Rasta Improvement Association.** A Rasta organization of St. Lucia.

# J

**Jackie Mittoo's Ragtime Band.**   *Mittoo's first band, formed when he was thirteen.  The band played rags and rhythm and blues.

**Jackson, Pipe Cock.**  Another name for Lee *Perry.

**Jackson, Siggy.**  Part owner of the original *Melodisc record label in England.

**Jackson, Vivian "Yabby You."**  Roots singer of sincere Rasta music. (D198)

**JAD.**  Record company formed by Johnny *Nash and Danny *Simms in 1964.

**Jaffee, Lee.**  North American friend of Bob *Marley; filmmaker and musician; worked on *Wailers' tours and with Peter *Tosh.

**Jagger, Mick.**  Rock superstar of Rolling Stones fame influenced by reggae music.  Jagger has worked with numerous reggae artists and recorded some of *Tosh's albums on his Rolling Stones label.

**Jah.**  (Jah Rastafari)  Name for the supreme deity of the Rastas.  Probably derived from the Hebrew god Yahweh or Jehova.  Rastas often quote Psalm 68:4 of the King James Bible to substantiate their choice of Jah: "Sing unto God . . . extol him that rideth upon the heavens by his name JAH, and rejoice before him."  Jah Rastafari is intoned by Rastas as an invocation, and as an expression of celebration.  Jah is often added to an individual's name as in "Jah Youth," "Jah Jerry," etc.

**Jah Love.**  One of the best known *soundsystems in Jamaica.

**Jah Malla.**  New York based reggae band composed of lead vocalist Cleon *Douglas, drummer Noel *Alphonso, keyboardist Michael *Ranglin, bassist Ronald "Boogsie" *Morris, and lead guitarist Brian *Montiro. (D090)

**Jah Negus.**  *Amharic title meaning "Jah King" which is attached to Haile *Selassie's name by Rastas.

**Jah Stitch.**  Jamaican *deejay artist.

**Jahson, David "Black Spy."**  Percussionist with *Inner Circle early on.

**Jamaica Broadcasting Company (JBC).**  One of two main radio stations in Jamaica.

**Jamaica Labor Party (JLP).** One of two main political parties in Jamaica.

**Jamaica Recording Studios.** One of three major studios in Jamaica in the 1960s.

**Jamaica Dangerous Drug Law.** Jamaican law used in the 1950s to harass and arrest Rastas.

**Jamdown.** A nickname for Jamaica.

**Jamma Songs.** (Rags) Work songs of African Jamaican slaves used while planting crops. Related in rhythm to the later boogie woogie.

**Jammy, Prince.** Highly respected and popular Jamaican recording engineer.

**Jarrett, Irvin "Carrot."** Persussionist for *Third World.

**Jazzbo, Prince.** Rootsy, bass heavy *deejay artist who became popular in the mid 1970s with his social commentary. (D091)

**Jerry, Brigadier.** Creative and conscious Jamaican *deejay artist who has worked extensively with *Jah Love. (D031;V04)

**Jerry, Jah.** See *Hines, Jerry.

**Jinnal.** (Jinnalship) A trickster, deceiver.

**Jivin' Juniors.** A popular vocal group in Jamaica during the rhythm and blues era of the 1950s.

**JLP.** See *Jamaica Labor Party.

**Jobson, Dickie.** Occasional *Wailers' manager.

**Joe Gibbs Recording Studio.** Jamaican studio owned by producer Joe *Gibbs.

**John Canoe.** See *Jonkonnu.

**John Cunnu.** See *Jonkonnu.

**John, Little.** *Deejay *dancehall artist. (D176;V10)

**Johnson, Harry "Harry J."** Jamaican reggae producer; owner of *Harry J's Studio in Kingston.

**Johnson, Linton Kwesi "LKJ."** Internationally known *dub poet. Also a poet, writer, and editor. Johnson was born in Jamaica, but resides in London. Known for his cutting and straightforward political, economic, and cultural critiques. (B164-169;D092-093;V15)

**Johnson, Michael E.** Leader, percussionist, and vocalist with *Killer Bees.

**Johnson, Roydel "Congo Ashanti Roy."** Early on tutored by Ernest *Ranglin, Johnson has worked with *Ras Michael and The Sons of Negus, The Rightful Brothers, and The Arabs. He was a founding member of the original *Congos and later moved on to solo work. (D055)

**Johnson, Steely.** (Stille Johnson) Reggae keyboardist and member of The *Roots Radics.

**Johnson, Webster "Tasmanian."** Keyboardist with *Matumbi.

**Jones, Desmond.** Drummer and percussionist with *Chalice.

**Jones, Fergus.** Percussionist with *Matumbi.

**Jones, Frankie.** Jamaican *dancehall style vocalist. (D094)

**Jones, Grace.** African American rock singer influenced significantly by reggae music. (V22)

**Jones, Sam.** Founding member of *Brimstone.

**Jones, Sandra "Puma."** African American social worker who emigrated to Jamaica in 1977 and later began performing with *Ras Michael and The Sons of Negus. She is best known as harmony vocalist with *Black Uhuru (from 1978 until her death in 1990).

**Jones Town.** A West Kingston ghetto.

**Jonkonnu.** (John Cunnu, John Canoe, Konny) 1. A seventeenth century Jamaican dance form. 2. A festival using drums, masks, and dance which is still performed in Jamaica over the Christmas holiday. Originally a religious festival, by the nineteenth century Jonkonnu became more European in character and more secular in function.

**Joseph.** Bob *Marley's name in the *Twelve Tribes of Israel. Within this group, the Aquarian birth sign is associated with the biblical Tribe of Joseph.

**Joshua.** Biblical name adopted by Michael *Manley during the 1976 presidential campaign in Jamaica.

**Judah Coptic.** One of many Rasta organizations.

**Junior Byles.** See *Byles, Junior.

# K

**Kali.** (Callie, Collie) One of many Rasta names for *herb or *ganja.

**Kamose, Ini.** Distinctive Jamaican *reggae artist who first gained notice in the early 1980s. (D095-096)

**Kan.** An *Amharic word for *herb or *ganja.

**Kata-tik.** See *Katta.

**Katta.** (Kata-tik, Catta-stick) Name for the stick and the rhythm created in *kumina by hitting the open end of the drum with sticks.

**Kay, Janet.** A popular British *lovers rock vocalist.

**Kaya.** One of many Rasta names for *herb or *ganja.

**Kbandu.** One of the two drums used in *Kumina, the kbandu functions as bass drum.

**Kelso, Beverly.** Female vocalist who worked with the original *Wailers in the 1960s.

**Kemit.** Ancient Egypt.

**Kerr Jr., Julian Hanson Marvin "Junior Marvin."** Blues guitarist and later lead guitarist with *Bob Marley and The Wailers (late 1970s). (D101)

**Kete.** Rasta hand drums.

**Khouri, Ken.** Founder of *Pioneer Record Company in Jamaica.

**Killer Bees.** (Michael E. Johnson and The Killer Bees) Successful Texas based reggae band which gained wider exposure with the release of several albums since the mid 1980s. The band is composed of Michael E. *Johnson (percussion, vocals), Malcolm *Welbourne (guitars, vocals), Stanton *Hoffman (keyboards, key bass, vocals), and Chuck *Norcom (drums). (D097)

**King Alpha.**   Rasta name for Haile *Selassie.  See also *Queen Omega.

**King Alpha and Queen Omega's Theocracy Daughters.**   A women's Rasta organization formed in 1980.

**King of Kings (KOK).**   One of several titles adopted by Haile *Selassie. Rastas use this title for the Ethiopian emperor and extend it to a kind of litany: "King of Kings, Lord of Lords, Conquoring Lion of the Tribe of Judah, Elect of God, and Light of the World."

**King  Sporty.**   Early  Jamaican  *deejay  artist  who  worked  with *Coxsone/Downbeat.

**King Stitt.**   *Deejay artist of the late 1950s to 1960s who worked with *Coxsone/Downbeat.

**King Tubby.**   See *Ruddock, Osborne.

**Kingston 12.**   Refers to a West Kingston area of ghettos and is derived from the postal zone numbering system.

**Kinsey, Donald.**   North American lead guitarist who worked periodically with *Bob Marley and The Wailers.

**Klick Records.**   Shortlived, small, but creative British record company which recorded reggae in the 1970s.

**Knibbs, Lloyd.**   Drummer for The *Skatalites.

**Knotty Dread.**   (Natty Dread)  A common nickname for *dreadlocked Rastas.

**Koffi.**   See *Cofi.

**KOK.**   See *King of Kings.

**Kong, Leslie.**   Successful, well known Jamaican record producer and owner of *Beverley's Records.  Kong died in 1971.

**Konny.**   See *Jonkonnu.

**Korchak, Scott "Karky."**   Member of *Blue Riddim Band.

**Koro.** *Maroon drums.

**Kotchie.** See *Cutchie.

**Kutchie.** See *Cutchie.

**Kumina.** (Cumina) 1. An African dance form in Jamaica. 2. An African folk religion traditional to African Jamaicans. The origin of Kumina is uncertain. Morrish and Barrett suggest the word is taken from the *Twi language of the *Ashanti. Clarke traces Kumina to the Angolan word "Kumona." Both the Ashanti and the Angolan words refer to possession, as in possession by the spirits of the ancestors. The religion finds its expression in singing, drumming, and dancing. See B014 B020, B078, B223. See also *Pukkumina, *Kbandu, *Playing Cast, *Katta.

**Kush.** (Kushites) See *Cush.

# L

**Laing, Cleveland "Lt. Stitchie."** *Deejay artist.

**Lamb-man.** Another name for a Rasta.

**Lambsbread.** A Jamaican and Rasta name for an especially fine variety of *herb or *ganja. 2. A New England based reggae band.

**Lamont, Eric "Bingy Bunny."** Reggae session musician. Rhythm guitarist for The *Roots Radics. Also a founding member of The *Morwells.

**Lara, Derrick.** Member of The *Tamlins.

**LaVilla, Louis.** Drummer with The *Majestics.

**Laurel and Hardy.** British *deejay duo.

**Lawrence, Larry.** Jamaican vocalist who created *Ethnic-Fight records.

**Lee, Bunny.** Veteran Jamaican record producer.

**Lee, Byron, and The Dragonaires.** Early on called The *Ska Kings. A well known Jamaican calypso-soca-ska band of the 1960s, popular with the middle and upper classes and sometimes criticized for coopting elements of the people's music which Byron had earlier scorned for economic gain. Part of the group of musicians who represented Jamaica at the 1964 World's Fair in New York City. (V03;B078:63,75-78)

**Lee Enterprises Limited.** Production company formed by Byron *Lee (along with Victor Sampson and Ronnie Nasralla) in 1961 principally to offer live shows islandwide.

**Lee, Neville.** Owner of *Sonic Sound.

**Lepke, Louie.** (Lui Lepke) Jamaican *deejay artist. (V24)

**Levi, I Jah Man.** See *Sutherland, Trevor.

**Levy, Barrington.** Popular Jamaican vocalist since the late 1970s. (D098)

**Lewis, Alva.** Reggae guitarist. Member of The *Hippy Boys and The *Upsetters.

**Lewis, George.** African born American slave who later joined George *Liele and others in Jamaica to establish the *Native Baptist Church there in the late 1700s.

**Lewis, Ian.** Founding member (bassist) of *Inner Circle.

**Lewis, Roger.** Founding member (guitarist) of *Inner Circle.

**Lick.** 1. Within general usage in Jamaica "lick" is a verb referring to a fight or assault (physical or psychological) as in "he lick me down." 2. A Rasta word for smoking the *chalice, as in "lick the chalice."

**Liele, George.** (George Lisle, George Sharpe) An African American preacher who founded the *Ethiopian Baptist Church in Jamaica in 1784, successfully blending African traditions and religious practices with Christianity.

**Light of Love.** Jamaican female harmony trio composed of Annicia *Banks, Sharon *Tucker, and Joy *Tulloch.

**Light of Saba.** Rasta band led by Cedric 'I'M' *Brooks.

**Light of the World.** One of several titles attached to Haile *Selassie's name by Rastas.

**Lincoln, Junior.** Director of Clement *Dodd's record labels and British representative for Jamaican music businessman, Tommy *Cowan. Lincoln formed *Ashanti Records. He also formed *Bamboo Records with Clement Dodd.

**Lincoln, Prince.** See *Thompson, Lincoln.

**Lindo, Earl "Wire."** Famous reggae keyboardist. Early on Lindo played for the Jamaican show band *Now Generation. He replaced Tyrone *Downie as keyboardist for *Bob Marley and The Wailers in 1973, just before The *Wailers began their "Catch a Fire" U.S./England tour.

**Lindo, Willie.** Well known veteran reggae guitarist.

**Lion.** (Lion of Judah) 1. An important symbol in Rastafari drawn from a variety of sources which illuminate the importance of the lion as a powerful symbol and ancient totem: biblical imagery (eg. the lion and the lamb); association with courage, wisdom, and royalty; association with African symbols, especially within the Ethiopian court of *Selassie; and association in physical appearance between the lion's mane and the Rasta's *dreadlocks. 2. A physical image used to symbolize the Rasta movement. It is often pictured in  profile as a standing or walking crowned lion holding a banner of red, gold, and green (see *Ethiopian Flag). The lion symbol as such is sometimes located within the larger tri-colored flag, and sometimes pictured within the center of the *Star of David. 3. A nickname for a Rasta (eg. *Lion-man). (B120:76-78)

**Lion, Jah.** Jamaican *deejay artist.

**Lion of Judah Time.** Early Rasta radio show (*JBC) taken off the air in 1963.

**Lion of The Tribe of Judah.** One of several titles adopted by Haile *Selassie. Rastas refer specifically to Revelation 5:2-5 to affirm the religious significance of this title. Hence the typical Rasta phrases: "Lion of Judah" and "Conquoring Lion of The Tribe of Judah." (B120:76-78) See *Lion.

**Lisle, George.** See *Liele, George.

**Liul Hayila Sillase.**  An *Amharic title meaning "Most High Might of the Trinity."  This title is attached to Haile *Selassie's name by Rastas.

**Livingston, Carlton.**  Jamaican *dancehall vocalist and songwriter.

**Livingston, Danny.**  Jamaican vocalist of the *rude boy period (1960s). Formerly one half of the duo Sugar and Dandy.

**Livingston, Neville O'Riley "Bunny Wailer."**  (Jah Bunny, Jah B)  The sole surviving member of the original three *Wailers.  A lifelong, close friend with Bob *Marley, Wailer worked with Marley and *Tosh until January 1975, when he left the band after their first U.S./England tour.  An enigmatic character, Wailer then retired to his farm and recorded a number of fine solo albums. His decision to return to the concert stage in 1982, to tour internationally in 1986, and to perform free throughout Jamaica in the late 1980s has ensured his continued role as a major figure, if not a prime mover in reggae music. See also *Youth Consciousness. (D181,D186-193;V04,V22)

**Livity.**  A central concept in Rasta.  Forsythe relates it to "everliving life," an essentially African concept in which all people have the right to a "complete and happy life." (B119:90)

**LKJ.**  See *Johnson, Linton Kwesi.

**Llewellyn, Barry.**  Harmony vocalist with the original *Heptones.

**Lloyd, Ervin "Allah."**  Vocalist and keyboardist with *Chalice.

**Local Hero.**  An Oklahoma based reggae band.

**Locks.**  See *Dreadlocks.

**Locks, Fred.**  Rasta oriented reggae vocalist.  See B130.

**Locksman.**  (Locksmen)  Name for a *dreadlocked Rasta.

**Lodge, June.**  A successful Jamaican female vocalist.

**LOL.**  See *Lord of Lords.

**Lone Ranger.**  Jamaican solo vocalist since the 1960s who has become quite popular with his *deejay, *toasting style.

**Lord Creator.**  See *Patrick, Kentrick.

**Lord Fly.** See *Fly, Lord.

**Lord Tanamo.** See *Gordon, Joseph.

**Lord of Lords (LOL).** One of several titles attached to Haile *Selassie's name by Rastas.

**Love, Dr. Robert.** An African Jamaican physician and publisher who led an islandwide protest against the British invasion of West Africa in the late 1800s. The founder of the National Club in Jamaica.

**Lovers Rock.** A subgenre of reggae music featuring smooth lilting rhythms, sweet vocals, and romantic lyrics. Popular both in Jamaica and England. Dennis *Brown and Gregory *Isaacs are the best known representatives of the style.

**Lubolo, Juan.** (Juan De Bolas) An early *Maroon leader who assisted the Spanish against the British incursion into Jamaica in 1655. Lubolo was made a colonel by the British in 1663, but the Maroons saw the agreement as a move toward re-enslavement and subsequently killed Lubolo.

**Lugtons.** Independent record distribution company for *Melodisc in England.

**Lumba.** Traditional *Nyabinghi chant.

# M

**Macaw.** United States based reggae band.

**Maccabee.** The Book of Maccabees is a part of the Apocrypha and describes the times of Judah. It was not admitted into the official Bible collection. Hence, Rasta sayings and reggae lyrics referring to "the half that's never been told." Preoccupation with the Maccabee illustrates Rasta's suspicions with Western renderings of the Bible. (B247:31)

**Machouki, Count.** Early *deejay artist with the *Coxsone/Downbeat *soundsystem. Thought to be the originator of *toasting. Machouki was mentor to deejay King *Stitt.

**Mack, Douglas.** One of the *Three Wise Men.

**Macka B.** British reggae artist.

**Mad Professor.** See *Fraser, Neil.

**Madden, David.** Jamaican trumpet player and member of *Zap Pow.

**Madden, Philip.** Member of *Zap Pow.

**Madhane Alam.** An *Amharic title meaning "Savior of the World" which is attributed to Haile *Selassie's name by Rastas.

**Madness.** British *two-tone band.

**Magic Notes.** Jamaican band of the late 1950s which fused rhythm and blues with *mento and *ska.

**Mahal, Taj.** An African American musician influenced by reggae music, especially Bob *Marley's music. (V03)

**Mahoney, Desmond.** Drummer with *Black Slate.

**Majestics.** Backing band composed of Ron *Stackman (keyboards), Jim *Schwartz (bass), Louis *LaVilla (drums), Don *Grant (guitars), and "Gladdy" *Anderson (keyboards).

**Makonnen, Tafari.** Haile *Selassie's family name.

**Malcolm, Carlos.** Jamaican vocalist.

**Malcolm, Omeriah.** Bob *Marley's maternal grandfather. Malcolm played an influential role in Marley's life early on.

**Man/Men.** A semantic polarity asserted by some Rastas. Despite grammatical conventions, Rastas use "man" in both singular and plural contexts to refer to (an) authentic (sincere, good hearted) person(s). Similarly, "men" is used in both singular and plural contexts to refer to (an) inauthentic (superficial) person(s). See also *Woman/Women.

**Mancura.** East Indian percussive instrument sometimes used in *Pukkumina. (B163:41-42)

**Mango Records.** A division of *Island Records.

**Manley, Michael.** Leader of the *PNP, Jamaican Prime Minister in the 1970s and again in the late 1980s and into the 1990s. During his first campaign, Manley had the support of many reggae/Rasta musicians including Bob *Marley,

Delroy *Wilson, Max *Romeo, and Junior *Byles. (B089:108) See also B212, B318, B329.

**Manley, Norman.** First leader of the *PNP. Former Prime Minister of Jamaica and father of Michael *Manley. See B235.

**Manning, Carlton.** Jamaican *rock steady and reggae vocalist; leader of *Carlton and The Shoes.

**Manning, Donald.** Vocalist with The *Abyssinians.

**Manning, Linford.** Vocalist with The *Abyssinians.

**Mark, Louisa.** Popular British *lovers rock artist.

**Markham, Craig.** Saxophonist with *Ipso Facto.

**Markiss.** Guitarist with *Ipso Facto.

**Marley, Bob and The Wailers.** See *Bob Marley and The Wailers.

**Marley, Cedella.** Bob *Marley's daughter and member of The *Melody Makers.

**Marley, David "Ziggy."** Bob *Marley's son and leader of The *Melody Makers. In the late 1980s Ziggy gained international attention for his slick pop reggae.

**Marley, Norval Sinclair.** Bob *Marley's father, a white Jamaican overseer who was a captain in the British West Indian Regiment.

**Marley, Rita Anderson.** Internationally known reggae vocalist. Solo artist, leader of The *Soulettes, member of the *I-Threes and of *Bob Marley and The Wailers. Married Bob *Marley in 1966. Heir to Marley's estate currently in litigation. (D099-100;V17)

**Marley, Robert Nesta.** (Bob Marley, Tuff Gong) February 6, 1945-May 11, 1981. International reggae superstar. Undoubtedly influential in shaping reggae music worldwide. Arguably the most important name in reggae music. Marley's musical career began in 1960 when he and childhood friend Bunny *Wailer started singing together in *Trench Town. Soon after, Marley and Wailer met Peter *Tosh in Joe *Higgs' Trench Town yard, thus forming the most legendary singing trio in reggae history. As leader of The *Wailers, Marley was largely responsible for the international spread, recognition, and influence of reggae music and, via his lyrics, of basic Rasta concepts and socio-political commentary. A perfectionist and increasingly sophisticated and cosmopolitan musician, Marley led The Wailers to international success and legendary fame, writing, arranging, and performing many of the most classic songs in reggae history to date. In 1981, Marley died from cancer in Miami, Florida. His death was a traumatic loss for Jamaica and Jamaicans as well as for reggae music and the expression of Rasta concepts to a worldwide audience. See *Bob Marley and The Wailers. See also B001, B026, B050-051, B081, B088-089, B092, B121, B146, B151, B168-169, B176, B206, B213, B216, B228, B253, B268, B314, B327, B353, B356-359, B365.

**Marley, Sharon.** Bob *Marley's daughter and member of The *Melody Makers.

**Marley, Stephen.** Bob *Marley's son and member of The *Melody Makers.

**Marley, Ziggy.** See *Marley, David.

**Maroons.** From the Spanish *cimarron. Name given to Africans originally brought to Jamaica under Spanish slavery who fled to the hills and were joined later by other runaway slaves. Despite the persistent efforts of British troops in the seventeenth and eighteenth centuries, the Maroons maintained their own free Maroon nation within Jamaica until they were compromised by a Peace Treaty with the British in 1738. Although the treaty tainted the Maroons image as freedom fighters, they remain an important illustration of political resistance in Jamaican history. Maroon villages such as *Accompong still exist today. Maroon culture, religion, and music have influenced contemporary Jamaican pop music. (B014:30-38, B078:4-7,B163:18-25) See *Treaty of 1738. See also B035, B045, B054.

**Marshall, Bucky.** Activist in and henchman for the *PNP. Marshall and his *JLP counterpart Claudie *Massop formed the concept of the 1978 *One Love Peace Concert and travelled to London to solicit Bob *Marley's support for and participation in the concert.

**Marshall, Cornell.** Reggae drummer for *Zap Pow; formerly with *Third World.

**Martin, Phonso.** Percussionist with *Steel Pulse.

**Martin, Vincent Ivanhoe.** (Rhygin) Legendary young Kingston gunman of the 1940s from which the story of "Rhygin" and the movie The Harder They Come were derived. (V13)

**Marvin, Junior.** See *Kerr, Julian Hanson.

**Mash It Up.** A Jamaican phrase. When used in the context of music it means to succeed; similar to "bring the house down" in North American idiom.

**Mash Up.** (Mash Down) To beat, destroy.

**Maskel, Haile.** Solo artist and former member of *Ras Michael and The Sons of Negus and *Light of Saba.

**Massop, Claudie.** Activist in and henchman for the *JLP. Massop and his *PNP counterpart Bucky *Marshall formed the concept of the 1978 *One Love Peace Concert and travelled to London to solicit Bob *Marley's support for and participation in the concert.

**Matthews, Winston "Pipe."** Jamaican reggae vocalist. Lead vocalist with The *Wailing Souls. Early on he sang with The *Wailers in *Trench Town and later formed The Wailing Souls.

**Matumbi.** British reggae band formed in 1972. Founded by band leader and lead guitarist and vocalist, Dennis *Bovell. Matumbi was a successful reggae group until they disbanded in the late 1970s when Bovell left to pursue a solo career. The band consisted of Bovell, Glen "Bagga" *Fagan (vocals), Webster "Tasmanian" *Johnson (keyboards), Euton "Fergus" *Jones (percussion), Bunny *Donaldson (drums), Patrick *Tenrew (trumpet), Henry *Tenrew (tenor saxophone), and Eaton *Blake (bass). (D102)

**Matuzalem.** Los Angeles based reggae band.

**Maytals.** See *Toots and The Maytals.

**Maytones.** Jamaican vocal group. (D181)

**McCook, Tommy.** *Alpha Boys School graduate, instructor at the *Count Ossie Community and Cultural Centre, and tenor saxophonist with The *Skatalites. (D174)

**McDonald, Lloyd "Bread."** Harmony vocalist with The *Wailing Souls.

**McDonald, Stephen.** Rasta who ran for political office in Jamaica in 1980.

**McFarlane, Greg.** Drummer with *Ipso Facto.

**McFarlane, Juju.** Bassist and vocalist with *Ipso Facto.

**McFarlane, Julitta.** Drummer and vocalist with *Ipso Facto.

**McFarlane, Wain.** Leader and lead vocalist with *Ipso Facto.

**McGregor, Freddie.** Well loved Jamaican vocalist and an internationally known reggae star. McGregor began singing at age seven, joined The *Clarendonians in 1963, and later became a successful solo artist. His first album was not released until 1979. Since then, McGregor's music has been successful worldwide. (D103-105;V04)

**McIntosh, Winston Hubert.** (Peter Tosh) October 19, 1944-September 9, 1987. One of the three original *Wailers, Tosh worked with Bob *Marley and Bunny *Wailer until January 1975 when Tosh and Wailer left the band amidst increasing tensions among the three musicians as well as with Chris *Blackwell. As a solo artist Tosh remained an internationally known reggae superstar and an outspoken socio-political critic until his death in 1987 at the hands of armed intruders. (D160-163,D181;V14,V19,V23) See B270, B333-334, B360.

**McKay, Bertie.** Rhythm guitarist with *Misty In Roots.

**McKay, Freddie.** Veteran and popular Jamaican reggae vocalist since the *rock steady era. Best known for his hit song "Picture on The Wall" (1970). (D106)

**McKenzie, Calvin "Rasheed."** Drummer with *Inner Circle early on.

**McLean, Bertram "Ranchie."** Reggae bassist and member of The *Oneness Band.

**McLean, Steve "Duck."** Member of *Blue Riddim Band.

**McNaughton, Trevor.** Harmony vocalist with The *Melodians.

**McQueen, Ronnie.** Original bassist with *Steel Pulse.

**Meadowlark Records.** A division of *Shanachie.

**Meditations.** Successful Jamaican harmony trio who began recording in 1976-1977. Consists of Ansel *Craigland (lead vocalist) and Winston *Watson and Danny *Clarke (harmony vocalists). The Meditations occasionally worked as back-up vocalists for Bob *Marley. (V05)

**Meeks, Brian.** Jamaican *dub poet from Canada.

**Mellow Rose.** British *lovers rock band.

**Mellowlarks.** Jamaican band of the late 1950s which fused rhythm and blues with *mento and *ska.

**Melodians.** Classic Jamaican harmony trio originally associated with the *rock steady period. The Melodians began recording in the mid 1960s and are still active today. Composed of Tony *Brevett (lead and harmony vocals), Brent *Dowe (lead and harmony vocals), and Trevor *McNaughton (harmony vocals). Best known for their legendary hit "Rivers of Babylon." (D107,D175)

**Melodisc.** British record label which broke ground for black music. Established by Emile *Shalet in 1946.

**Melody Makers.** (Ziggy Marley and The Melody Makers) Jamaican reggae rock band composed of Bob *Marley's children: Ziggy *Marley, Stephen *Marley, Cedella *Marley, and Sharon *Marley. The Melody Makers became a hot international act by the late 1980s, partly due to some uncanny likenesses in style between Ziggy and his father, and partly due to the band's slick, commercial sound. (D108,D179,D200;V24,V28)

**Members.** A British band fusing reggae and punk music.

**Men At Work.** Australian band popular in the early 1980s and influenced significantly by reggae music.

**Menelik.** (Ben-Menelik) Son of King Solomon and Queen of Sheba. Ruler of Ethiopia around 900 B.C. *Selassie claimed to be a direct descendant of Menelik.

**Mento.** Traditional Jamaican folk music dated from the late 1800s and somewhat similar in sound to the calypso of Trinidad. Uses African, European, and Latin American musical elements. Mento is an early precursor to reggae music.

**Meredith, Christopher.** Bassist with The *High Times Players.

**Messenjah.** Canadian based reggae band popular since the late 1980s and composed of Rupert "Ojiji" *Harvey (lead vocals, guitar), Eric "Babyface" *Walsh (guitar), Hal "Saint" *Duggan (keyboards), Haile *Yates (percussion), Charles "Tower" *Sinclair (bass), and Crash *Morgan (drums). (D109)

**Michigan and Smiley.** (General Smiley and Papa Michigan) Respected and successful Jamaican *deejay duo since the late 1970s.

**Michigan, Papa.** See *Michigan and Smiley.

**Mighty Diamonds.** Classic Jamaican harmony trio. The Diamonds formed in 1969, but were not popular until the mid 1970s. The band consists of Donald

"Tabby" *Shaw (lead vocals) and Lloyd "Judge" *Ferguson and Fitzroy "Bunny" *Simpson (harmony vocals). (D110-112,D179;V02,V24,V26)

**Mighty Upsetter.** One of several nicknames for Lee *Perry.

**Militant.** Another name for *rockers.

**Miller, Jacob.** One of the most popular vocalists in Jamaica until his death in 1980 (auto accident). Miller was the leader of *Inner Circle and a star in the reggae movie <u>Rockers</u>. (D113,D181;V05,V14,V25,V26)

**Miller, Nelson.** Drummer with The *Burning Band.

**Minott, Echo.** Popular *dancehall style vocalist. (V10)

**Minott, Sugar.** Popular Jamaican vocalist and *deejay. Minott began recording at *Studio One in the 1960s. As a solo artist in the 1970s-1980s, Minott has been active and successful. (D114)

**Mission to Africa.** 1961 trip to Africa by Jamaican scholars, community leaders, and Rastas from which was drafted both a majority and a Rasta minority report. See *Three Wise Men. See also B004, B196, B204, B235, B269.

**Misty In Roots.** (Misty) Creative *roots band formed in England in 1975. Includes Tony *Henry (bass), Vernon *Hunte (organ), Julian *Peters (drums), Delvin *Tyson (vocals), Bertie *McKay (rhythm guitar), Barry *Facey (guitar), and Wolford *Tyson (lead vocals). (D115-116)

**Mittoo, Jackie.** An important figure throughout the history of Jamaican pop music, especially *rock steady. Mittoo is both composer and accomplished keyboardist. He formed *Jackie Mittoo's Ragtime Band. Mittoo also has worked with The *Soul Brothers and The *Soul Vendors.

**Mods.** British *blue beat band of the 1960s.

**Mohammed, Prince.** *Deejay artist.

**Mon.** *Patois and Rasta word for "man."

**Montiro, Brian.** Lead guitarist with *Jah Malla.

**Moodie, Harry.** Jamaican record producer.

**Moore, Johnny "Dizzy."** Trumpet player for The *Skatalites.

**Moore, Junior.** Member of The *Tamlins.

**Morant Bay Rebellion.** Post emancipation rebellion of 1865 led by Paul *Bogle and George William *Gordon in demonstration against government corruption and continued poor treatment of African Jamaicans. While the incident began as a peaceful protest rally, some three hundred government forces and volunteers opened fire on some four hundred protesters. Many area people were imprisoned or killed. See B035.

**Morgan, Crash.** Drummer with *Messenjah.

**Morgan, Derrick.** Jamaican vocalist who covered North American rhythm and blues tunes in the early 1960s and later devoted his lyrics to the social commentary of the *rude boy era.

**Morgan, Earl.** Harmony vocalist with the original *Heptones.

**Morris, Nago.** Replaced Leroy *Sibbles as lead vocalist with The *Heptones in the 1970s.

**Morris, Ronald "Boogsie."** Bassist with *Jah Malla.

**Morrison, Leebert "Gibby."** Bassist with The *High Times Players.

**Morwells.** Jamaican harmony group formed in 1973 by Bingy *Bunny and Morris "Blacka Morwell" *Wellington.

**Moses, Pablo.** Distinctive Rasta reggae vocalist popular throughout the 1980s. (D117-119)

**Mount Zion.** See *Zion.

**Movement.** British reggae band of the 1970s.

**Mowatt, Judy.** Jamaican female vocalist. Sometimes called the Queen of Reggae. Originally a dancer, Mowatt sang with The *Gaylettes early on. In the 1970s Mowatt joined Rita *Marley and Marcia *Griffiths, forming The *I-Threes (Bob *Marley's background vocalists). Since Marley's death, Mowatt has worked primarily as a solo artist, releasing international hit albums like the classic Black Woman. (D120-122;V14,V24)

**Moyne Report.** The result of strikes and rebellion in the 1930s, the Moyne Report discovered that wages for the poor in Jamaica had not increased since emancipation, one hundred years earlier.

**Mundell, Hugh.** Young Rasta vocalist who delivered conscious and political lyrics. His work was produced by Augustus *Pablo. Mundell died in 1983. (D123)

**Murderer.** A popular Jamaican term used in the context of music in the 1980s to refer to an excellent musician, or a performance which overwhelms the audience.

**Murvin, Junior.** Jamaican vocalist since the late 1960s. (D181)

**Music Mountain.** Kingston recording studio.

**Musical Youth.** Popular British youth reggae band in the early 1980s. (D124;V27)

**Mutabaruka.** See *Hope, Allan.

**Myal.** (Myalism) An African Jamaican traditional religion and healing cult derived from *Ashanti tribal religions and initially preserved and practiced in Jamaica by the *Maroons. Often described as the positive counterpart to *Obeah (as a "white" magic in opposition to "black" magic). *Kumina, the Myal dance form, and its accompanying drumming rhythms are important precursors to reggae music. (B078:11,B163:12-36,B223:45-48)

**Myal Procession of 1842.** Post emancipation religious event which marked a resurgence of African derived, traditional Jamaican religions. It was a precursor to the *Great Revival.

**Myers, Andy "Drew."** Member of *Blue Riddim Band.

**Mystic Man.** A name applied to some Rastas. Assumes an intimate relationship between the individual and spiritual, psychic, or magical forces.

**Mystic Revelation of Rastafari.** 1. A *Nyabinghi/Rasta music group formed in the late 1960s. See *Count Ossie and The Mystic Revelation of Rastafari. 2. Another name for the *Rastafarian Repatriation Association.

**Myton, Cedric.** Reggae vocalist and founding member of The *Congos (1975). He also worked with The Tartons and The Royal Rasses. (D046;B078:192)

# N

**Nabbie, Navvie.** *Dub poet. (D184)

**Nanny.** See *Accompong Nanny.

**Nash, Johnny.** African American musician and actor. Originally Nash worked within the North American pop music industry, but was later influenced by soul and then reggae music. Nash, along with Danny *Simms, formed *JAD Records.

**Native Baptists.** Followers of African influenced Christianity first brought to Jamaica by George *Liele in 1784.

**Natty Dread.** (Knotty Dread) A common nickname for *dreadlocked Rastas.

**Nazarites.** Ascetics of biblical times to which some Rastas claim association.

**Negro World.** A newspaper sponsored by Marcus *Garvey.

**Negus Negast.** (Negus Negasti) An *Amharic title meaning "King of Kings," attributed to *Selassie's name by Rastas.

**Negusa Negast.** *Big Youth's record label.

**Nelson, Errol.** At one time a harmony singer for *Black Uhuru.

**Nelson, Errol "Tarzan."** Keyboardist with The *High Times Players.

**Neville Brothers.** Successful, creative, and politically progressive New Orleans based band which combines elements of rock, blues, jazz, cajun, and reggae music. (V17,V22)

**Nicodemus.** Jamaican *deejay artist. (D182)

**Nighthawk Records.** St. Louis based record company specializing in blues and reggae. Owned by Robert *Shoenfield and Leroy *Pierson, Nighthawk demonstrates a sensitivity to and respect for reggae and offers an auction for collectors of rare Jamaican singles.

**Nisbett, Steve "Grizzly."** Drummer with *Steel Pulse.

**No True?** A *patois and Rasta phrase meaning "isn't it true?" or "don't you see?"

**Norcom, Chuck.** Drummer with *Killer Bees.

**Now Generation.** Jamaican show band for which several important reggae musicians worked including Earl "Wire" *Lindo and Dennis *Brown.

**Nowlin, Bill.** Head of *Heartbeat Records.

**Nubia.** Also referred to as *Cush and Meroe in the Bible, Nubia most probably was the ancient, biblical site of Ethiopia.

**Nyabinghi.** (Nyabingi, Niabingi, etc.) 1. A religious-spiritual movement in Rwanda from the 1700s to the early 1900s named after Queen Nyabinghi, led by a series of spiritually influential women, and focused on military actions against white imperialists and colonialists. 2. An orthodox, primarily religious-spiritual faction of Rastafari. See B149. 3. A Rasta ritual/convention also called a *grounation. 4. A name for Rasta music consisting of chants and drumming used at grounations. 5. A nickname (Nyabinghi, Nya, Bingi) for male Rastas, usually *dreadlocked. See B020, B149.

**Nyankopong.** (Nyankonpon, Nyame) Supreme deity of the *Ashanti who was worshipped by the original *Maroons of Jamaica and from which the Maroon village and the *Myal deity take their names. See also *Accompong.

# O

**Oban, George.** Founding member and bassist for *Aswad. Oban left Aswad around 1978-1979 and began solo work recording his own distinctive reggae, funk, and jazz influenced fusion music.

**Obeah.** (Obiah, Obia, Obi) Derived from the *Ashanti word Obayi, Obeah is associated with sorcery, magic, and voodoo. In Jamaica, Obeah is a form of magic using herbs, charms, and amulets to protect from or inflict injury upon an enemy. See B223.

**Old Testament.** A text which has had significant influence on Rastas' beliefs, especially the books of Daniel, Deuteronomy, Isaiah, Leviticus, and Numbers. See B036, B247.

**Olson, Peter.** See *Austin, Peter.

**One Drop.** Generally speaking, the reggae drumming style in which the bass drum enters on beats two and four. More specifically, according to reggae musician Terry "Truthawk" Hale, one drop is a reggae drumming style in which the bass drum is emphasized only on beat four, thereby leaving "space" for other percussive instruments.   Carlton *Barrett, who is often cited as the reggae drummer who perfected this style, also simplified the role of the high hat by using 1/4 instead of 1/8 note timing.

**One God, One Aim, One Destiny.**   Slogan of the *Garvey movement often used by Rastas as well.

**One Love.**   Common Rasta salutation of unity.

**One Love Peace Concert.**   1978 Kingston concert organized by Bucky *Marshall and Claudie *Massop to foster political unity in Jamaica.   *Marley's participation in the concert marked his first return to Jamaica after he had been shot in 1976, and it was at this concert that Marley coaxed Prime Minister Michael *Manley and opposition leader Edward *Seaga on stage for a symbolic handshake. (V14)

**One Vibe.**   Jamaican backing band for stage shows.

**Oneness Band.**   Backing band for Jimmy *Cliff.   Composed of Earl "Chinna" *Smith and Ras "Dougie" *Bryan (guitars), Ansell *Collins (keyboards), Uzziah "Sticky" *Thompson (percussion), Ranchie *McLean (bass), and Michael "Boo" *Richards (drums).

**Onuora, Oku.**   See *Wong, Orlando.

**On-xyz.**   Detroit based reggae funk fusion band formed in the late 1970s. There have been major personnel changes in the past few years and the recent addition of Sistah, a group of female backing vocalists and dancers. Throughout its history On-xyz has offered a clean, creative, compelling fusion music which has gained the attention of many Jamaican musicians.

**Ooman.**   *Patois and Rasta word for "woman."

**Opel, Jackie.**   Popular rhythm and blues singer in Jamaica originally from Trinidad.

**Osahene.**   Bob *Marley's *Ashanti title meaning "redeemer."

**Osbourne, Johnny.**   Popular Jamaican reggae soul vocalist. (D130,D176;V10)

**Ossie, Count.**   See *Williams, Oswald.

**Overstand.**   Rasta word which is believed to illustrate more accurately the intent of the word "understand."

# P

**Pablo, Augustus.** See *Swaby, Horace.

**Paley, Kenneth.** Harmony vocalist with *Culture.

**Palma, Tristan.** (Tristan Palmer) Popular Jamaican vocalist.

**Palmer, Michael.** Popular Jamaican *dancehall style vocalist. (D094)

**Pama, Carl.** See *Pama Records.

**Pama, Harry.** See *Pama Records.

**Pama Records.** British reggae label of the 1960s owned by Carl and Harry Pama.

**Paragons.** Popular and legendary *rock steady band formed in 1964 and led by John *Holt. Also consisted of Tyrone *Evans, Howard *Barrett, Roslyn *Sweet, and Bob *Andy. (D133)

**Parkes, Lloyd.** (Lloyd Parks) Reggae bassist and leader of *We the People. (V02-03,V14)

**Patois.** Name given to the Creole English spoken in Jamaica and developed from a mix of English and African linguistic influences.

**Patrick, Kentrick "Lord Creator."** Popular Jamaican vocalist of the *ska and early *soundsystem period.

**Patterson, Alvin "Seeco."** Early on a Rasta hand drummer (1960s), Patterson was percussionist for Bob *Marley from 1975-1980. (B089:37)

**Patterson, Carl.** Record producer and member of *Carlton and The Shoes.

**Paul Blake and Bloodfire Posse.** Popular *dancehall group best known for their 1984 hit "Get Flat." (V04)

**Paul, Frankie.** *Lovers rock style vocalist popular since the mid 1980s.

**Peace Concert.** See *One Love Peace Concert.

**Peace and Love.** A Rasta salutation.

**Peace Treaty of 1738.** See *Treaty of 1738.

**Pearce, Patrick "Betty."** Member of *Blue Riddim Band.

**Peart, Robi.** Lead vocalist with *Chalice.

**Penn, Admiral William.** Penn, along with General Robert *Venables, launched the first British invasion of Jamaica at Spanish Town on May 10, 1655. (B223:9)

**Peoples National Party (PNP).** One of two main political parties in Jamaica.

**Peoples Political Party (PPP).** *Garvey's political party, re-established by Millard Johnson in the 1960s.

**Perkins, Lascal.** Jamaican rhythm and blues vocalist of the late 1950s.

**Perry, Lee "Scratch."** Originally a sound engineer for *Coxsone, Perry established his own *Black Ark Studios and the studio band The *Upsetters. Perry is well known and respected for producing some of The *Wailers' most interesting early work, and for his eccentric brillance as a creative producer, engineer, and musical artist. (D134;V26)

**Perry, Pauline.** Independent record producer and former wife of Lee *Perry.

**Peters, Julian.** Drummer with *Misty In Roots.

**Phillips, Gus.** Founding member of *Brimstone.

**Pinkney, Dwight.** ( Dwight Pickney) Co-founder and guitarist for *Zap Pow.

**Pierson, Leroy.** Part owner of *Nighthawk Records.

**Pinchers.** Jamaican *deejay *dancehall artist.

**Pinnacle.** Rasta commune near Sligoville led by Leonard *Howell from 1940 through a number of police raids until 1954, when it was finally destroyed by police, thus displacing many members who resettled in West Kingston.

**Pint, Half.** See *Roberts, London Andrew.

**Pioneer Company.** Jamaican record company established by Ken *Khouri in 1954 out of which developed *Federal Records.

**Pioneers.**  British Jamaican reggae band of the 1960s more recently based in Toronto.

**Pipe and The Pipers.**  Name used by The *Wailing Souls when they recorded for *Tuff Gong in order to avoid confusion with The *Wailers.

**Pipe Cock Jackson.**  See *Jackson, Pipe Cock.

**Planitone Records.**  British Jamaican record company formed in the 1960s and owned by Sonny *Roberts and Lloyd *Harley.

**Planno, Mortimer.**  Respected Rasta elder and spokesperson; one of the *Three Wise Men; spiritual mentor of Bob *Marley.

**Playing Cast.**  One of the two drums of *Kumina.  The Rasta *repeater drum resembles the playing cast.

**PNP.**  See *Peoples National Party.

**Poco-Yards.**  Open air yards in which *Pocomania is practiced.

**Pocomania.**  See *Pukkumina and *Kumina.

**Police.**  Internationally known British rock-reggae fusion band.

**Politricks.**  Rasta word for "politics."

**Polyrhythm.**  A characteristic common to African music in which more than one rhythm is maintained at any given time.  Polyrhythmic elements are used in reggae music.

**Pope.**  In Rastafari, the Pope is a symbol of white Western civilization, representing religious and political repression and the legacy of slavery.

**Porter, Keith.**  Lead vocalist for The *Itals.

**Pottinger, Sonia.**  Reggae producer, owner of *Tip Top Records and later of the *High Note label.  Part owner of the *Sky Note label.  Pottinger inherited *Treasure Isles Studios from her husband, Duke *Reid.

**PPP.**  See *Peoples Political Party.

**Priest, Maxi.**  Popular British Jamaican reggae vocalist (1980s). (D135)

**Prince Buster.**  See *Campbell, Cecil.

**Prince Far I.** See *Far I, Prince.

**Prince Jammy.** See *Jammy, Prince.

**Prince Jazzbo.** See *Jazzbo, Prince.

**Prince Lincoln.** See *Thompson, Lincoln.

**Prophet, Michael.** Jamaican vocalist.

**Pukkumina.** (Pocomania) African Jamaican Christian religion which developed out of the *Great Revival and is related to *Kumina.

**Putmon, Louis.** Keyboardist and lead vocalist with *House of Assembly.

# Q

**Quaco.** *Maroon captain under *Cudjoe. Quaco later supervised the *Treaty of 1738 between the British and the free *Maroons of Jamaica.

**Quadrille.** European ballroom set dance practiced by the Jamaican plantation class and later adopted and Africanized by African Jamaican slaves.

**Quasar.** Indiana based reggae band.

**Queen.** Rasta name for a female companion or mate.

**Queen Omega.** In Rasta, the counterpart of *King Alpha. The female aspect of *Jah.

**Queen of Sheba.** Egyptian queen who for Rasta symbolizes Africa and to whom Haile *Selassie claims to be a direct descendant.

# R

**Radio Jamaica Rediffusion (RJR).** One of Jamaica's two main radio stations.

**Rags.** See *Jamma songs.

**Randy's Records.** Well known reggae record shop on the Parade in downtown Kingston. (V26)

**Ranger, Lone.** Popular veteran Jamaican *deejay artist.

**Ranglin, Ernest.** Legendary Jamaican musician; consummate guitarist active since *ska's heydays.

**Ranglin, Michael.** Keyboardist with *Jah Malla; Ernest *Ranglin's son.

**Rankin, Louie.** Jamaican *deejay artist. (D182)

**Ranking Dread.** Jamaican *deejay artist.

**Ranking Taxi.** Japanese reggae *deejay artist. (V04)

**Ras.** 1. Ethiopian title (like "sir") adopted by many Rastas. 2. Used in Jamaican profanity, as in *ras clot.

**Ras Brass.** (Rass Brass) Horn section composed of Dean *Frazer (saxophone), Nambo *Robinson (trombone), and Junior "Chico" *Chin (trumpet).

**Ras Clot.** (Ras Claat) Common Jamaican and Rasta profanity. See *Bumba Clot and *Blood Clot.

**Ras Daniel Heartman.** See *Heartman, Ras Daniel.

**Ras Dizzy.** See *Dizzy, Ras.

**Ras-J Tesfa.** See *Tesfa, Ras-J.

**Ras Michael.** See *Ras Michael and The Sons of Negus.

**Ras Michael and The Sons of Negus.** Ras Michael and his various and many drummers are the most well known musicians playing and recording Rasta or *Nyabinghi music. For many years the group has offered distinctive, inspired hand drumming, chants, and *roots jazz fusion music. (D136-138;V05,V26)

**RAS Records.** (Real Authentic Sounds) Washington D.C. based reggae record company owned and operated by *Doctor Dread.

**Ras Tafari.** Another name for Haile *Selassie. "Ras" is an Ethiopian title and "Tafari" is Selassie's family name. It is from this name that Rastas titled their movement Rastafari.

**Rasta.** 1. A shortened name for Rastafari. 2. A name used to refer to Rastafari's members.

**Rasta Man.** A name used to refer to members of Rastafari.

**Rasta Music.** The essentially noncommercial religious drumming and chanting of Rastafari. It incorporates instruments and idioms of reggae and traditional jazz. See also *Nyabinghi.

**Rasta Talk.** (Dread Talk) The subcultural language of Rastafari which reflects the group's metaphysical and political world view. See *I-Words. See also B077, B082, B258-259, B313, B338.

**Rastafari.** Pronounced with a long "i" at the end and derived from Haile *Selassie's family name *Ras Tafari. Rastafari is the primary derivative of the word used by Rastas. Rastafarite, Rastafarian, and Rastafarianism are generally rejected by Rastas themselves as these terms connote a rigidity, dogmatism, and institutionalization negatively associated by Rastas with terms like "capital<u>ism</u>" or "commun<u>ism</u>." Rastafari is a social, cultural, political, and religious movement founded in Jamaica in 1930 and based in *Garvey's legacy, *Ethiopianism, Pan-Africanism, and Black Consciousness. On the surface, Rastafari is a religious-cultural movement which subscribes to the belief that Haile *Selassie is God reincarnated and which focuses on traditional African culture as well as a communal and natural life style. More important, Rastafari has functioned to create a new, positive identity for many African Jamaicans and, to a certain extent, has forced the Jamaican society and polity to confront their own African origins. Rastafari has spread worldwide since the late 1960s, primarily through the medium of reggae music.

**Rastafarian.** See *Rastafari.

**Rastafarian Melchizedek Orthodox Church.** Rasta organization led by Prince Edward *Emmanuel.

**Rastafarian Movement Association (RMA).** Well organized socially and politically active Rasta organization headquartered in Kingston. The RMA offers a liberal, more secular interpretation of Rastafari which allows work within the wider society rather than advocating cultural and social separatism. See B266.

**Rastafarian Repatriation Association (RRA).** One of a number of Rasta organizations, the RRA focuses on education about Ethiopia and African cultures. Led by the *Three Wise Men and sometimes called the *Mystic Revelation of Rastafari.

**Rastafarianism.** See *Rastafari.

**Rastafarite.**  See *Rastafari.

**Reasoning.**  Informal, but assertive discussion sessions in Rastafari emphasizing open dialectic on current issues, politics, culture, and religion.  Reasoning is a central practice within Rastafari.  See *grounation.

**Rebels.**  Colombian reggae band formed in 1982.

**Red Cloud.**  British reggae band.

**Reed, Altamont.**  An early spokesperson of the Rasta movement.

**Reggae.**  A genre of pop music indigenous to Jamaica which emerged around 1968 (Toots *Hibbert is said to have coined the word).  Its immediate precursors were *ska and *rock steady.  Reggae is an eclectic urban pop music influenced by rock and roll, rhythm and blues, soul, Latin American music, traditional Jamaican religious and secular music, and African musical idioms. Reggae is characterized primarily by its unique rhythmic structure in which beats two and four (in 4/4 time) are accented rather than beats one and three, and by its generally slow tempo.  The bass and drums maintain the relatively simple and clean rhythmic foundation in reggae, while other instruments serve a characteristically African role by offering further rhythmic and percussive elaboration. Reggae was conceived primarily as a recorded dance music, usually lyrical.  Variants of reggae music include *deejay music, *dancehall music, *rockers, *lovers rock, *dub music, *dub poetry, and *Rasta music.  When associated with Rastafari, the reggae rhythm is accompanied by socially, politically, culturally, and religiously critical lyrics and as such functions as a form of protest or resistance music. (B224)  Origins of the word "reggae" are unclear.  Some claim it is an onomatopoeia for the sound of the reggae rhythm guitar; others say it is derived from a kind of "sex-talk."  The most popular explanation is that the word means "raggedy," "everyday," or "from the people." (B092:45)

**Reggae Philharmonic Orchestra.**  Innovative British based reggae band (late 1980s) which combines reggae rhythms with jazz and classical music idioms. Includes Mykaell S. *Riley (vocals, drums); Ellen Blair, Johnny T., Steve Bradshaw, Simon Walker (violins); Faye Clinton (cello); Ellen Blair, Steve Bradshaw (violas); Sara Lowenthal (double bass); Yolisa Phahle, Deirdre Pascall (keyboards); Wayne Batchelor, Winston Blissett (bass guitars); Kushite (saxophone); Marc D'Aieur, Nick Page (acoustic guitars); Tim Atkins (drums), and others. (D140)

**Reggae Sunsplash.**  An annual international reggae festival held in Montego Bay, Jamaica.  The traditional site for Sunsplash is Jarrett Park, although the festival has periodically moved to the *Bob Marley Performing Arts Centre.  A major Jamaican tourist event, Sunsplash typically attracts a large international audience and from it a number of live festival albums and videocassettes have been produced. (D179;V02-04,V23-24)  See B218.

**Regulars.**  British reggae band of the early to mid 1970s.

**Reid, Duke.**  Veteran *soundsystem operator and Jamaican reggae producer. Reid was founder and owner of *Treasure Isle Studios.

**Reid, Junior.**  Vocalist with *Black Uhuru since the mid 1980s.

**Reid, Roy "I-Roy."**  Jamaican *deejay artist since 1970.  Sometimes accused of being an imitator of the famous *U-Roy. (D080)

**Reincarnation.**  An important concept in Rastafari derived from African as well as other traditional Eastern metaphysical systems.  Some Rastas specifically cite seventy-two reincarnations of *Jah, with *Selassie as the seventy-second. (B119:90)

**Religion.**  In Rasta, a suspect word associated with colonialism, slavery, and missionary attempts to appease and repress African Jamaicans.  Contemporary organized religion is met by Rastas with the same distain, as they feel the original intent of Christianity has been so distorted by political motives as to render it useless or harmful.

**Repairer of the Breach.**  Self styled title of Claudius *Henry.

**Repatriation.**  Physical repatriation of Africans to their home continent was an original demand of Rastafari.  Although some Rastas have relocated to Africa and others still desire repatriation, the term is now also associated with the desire to retrieve African traditions and culture, thereby Africanizing Jamaica. (B014:172)  See also B126, B159, B201, B235-236, B251, B339.

**Repeater.**  One of the three Rasta drums, the repeater functions as lead and is similar to the *Playing Cast in *Kumina and the *Akette in *Burru.

**Revival Religion.**  A general concept referring to the resurgence of African influenced religion in Jamaica after the *Great Revival.

**Revolution.**  In Rasta, revolution usually refers to a spiritual or metaphysical revolution rather than an armed struggle to replace one political system with another.

**Revolutionaries.**  A *Channel One studio band including Sly *Dunbar (drums), Robbie *Shakespeare (bass), and Ansell *Collins (keyboards). (D145)

**Rhumba Box.** A percussive instrument traditional to *Burru music and similar to the African kalimba or thumb piano.

**Rhygin.** (Rhyging) Nickname (which means "raging") for the legendary Jamaican rebel and gunman, Vincent *Martin, whose story is told in the film The Harder They Come. (V13)

**Rhythm Force.** One of several names the *Barrett brothers used as session musicians.

**Richards, Chip.** Promoter for *Trojan Records, part owner with Sonia *Pottinger of the *Sky Note record label.

**Richards, Michael "Boo."** Veteran and well known reggae drummer. Drummer with the reorganized *Wailers (late 1980s).

**Ricketts, Ferdinand.** A *Garveyite and one of several spokespersons of the early Rasta movement of the 1930s.

**Rick's Cafe.** Well known Negril hangout for musicians, Rastas, and travellers enamored with the movement and its music.

**Riddims.** Because the bass guitar functions as a percussive instrument in reggae music, bass lines are called "riddims" in reggae. (B092:53)

**Riddim Solo.** Rhythm tracks laid without horns and melody; a precursor to the development of *dub music.

**Riley, Jimmy.** Important reggae vocalist of the late 1960s. Early on Riley worked with the *Sensations, The *Uniques, and later as a solo artist.

**Riley, Mykaell S.** Lead vocalist, producer, and arranger for the *Reggae Philharmonic Orchestra. Also a founding member of *Steel Pulse.

**Rivals.** Jamaican band formed by Ansel *Smart in the early 1960s.

**RJR.** See *Radio Jamaica Rediffusion.

**Roberts, London Andres "Half Pint."** Popular and award winning Jamaican vocalist and songwriter.

**Roberts, Sonny.** Part owner of *Planitone Records.

**Robinson, Nambo.** Veteran Jamaican trombone player. Member of *Ras Brass.

**Robinson, Tony "Tony Gad."** Bassist for *Aswad.

**Rock Against Racism.** An organization working against racism which has promoted a number of punk and reggae concerts.

**Rock Steady.** (Rocksteady) An indigenous Jamaican pop music and relaxed dance rhythm which grew out of *ska in the mid 1960s. While the rhythm in rock steady is similar to that of ska, the tempo is slower and the lyrics are imbued more with social commentary. A precursor to reggae music.

**Rockers.** (Militant) A style of reggae music originated by *Sly and Robbie when, in the mid 1970s, Sly changed his drumming style from *one drop to an eight to the bar bass drum rhythm. The music felt faster in tempo due to the new high hat style, even though the overall tempo had slowed down somewhat.

**Rod of Correction.** The name Michael *Manley gave to a token gift from Haile *Selassie (a walking stick) which Manley used to court the Rasta population during the 1972 elections. See B318.

**Rodney, Walter.** An African studies scholar originally from Guyana. Rodney worked extensively in Jamaica in the 1960s to educate Rastas about African history from a materialist perspective. The message took hold for some Rastas who rejected sentimental notions of repatriation and *Selassie's divinity, and instead focused on practical political and social critiques and actions. For his powerful community teaching sessions or *groundings, Rodney was banned from Jamaica. (B053:128-133) See also B054, B273.

**Rodney, Winston "Burning Spear."** Rodney originally formed the Burning Spear band in 1968 as a vocal trio including harmony singers Rupert *Hines and Delroy *Wilmington, who later left the band. Spear has become an internationally recognized reggae artist known for his characteristic blues vocal style, his innovative compositions and arrangements, and his sincere allegiance to *roots music, historical analysis, and Black Consciousness themes. (D037-042;V02,V11,V15,V23)

**Rodriquez, Rico.** An accomplished Jamaican trombonist based in England. An *Alpha Boys School graduate who worked with *Count Ossie and The Mystic Revelation of Rastafari in the *Wareika Hills in the late 1950s and early 1960s. (D141)

**Roger, Cledwyn.** Rhythm guitarist with *Black Slate.

**Roland Alphonso's Alley Cats.** A studio band led by *Alphonso which was also known as The *Soul Brothers.

**Rome.** In Rasta, a pejorative symbol for modern day *Babylon. See also *Pope.

**Romeo, Max.** An important Jamaican reggae singer, Romeo first gained commercial success with sex and romance songs in the late 1960s, but later in the 1970s recorded important and controversial politically oriented reggae songs. (D142)

**Roots.** 1. A common Rasta term referring to things natural and emphasizing historical links with Africa, the legacy of slavery, and the African diaspora. 2. A nickname of affection for Rastas. 3. A Rasta greeting. 4. Reggae music which maintains an allegiance, both instrumentally and lyrically, to the roots concept.

**Roots Radics.** (Roots Raddics, Radix) Veteran and well known reggae session band composed of Errol "Flabba" *Holt (bass), Lincoln "Style" *Scott (drums), Eric "Bingy Bunny" *Lamont (guitar), and Stille *Johnson (keyboards). The Radics function as backing band for a variety of Jamaica's best vocalists.

**Rose, Michael.** Best known as the lead singer for *Black Uhuru, Rose left the band in the mid 1980s to pursue a solo career. More recently he has adopted the name Mykal Roze. (V17)

**Rotten, Johnny.** Leader of the British punk band, The Sex Pistols, whose work was influenced by reggae music.

**Roy, Congo Ashanti.** See *Johnson, Roydel.

**Royal Rasses.** Reggae harmony trio of the mid 1970s.

**Roze, Mykal.** See *Rose, Michael.

**Rub-A-Dub.** 1. A reggae rhythmic style which Davis and Simon say was developed by Sly *Dunbar in 1979-1980. The style is characterized by a tempo similar to *rock steady and a bass drum that plays off beats two and four. (B092:130) 2. A style of *deejay music. 3. A rather suggestive style of reggae dancing.

**Ruby, Jack.** Legendary Jamaican *soundsystem operator, studio owner, and record producer headquartered in Ocho Rios. (V26)

**Ruddock, Osborne "King Tubby."** Electrician, legendary veteran Jamaican *soundsystem engineer, and studio owner. King Tubby was a pioneer in the development and recording of *dub music.

**Rude Boys.** 1. Rough, rebellious youths who reacted to widespread political and economic tension in Jamaica in the 1950s-1960s by emulating Hollywood gangster characters. 2. Popular Jamaican music of the time which was influenced by and addressed the perspective of the rude boys. See B141-142, B330, B355.

**Rudie.** A nickname for *rude boys.

**Ruts.** A British reggae punk fusion band.

# S

**Sam Sharpe Rebellion.** One of the biggest slave rebellions in Jamaica (1831-1832). Led by Sam *Sharpe, it hastened emancipation in Jamaica.

**Sandii and The Sunsetz.** Japanese reggae vocalist and backing band. (D178;V04)

**Sassafras.** Deejay artist.

**Satta Massagana.** (Satta Amassagana, Satta Massegana) 1. A classic reggae song by the *Abyssinians. The title translates to "give thanks and praises." (D001) 2. Now a conventional rhythm used in reggae music.

**Schwartz, Jim.** Bassist with The *Majestics.

**Scorcher.** Jamaican *deejay artist.

**Science.** A Jamaican term referring to *Obeah.

**Scientist.** See *Brown, Overton.

**Scott, Lincoln "Style."** Legendary reggae drummer and member of The *Roots Radics.

**Scott-Heron, Gil.** An African American musician influenced by reggae music.

**Scrape-The-Earth Campaign.** A government initiated action (1966) to drive Rastas from West Kingston areas. *Back O' Wall was bulldozed as part of the campaign.

**Scully and Bunny.** Popular Jamaican vocalists of the rhythm and blues era.

**Seaga, Edward.** Anthropologist, record producer, leader of the *JLP, and former Prime Minister of Jamaica.

**Seen.** A Rasta word meaning "to know, to *overstand." It is often used as an interrogative tag word at the end of a sentence to ask, in essence, if the auditor comprehends what the speaker has said (eg. "It dread all over, seen?").

**Selah.** A Rasta word used at the end of prayers and psalms which functions as a substitute for "Amen."

**Selassie, Haile.** (Haile Selassie I) The name taken by Tafari *Makonnen, or *Ras Tafari when he was crowned emperor of Ethiopia in 1930. The coronation of Selassie was interpreted by some Jamaicans as a fulfillment of *Garvey's 1916 prophecy, thus causing the inception of the Rasta movement. In orthodox Rasta, Selassie is seen literally as a reincarnation of *Jah; in more secular and political Rasta circles, Selassie is seen as a symbol of African identity, pride, power, and self worth. See B022, B102, B156, B329, B361.

**Selecter.** A British punk reggae or *two-tone band.

**Selectra.** An independent British record distributor.

**Sensations.** A Jamaican stage show band.

**Sensimilla.** Another name for *herb or *ganja, especially high quality seedless herb.

**Set Girls.** Originally women dancers in Jamaica who entertained visiting military personnel. The Set Girl dance form later influenced the *Jonkonnu, diluting and secularizing it.

**Shaka Man.** A California based reggae vocalist and songwriter.

**Shakers.** A white, United States based reggae band.

**Shakespeare, Robbie.** Legendary, internationally famous reggae bassist. Best known for his work with drummer Sly *Dunbar. See also *Sly and Robbie.

**Shaka, Jah.** British producer and *soundsystem operator.

**Shakka.** (Shaka) A percussive instrument used in *Burru music.

**Shalet, Emile.** Founder of *Melodisc Records.

**Shanachie.** New Jersey based record label, originally focusing on Irish folk music. Shanachie began handling a variety of top reggae acts in 1980.

**Sharpe, George.** See *Liele, George.

**Sharpe, Samuel.** A charismatic African Jamaican slave from Montego Bay who was the principal leader in the *Sam Sharpe Rebellion.

**Shashemane.** (Shashamani; Sheshemani) A farm at Shashemane, Ethiopia given to the *Ethiopian World Federation by Haile *Selassie. It is a religious commune which several Jamaican Rastas have settled in, and it has been visited by various reggae artists. See B186.

**Shaw, Donald "Tabby."** Lead singer of The *Mighty Diamonds.

**Sheba, Queen.** Ancient Egyptian queen to whom *Selassie claimed to be a direct descendant.

**Sheiks, The.** A Jamaican band (circa 1960s) composed of Dobbie *Dobson, Lloyd *Spence, Jackie *Mittoo, Tony *DaCosta, and others.

**Shelley, Count.** See *Barrett, Ephraim.

**Shelley Records.** A British record label formed by Count *Shelley in the early 1970s.

**Shinehead.** A *deejay *dancehall artist based in New York.

**Shoenfield, Robert.** Part owner of *Nighthawk Records.

**Sibbles, Leroy.** (Leroy Sibblas) A popular and famous Jamaican reggae vocalist, Sibbles originally was lead singer for The *Heptones, leaving the band in the late 1970s to pursue a solo career. (D143;V05,V27)

**Simms, Danny.** (Danny Sims) U.S. born music promoter and business partner with Johnny *Nash. Simms was part owner (with Nash) of the *JAD label.

**Simms, Zoot "Skully."** Jamaican percussionist.

**Simon, Paul.** A United States folk rock singer influenced by reggae music in the 1970s.

**Simon, Tito.** British reggae artist of the 1970s.

**Simpson, Derek "Duckie."** Harmony vocalist with *Black Uhuru.

**Simpson, Fitzroy "Bunny."** Harmony vocalist with The *Mighty Diamonds.

**Sinclair, Charles "Tower."** Bassist with *Messenjah.

**Sip.** A Rasta word referring to the act of smoking *herb or *ganja, particularly from a *chalice or *chillum (eg. "sip your cup").

**Sir Cavalier's Combo.** Another name under which The *Soul Brothers worked.

**Sir Lord Comic.** A Jamaican *deejay artist whose mentor was Count *Machouki.

**Sistren.** A Rasta term for women as well as a term for Rasta women. Sistren's usage is both singular and plural and is the counterpart of the Rasta word *bredren. 2. A Jamaican Rasta women's organization. Sistren operates theatre and textile collectives.

**Ska.** The first commercial indigenous pop music of Jamaica. Ska developed in the 1950s and incorporated elements of *mento, boogie woogie, and rhythm and blues to form a people's music at first rejected by middle and upper class Jamaicans. A precursor to reggae music.

**Ska Kings.** Name used early on by Byron *Lee and The Dragonaires.

**Skank.** Reggae dance. With various nuances (defiance, confidence, sensuality, etc.), the skank focuses primarily on expression of the drum and bass line. Louise *Bennett associates it with the "weak-kneed" *yanga step indicative of mento dancing. (B163:47,B224:152-160)

**Skatalites.** (1963-1965) Legendary *ska band consisting of Jamaica's finest musicians, many of whom had studied at the *Alpha Boys School and had already become famous jazz musicians. The band consisted of Tommy *McCook (tenor sax), Roland *Alphonso (tenor sax), Lester *Stirling (alto sax), Don *Drummond (trombone), Johnny "Dizzy" *Moore (trumpet), Jah *Gerry (guitar), Lloyd *Brevette (bass), Lloyd *Knibbs (drums), and Lord *Tanamo and Tony *DaCosta (vocals). (D144;V27)

**Sheiks.** Jamaican band of the early 1960s which included Jackie *Mittoo, Tony *DaCosta, and others.

**Skin, Flesh, and Bone.** A Jamaican road band and backing band formed by Lloyd *Parkes. (D174)

**Sky Note.** A Jamaican record label owned by Sonia *Pottinger and Chip *Richards.

**Slide and Slur.** An African musical technique used in reggae.

**Slim and The Uniques.** A locally popular Jamaican vocal group of the 1970s.

**Slits.** A punk band influenced by reggae music.

**Sly and Robbie.** Drummer Sly *Dunbar and bassist Robbie *Shakespeare, according to many authors and reggae fans, are the definitive personification of reggae music. The most famous rhythmic foundation in reggae history, Sly and Robbie also record their own solo albums and work with the finest musicians in a variety of pop music genres around the world. (D145-146)

**Small, Minnie.** A popular Jamaican singer with the international hit "My Boy Lollipop" in 1964. Small was part of the group of musicians who represented Jamaica at the 1964 World's Fair in New York City.

**Smart, Ansel.** Founder of The *Rivals.

**Smart, Leroy.** Popular Jamaican reggae vocalist. See B130.

**Smile Jamaica.** A free concert in Kingston at the National Stadium on December 5, 1976, planned by Bob *Marley. Marley was able to perform at the concert even though he had been shot by intruders at his home on Hope Road at the beginning of that week. (B357:287)

**Smiley, Emillo.** Harmony vocalist with *Foundation.

**Smiley, General.** See *Michigan and Smiley.

**Smith, Carlton.** Member of The *Tamlins.

**Smith, Cherry.** Background vocalist with The *Teenagers.

**Smith, Dennis "Alcapone."** Part owner of the *soundsystem "El Paso" in the 1960s; Jamaican *deejay artist.

**Smith, Earl "Chinna."** Legendary reggae guitarist. One of the finest reggae musicians in Jamaica, Smith has worked with a myriad of musicians and bands, including *Bob Marley and The Wailers.

**Smith, Malachi.** Jamaican *deejay and *dub poet. (D184)

**Smith, Michael "Mickey."**  A brilliant Jamaican *dub poet whose political poetry was highly controversial.  Smith was murdered on the streets of Kingston in 1983.  (D147;B308-311)  See B254.

**Smith, Oliver.**  *Dub poet. (D184)

**Smith, Patti.**  Rock singer and rock group influenced by reggae music.

**Smith, Slim.**  Jamaican ballad singer of the *rock steady era; leader of The *Uniques.

**Smith, Vivian.**  Jamaican vocalist and member of The *Deccas.

**Smith, Warren.**  Head of *Epiphany Records.

**Smith, Wayne.**  Jamaican vocalist popular since the mid 1980s.

**Solar System Band.**  Backing band for Alpha *Blondy.

**Solomon, King.**  Ancient Ethiopian king to whom *Selassie claimed to be a direct descendant.

**Solomonic Records.**  Bunny *Wailer's record label.

**Solution.**  Colombian reggae band.

**Sonia.**  A British *lovers rock artist.

**Sonic Sound.**  Jamaican record company owned by Neville *Lee.

**Sons of Jah.**  British reggae band of the 1970s.

**Soon Come.**  A well known Jamaican saying which indicates that something will occur at an undetermined time in the future.

**Soul Brothers.**  Studio band led by Roland *Alphsono and formed by Coxsone *Dodd immediately after The *Skatalites broke up in 1965.  Later it was directed by Jackie *Mittoo.

**Soul Defenders.**  One of *Coxsone's studio bands.

**Soul Mates.**  One of several names under which The *Barrett brothers did session work. (D174)

**Soul Syndicate.** Veteran Jamaican road and session band. Composed of leader Earl "Chinna" *Smith (guitar), Carlton "Santa" *Davis (drums), George "Fully" *Fullwood (bass), and Tony *Chin (guitar).

**Soul Vendors.** (Soul Vendours) Another name used by The *Soul Brothers. (D180)

**Soulettes.** A vocal group formed by Rita Anderson *Marley early on which included Constantine "Dream" *Walker and Marlene "Precious" *Gifford.

**Soundsystem.** (Sound System) Mobile discotheques which first appeared in Jamaica after World War II. The soundsystems are a vitally important institution in Jamaican pop music. While the systems originally played North American music and rhythm and blues, the American move to rock and roll in the 1950s pressured the system operators to promote local talent (since the Jamaican audiences were not taken with rock, the operators were forced to look closer to home for material). Hence, tense competition among systems in large part influenced the development of *ska, *rock steady, and reggae. The systems also served to establish important producers, sound engineers, and *deejay artists.

**Special AKA.** See *Specials.

**Specials.** 1. Rhythm track recordings used in *soundsystem competitions or clashes. 2. A British punk reggae fusion or *two-tone band. Early on called the Special AKA.

**Spence, Cecil "Skeleton."** Vocalist with *Israel Vibration.

**Spence, Lloyd.** Jamaican bassist who has worked with The *Sheiks, The *Soul Brothers, etc.

**Spliff.** Name for the large *herb or *ganja cigarettes characteristic in Jamaica.

**Sporty, King.** Early Jamaican *deejay artist who worked with *Coxsone/Downbeat.

**Stackman, Ron.** Keyboardist with The *Majestics.

**Star of David.** Judaic symbol adopted by Rastas due to their belief that they are the true Israelites. (B120:76-78)

**Steel Pulse.** Internationally successful British based reggae band founded in 1972. Originally composed of leader David *Hinds (lead vocals, guitar), Basil

*Gibbidom (lead guitar, vocals), and Ronnie *McQueen (bass). Steel Pulse now also includes Selwyn "Bumbo" *Brown (vocals, keyboards), Phonso *Martin (vocals, percussion), Steve "Grizzly" *Nisbett (drums), and Alvin *Ewen (bass). (D148-150,D179;V02,V12,V24)

**Steir, Tony.** Keyboardist with The *Twinkle Brothers.

**Sterling, Keith.** Reggae keyboardist.

**Sterling, Michael.** Lead guitarist for the newly reorganized *Inner Circle.

**Steward, Elbert.** Member of The *Cables.

**Stewart, Anita.** *Dub poet. (D183)

**Stewart, Willie.** Drummer for *Third World.

**Sting.** See *Sumner, Gordon.

**Stirling, Lester.** Alto saxophonist for The *Skatalites. (D174)

**Stitch, Jah.** *Deejay artist.

**Stitchie, Lt.** See *Laing, Cleveland.

**Stitt, King.** Jamaican *deejay artist of the late 1950s and the 1960s who worked with *Coxsone/Downbeat.

**Stoddard, Vincent.** Member of The *Cables.

**Strawberry Hill.** An old estate in the Blue Mountains outside Kingston which is owned by Chris *Blackwell and was frequented by Bob *Marley and other musicians.

**Studio One.** A dominant Jamaican recording studio in the 1960s. Owned by Clement *Dodd, Studio One has been vitally important to the history and development of reggae music.

**Sufferer Sound.** A British *blues dance sound engineer.

**Sumner, Gordon "Sting."** Influenced significantly by reggae music, Sting is the leader of the British rock fusion band *Police.

**Sunsplash.** See *Reggae Sunsplash.

**Supersonics.** Band formed by Tommy *McCook after The *Skatalites disbanded in 1965.

**Suru Board.** The wooden board upon which Rastas prepare *herb or *ganja for the *chalice.

**Sutherland, Dallimore.** Vocalist with The *Gladiators.

**Sutherland, Nadine.** Jamaican reggae vocalist who was a protege of Bob *Marley.

**Sutherland, Trevor "I Jah Man Levi."** British Jamaican reggae rock musician. (D076)

**Swaby, Horace "Augustus Pablo."** Distinctive and successful keyboardist and melodica player who works solely in the *dub genre. (D131-132,D174)

**Sweet, Roslyn.** Vocalist with The *Paragons.

**Swelele.** United States based reggae band.

**Swinging Cats.** British punk reggae or *two-tone band.

# T

**Tabla.** East Indian percussive instrument sometimes used in *Pukkumina drumming.

**Tacky.** A *Coromantee slave in Jamaica and leader of *Tacky's Rebellion in the sixteenth century.

**Tacky's Rebellion.** Jamaican rebellion in 1760 involving over one thousand slaves and led by *Tacky. The results of the rebellion included the death of Tacky and the murder or suicide of some three to six hundred slaves.

**Talking Drums.** African drums used in Jamaica by the slave population to communicate messages among themselves in secret. Realizing the power of the drums, the British banned talking drums, threatening a death sentence to violators.

**Tam.** Knitted hats (similar to berets, but larger) often in Rasta colors of red, green, and gold. Worn originally by *dreadlocked Rastas to conceal their locks when moving within the larger Jamaican society. Today, tams are more a matter of style for many.

**Tamlins.** Popular Jamaican harmony trio since 1968. Originally composed of Junior *Moore, Carlton *Smith, and Winston *Morgan. Morgan was later replaced by Derrick *Lara. (D151)

**Tanamo, Lord.** See *Gordon, Joseph.

**Taylor, Don.** Bob *Marley's personal manager.

**Taylor, Otis.** Reggae coordinator for *Flying Fish Records.

**Taylor, Tyrone.** Jamaican vocalist best known for his hit "Cottage in Negril."

**Techniques.** Jamaican group of the *rock steady period.

**Teenagers.** *Trench Town vocal group formed early on by Bunny *Wailer, Peter *Tosh, Junior *Braithwaite, Beverly *Kelso, and Cherry *Smith.

**Tenor Saw.** Jamaican vocalist first popular in 1985.

**Ten Point Moral Code.** List written by Sam *Brown explicating the doctrine of Rasta. (B014:148-150,B043)

**Tenrew, Henry.** Tenor saxophonist with *Matumbi.

**Tenrew, Patrick.** Trumpet player with *Matumbi.

**Terrorists.** New York based white reggae band.

**Tesfa, Ras-J.** Rasta poet, writer, actor, and singer based in New York. (D139;B325)

**Tetrack.** Harmony trio first popular in the late 1980s.

**Third World.** An internationally acclaimed reggae rock fusion band. First formed in 1973 by former *Inner Circle members Michael *Cooper and Stephen *Coore. Highly popular and well known for its creative arrangements and sophisticated, professional musicianship. Third World is composed of Bunny "Rugs" *Clarke (lead vocals), Michael "Ibo" *Cooper (keyboards), Stephen "Cat" *Coore (lead guitar), Willie *Stewart (drums), Richard *Daley (bass), and Irvin "Carrot" *Jarrett (percussion). (D152-157,D179,D181;V02,V11,V15,V23-24,V26)

**Third World Records.** British record company formed by Count *Shelley after his earlier *Shelley Records went out of business.

**Thomas, Elaine.** *Dub poet. (D183)

**Thomas, Euston.** Harmony vocalist with *Foundation.

**Thomas, Jah.** Jamaican *deejay artist.

**Thomas, Nicky.** Reggae artist who recorded for *Trojan Records.

**Thompson, Carroll.** British *lovers rock vocalist.

**Thompson, Errol "Errol T."** One of the finest *dub engineers and producers in Jamaica. Early on Thompson hosted a Rasta oriented radio show, *Culture Corner, which was initiated by Bob *Marley. Thompson engineers for *Joe Gibbs Studio.

**Thompson, Lincoln "Prince Lincoln."** Jamaican reggae vocalist.

**Thompson, Linval.** Jamaican vocalist.

**Thompson, Orvin.** Keyboardist and vocalist with *Ipso Facto.

**Thompson, Uzziah "Sticky."** Veteran Jamaican reggae percussionist.

**Thompson, Winston James "Doctor Alimantado."** Jamaican *deejay who began recording in the late 1960s.

**Three Wise Men.** Name for the Rasta delegation included in Jamaica's 1961 *Mission to Africa. The Three Wise Men (Mortimo *Planno, Douglas *Mack, and Filmore *Alvaranga) filed their own minority report. See B004.

**Tiger.** *Deejay artist.

**Tip Top Records.** Sonia *Pottinger's record label.

**Toasting.** A *deejay art form which transformed the role of the deejay from one who plays records to one who plays an important creative role in *soundsystem and *dancehall music. Thought to have been originated by deejay Count *Machouki, toasting refers to the deejay talking or chanting over the recorded music at soundsystem dances.

**Tomlin, Ellis.** *Dub poet. (D184)

**Toots and The Maytals.** Led by blues soul vocalist Toots *Hibbert, the band is known internationally for its enduring and foundational role in the development of Jamaican pop music. Originally singing spirituals and then *ska, Toots is also credited for coining the term "reggae" with his 1968 song "Do the Reggay." Toots and The Maytals have survived the various phases through which Jamaican music has developed to become a classic and legendary reggae band. (D158-159,D175;V03,V11-12,V15,V22,V26)

**Tosh, Peter.** See *McIntosh, Winston Hubert.

**Tradition.** British reggae band of the 1970s.

**Treasure Isle Records and Studio.** Duke *Reid's recording studio and company. Later Sonia *Pottinger took over the business.

**Treaty of 1738.** (Blood Treaty) The treaty between the free *Maroons of Jamaica and the British government in which the Maroons were granted some fifteen hundred acres of land and some superficial political autonomy. Yet, under the treaty's terms, the Maroons became mercenary forces required to capture runaway slaves for the British. Hence, the treaty tainted the Maroons' image as freedom fighters and revolutionaries. (B014:34-36)

**Trench Town.** West Kingston ghetto in which many Rastas settled and where many of Jamaica's musicians (including *Marley) began their careers.

**Trinity.** See *Brummer, Wade.

**Trod.** Rasta word meaning "to walk, to travel, to move forward (physically or spiritually)."

**Trojan Records.** A major British reggae record company formed by Chris *Blackwell and Lee *Goptal in 1968.

**Tubby, King.** See *Ruddock, Osborne.

**Tucker, Jimmy.** A popular Jamaican singer of the rhythm and blues era.

**Tucker, Sharon.** Member of *Light of Love.

**Tuff Gong.** *Marley's record label, deriving its name from his *Trench Town nickname. Tuff Gong is a multi-million dollar third world recording company.

**Tuff, Tony.** Jamaican vocalist.

**Tulloch, Joy.** Member of *Light of Love.

**Twelve Tribes of Israel.** A hierarchically organized Rasta organization founded in *Trench Town by Vernon *Carrington in 1968. See B130, B186.

**Twenty-One Families.** Refers to an old Jamaican story that twenty-one families hold all the economic and political power in Jamaica. See B357:84-85 for a list of the family names.

**Twenty-One Points.** Campaign platform of Sam *Brown in 1964 which represents a further elaboration of his earlier *Ten Point Moral Code. (B014:148-149)

**Twi.** Language of the *Ashanti from which many Jamaican *patois words are derived.

**Twinkle Brothers.** Self contained *roots reggae band heavily influence by Rasta and based in the northcoast town of Falmouth. Composed of Norman *Grant (lead vocals), Derrick *Brown (bass), Ralston *Grant (rhythm guitar), John *Wheatley (drums), Tony *Steir (keyboards), Bongo *Asher (percussion), Aston *Grant (lead guitar), and Karl *Hyatt (percussion). (D165-166;V03)

**Two-Tone.** A fusion music incorporating elements of *ska, reggae, rock, and punk, and developed by British musicians in the 1970s.

**Tyson, Delvin.** Vocalist with *Misty In Roots.

**Tyson, Wolford.** Lead vocalist with *Misty In Roots.

# U

**UB40.** Prolific and slick British reggae band. UB40, named after the British unemployment benefits form number, began its recording career with creative original compositions blending reggae and British urban influences. More recently, the band has concentrated on reggae and *deejay versions of pop songs. (D167-170;V17)

**U-Brown.** *Deejay artist.

**Undivided.** A British reggae band of the 1970s.

**UNIA.** See *Universal Negro Improvement Association.

**Uniques.** A Jamaican *rock steady and reggae band led by singer Slim *Smith.

**Universal Convention.** Name of the first islandwide Rasta *grounation held in *Back O' Wall in March, 1958. To force a confrontation with the police, Rastas then converged on *Victoria park in a symbolic capture of Kingston. They were eventually removed by the police.

**Universal Negro Improvement Association (UNIA).** Organization established in Jamaica by Marcus *Garvey in January of 1914. Later Garvey introduced the organization to African Americans in New York. Popularly called the *Back-to-Africa movement, Garvey's work with the UNIA served to uplift the self-image of Africans around the globe.

**Upsetter.** A nickname for Lee *Perry.

**Upsetters.** Lee *Perry's studio band. (D174;V26)

**Upsetter Records.** Record company founded by Lee *Perry in the late 1960s.

**U-Roy.** See *Beckford, Ewart.

**UWI Report.** Refers to the 1960 University of West Indies report on the Rastafarian movement requested by Rastas, written by UWI scholars M.G. Smith, Rex Nettleford, and Roy Augier, and submitted to the government. The report did much to erode the then widespread negative perception of Rastas as criminally insane. The authors' recommendations facilitated some improvements in treatment of Rastas by the government and society in general. (B307)

# V

**V-Rocket.** Jamaican *soundsystem operator.

**Velez, Martha.** U.S. rock singer who worked with Bob *Marley in 1975.

**Venn, Gladstone.** Vocalist with *Matumbi.

**Version.** In Jamaican music, the flip or "B" side of a single record. The version side is a *dub instrumental of whatever lyrical recording is on the "A" side. Versions played an important role in the development of *deejay and *dub music.

**Viceroys.** Jamaican harmony trio who first recorded in the late 1960s.

**Virgin Records.** British record label which handles reggae.

**Vision.** See *Walker, Constantine.

**Vulcan/Grounation Records.** British reggae label.

# W

**Wail'N'Soul'M.'** *Wailing Souls (*Wailers) record label from 1967-1970. See Leroy Pierson's discography of the label in <u>Reggae and African Beat</u>, 7, 3, 1988: 10-11/57-58.

**Wailer, Bunny.** See *Livingston, Neville O'Riley.

**Wailers.** (Wailing Wailers, Wailing Rude Boys, The Teenagers) Foundational and legendary reggae band originally composed of Bob *Marley, Bunny *Wailer, Peter *Tosh, Junior *Braithwaite, Beverly *Kelso, and Cherry *Smith (early 1960s). In the mid 1960s the group was reduced for a time to the classic Marley-Wailer-Tosh trio. Later, various musicians were added and, in 1975, Wailer and Tosh left the band. By this time, and sometimes earlier, the band used the name *Bob Marley and The Wailers. See personnel listed under *Bob Marley and The Wailers. More recently at least two reorganized Wailers bands have emerged. (D129,D194-195)

**Wailers Band.** See *Wailers.

**Wailing Rude Boys.** See *Wailers.

**Wailing Souls.** *Roots reggae harmony quartet together since the 1960s, but more popular since the early 1980s. Composed of Winston "Pipe" *Matthews (lead vocals), Lloyd "Bread" *McDonald (harmony vocals), George "Buddy" *Haye (harmony vocals), and Rudolph "Garth" *Dennis (harmony vocals). See also *Pipe and The Pipers. (D196-197)

**Wailing Wailers.** See *Wailers.

**Wales, Jose.** Popular Jamaican *deejay artist. (V04)

**Walker, Albert.** Harmony vocalist with *Culture.

**Walker, Bagga.** Reggae bassist.

**Walker, Constantine "Dream."** (Constantine "Vision" Walker)  Member of The *Soulettes.

**Wallace, Leroy "Horsemouth."** Legendary and distinctive reggae drummer and star of the reggae movie Rockers. (D181;V25)

**Wallace, Mickey.** Bassist and percussionist with *Chalice.

**Walsh, Eric "Babyface."** Guitarist with *Messenjah.

**Wareika Hills.** Location of *Brother Issie Boat's Rasta Camp, later *Count Ossie's home. Many fine musicians worked together at Wareika Hills in the early 1960s.

**Washington, Delroy.** British reggae artist.

**Watson, Winston "Mighty Dread."** Harmony vocalist with The *Meditations.

**Waul, Franklyn "Bubbler."** Reggae keyboardist and bassist.

**We The People.** Reggae backing band led by bassist Lloyd *Parkes.

**Webber, David.** Vocalist with The *Gladiators.

**Welbourne, Malcolm.** Guitarist and vocalist with The *Killer Bees.

**Welch, Tony.** *PNP ghetto representative and friend of Bob *Marley who, with Marley and Bucky *Marshall, negotiated a peace pact between the PNP and the *JLP and planned the *One Love Peace Concert.

**Wellington, Morris "Blacka Morwell."** Founding member of The *Morwells.

**Wheatley, John.** Drummer with The *Twinkle Brothers.

**Whoosh, Jah.** *Deejay artist.

**Wicked and Wild.** A popular Jamaican saying in the mid to late 1980s used to express appreciation for and satisfaction with a song or a band's performance.

**Williams, Michael.** Bassist with *Zap Pow.

**Williams, Oswald "Count Ossie."** Foundational and legendary *Nyabinghi drummer. The late Count Ossie worked with and influenced numerous drummers and other musicians in Kingston and in the *Wareika Hills. As leader of The *Mystic Revelation of Rastafari, Ossie was one of the first and few Rasta drummers to record Nyabinghi music. Ossie also worked to establish and maintain African and Rasta culture in Jamaica. (D127)

**Wilmington, Delroy.** Harmony singer with the original *Burning Spear group.

**Wilson, Delroy.** Popular Jamaican singer since the 1960s. Best known for his *PNP campaign theme song "Better Must Come" (1971). (V10)

**Wilson, Roy.** Part of the singing duo *Higgs and Wilson.

**Wisdom Weed.** A Rasta phrase referring to *herb or *ganja.

**Woman/Women.** See *Man/Men.

**Wonder, Stevie.** African American musician and international superstar influenced by reggae music.

**Wong, Dickie.** Jamaican record producer.

**Wong, Orlando "Oku Onuora."** Jamaican social and political activist. While in jail in the early 1970s, Orlando began writing poetry and has become a talented and well known *dub poet. (D128;B246)

**Word Sound and Power.** (Word Sound Have Power, Word Sound Is Power) 1. A saying or trinity in Rasta representing the belief that the Word is God; hence, words are the greatest form of power. 2. A session band and backing band for Peter *Tosh.

**World Beat.** Currently used to refer to eclectic forms of international pop music which incorporate elements of various musical idioms worldwide, especially African or Latin American idioms.

**Wright, Delroy.** Jamaican record producer.

**Wright, Gladstone.** Reggae keyboardist.

**Wright, Winston.** Reggae keyboardist and session musician. Has worked with The *Supersonics, The *Sheiks, Byron *Lee, and others.

**Wynter, Ian.** Reggae keyboardist.

# X

**Xaymaca.** *Arawak name for Jamaica meaning "Isle of the Spring."

# Y

**Yabby You.** See *Jackson, Vivian.

**Yanga.** A dipping dance step in *mento which Louise *Bennett links to reggae dancing.

**Yard.** 1. In Jamaica, a reference to a person's home or yard. 2. In Rasta, a location where Rastas gather for ritual purposes. 3. For Jamaicans and Rastas living abroad, "yard" simply refers to Jamaica.

**Yates, Haile.** Percussionist with *Messenjah.

**Yellowman.** See *Foster, Winston.

**You, Yabby.** See *Jackson, Vivian.

**Youth Consciousness.** A Christmas night concert at the National Stadium in Kingston (1982). Historically important as the first live performance by Bunny *Wailer since he left *Bob Marley and The Wailers in 1975.

**Yukon, Howard.** Member of *Blue Riddim Band.

# Z

**Zap Pow.** Horn section formed in 1970 by David *Madden and Dwight *Pinkney. Works primarily in recording sessions, but has occasionally recorded as a band. Known for their experimental music. Composed of David *Madden (trumpet), Dwight *Pinkney (guitar), Glen *DaCosta (tenor sax), Michael *Williams (bass), Cornell *Marshall (drums), and Beres *Hammond (vocals). (D174)

**Zephaniah, Benjamin.** British *dub poet.

**Ziggy Marley and The Melody Makers.** Name used by The *Melody Makers subsequent to the release of their debut album. (D200;V28)

**Zion.** (Mt. Zion) Geographic center and symbol of Rasta spirituality, Rastas believe the true Zion is located in Ethiopia, not Jerusalem. (B120:76-78) See B382.

**Zion Revival.** One of two African Christian groups born out of the *Great Revival. Zion Revival maintains strong ties to Christianity, but incorporates traditional African ritual drumming and dancing.

**Zohn, Bob.** The late Bob Zohn was leader and lead vocalist with *Blue Riddim Band.

**Zukie, Tapper.** Jamaican *deejay, working mostly out of England.

**ANANCY**

# Annotated Discography

**D001**  The Abyssinians.  <u>Forward</u>.  Alligator, AL-8305, 1982.

This is the most accessible long playing recording of a crucially important roots reggae vocal trio.  Backed here by a litany of reggae's best musicians (including Sly Dunbar, Robbie Shakespeare, Earl "Chinna" Smith, Leroy "Horsemouth" Wallace, Leroy Sibbles, and Lloyd Parkes), this album includes the Abyssinians' original roots classic: "Satta Massagana."  "Satta," along with its dub version, "Mabrak," incorporates Rasta metaphysical images and the now classic chorus in Amharic.  "Satta Massagana" has since been recorded in various versions by a number of reggae artists.  All arrangements here exude a rather mystical quality indicative of the band's style.  Some tracks include snatches of exemplar early dub.

**D002**  Alpha Blondy.  <u>Apartheid is Nazism</u>.  Shanachie, 43042, 1987.

The new international reggae superstar from the Ivory Coast offers a first class production here with moving backup by his Solar System Band and brilliant compositions by Blondy sung in French, Mandingue, English, Dioula, and patois.  Superb reggae arrangements and backing lyrics in African languages form a stunning combination.  The French piece, "Jah Houphouet," is nostalgic of The Wailers, particularly Marley's "So Jah Seh." (D028)  Solar System, particularly lead guitarists Yao Mao and Christian Polloui, serve up unbeatable rockers on "Kiti."

**D003**  Alpha Blondy.  <u>Jerusalem</u>.  Shanachie, 43054, 1988.

Reggae journalist Stephen Davis and others have compared Alpha Blondy to Bob Marley.  Indeed, upon listening to the classic Wailers' backing in this album and in <u>Cocody Rock</u> (Shanachie, 64011, 1988) combined with Blondy's brilliant compositions and charismatic vocals, it is tempting to make the comparison.  Framed in classic and sophisticated reggae, the expression consistently is sincere, committed, and exciting. Recorded at Tuff Gong. A collector's item for those charting the cutting edge fusion of pop and folk musics into innovative international forms.

**D004** Amazulu. Amazulu. Mango, MLPS-9805, 1986.

A slick and engaging pop reggae rock album by this British female harmony trio. Distinctive, powerful vocals and interesting high energy arrangements. Mostly contains songs of romance. Includes "Excitable," "Montego Bay," "Cairo," "Upright, Forward," and others. Songs produced by Christopher Neil, Dennis Bovell, Andy Hill, and others.

**D005** Andy, Bob. Bob Andy's Song Book. Studio One, SOL-1121, n.d.

Compiled by Coxsone, this album contains twelve early recordings by the immensely popular and award winning Jamaican singer and songwriter, Bob Andy. Includes "Desperate Lover," "Life Could Be a Symphony," "I've Got to Go Back Home," "Going Home," "Let Them Say," and others. All songs written by Bob Andy. A collector's item.

**D006** Andy, Bob. Restrospective. Heartbeat, HB-32, 1987.

Veteran reggae musicians and fans are apt to name Bob Andy as "the best" or "one of the best" vocalists in Jamaica. Originally associated with the rock steady era, Andy's soulful vocals as well as his crisp lyrics of simple truths are well represented in this more recent album.

**D007** Andy, Horace. Best of Horace Andy. Studio One, SOLP-5565 (disc is stamped SOL-5555), n.d.

This Studio One production includes twelve songs by the veteran and highly popular Jamaican vocalist, Horace Andy. It illustrates Andy's soprano vocals and includes pop songs ("I Can See Clearly Now," "Knock three Times") as well as "Conscious Dreadlocks," "Born in The Ghetto," and others. Produced by Clement Dodd.

**D008** Aswad. Aswad. Mango, MLPS-9399, 1976.

A good roots reggae debut album by Aswad. Includes some fine early style dub elements (for example, "Red Up") prior to the band's later electronic sophistication. "Ethiopian Rhapsody" is a superb instrumental piece featuring harmonica, piano, and beautiful melodic folk guitar. "Back to Africa" is also a pretty tune with delightful harmony vocals and keyboard. Some moments are uninspiring, but it is interesting to compare this early work with Aswad's more recent, upbeat, soul infused sound. For example, compare their original version of "I A Rebel Soul" here with their later version on <u>Rebel Souls</u> (Mango, MLPS-9780, 1984).

**D009**  Aswad.  <u>Distant Thunder</u>.  Mango, MLPS-9810, 1988.

Professional, precise, and generally strong.  Plays with a mix of roots reggae and rhythm and blues more so than in the previous <u>Rebel Souls</u> (Mango, MLPS-9780, 1984).  Except for traditional bass and drum heavy rockers in songs like "I Can't Get Over You," "Tradition," and "Justice," other cuts blend rhythm and blues with reggae rhythms to create romantic, lilting dance tunes like "Feelings." In "The Message" Aswad incorporates energetic jazz elements  while "Give a Little Love" flirts with calypso.

**D010**  Aswad.  <u>Live and Direct</u>.  Mango, MLPS-9723, 1983.

An energetic collage of Aswad's many styles recorded live at the 1983 Notting Hill Gate carnival in England.  Smooth rockers on side one, particularly in the last two cuts ("Roots Rocking" and "Drum and Bass Line"), give way to an interesting assortment of styles on side two which includes a soca number, two heavy rockers cuts, and a delightful medley of classic dancehall pieces.

**D011**  Banton, Pato.  <u>Never Give In</u>.  Greensleeves, GREL-108, 1987.

Banton's fundamental deejay style mirrors conventional patterns used by Jamaican artists of this time, but he expands the boundaries of the genre by incorporating elements of dub poetry and melodic singing.  Creative and finely arranged reggae rhythms and consistently worthwhile lyrics also enhance Banton's work.  Includes "Absolute Perfection," "My Opinion," "Pato and Roger Come Again" (with Ranking Roger), "Hello Tosh," and others.  Backed by the Studio Crew and the Ever Ready Horn section.  Backing vocals by Venus. Recorded and mixed at Sine Wave Studio.

**D012**  Bennett, Louise.  <u>"Yes M' Dear"--Miss Lou Live</u>.  Island, n.n., 1983.

Louise Bennett's Jamaican folk poetry in patois paved the way for later dub poets.  This, her first live album, was recorded by Richard Digby Smith live at the Lyric Theatre in London for Imani Music and includes an introduction by Linton Kwesi Johnson.

**D013**  Big Youth.  <u>A Lluta Continua</u>.  Heartbeat, HB-28 (44142), 1985.

A superb recent album with backing vocals by Leroy Sibbles and The Tamlins. Illustrates well Big Youth's varied talents--as a conscious deejay and as a composer and vocalist of strong roots rockers.  The title cut, which translates to "the struggle continues," is an extraordinary tribute to the fight for freedom in South Africa.  The cut highlights Jah Youth's vocal abilities, exciting guitar work by Willie Lindo, and a fine horn section including Cedric Brooks, Dean Frazer, Byard Lancaster, and Micky Hanson.  A similar message is offered in the upbeat reggae piece, "Bush Mama"--dedicated to the women struggling for freedom in Namibia.  Also includes the catchy "K.K.K."  In "Sing Another Song," Jah Youth criticizes the recent monotony in deejay music.  A fine production with ten strong cuts reflecting the Youth's classic deejay style as well as his recent and successful move into roots reggae arrangements and vocals.

**D014**  Big Youth.  Isaiah First Prophet of Old.  Negusa Nagast, n.n., n.d.

Debut album of the incomparable Big Youth.  Recorded at Joe Gibbs in Kingston and distributed by Cash and Carry Records.  A true collectible for students and admirers of original, indigenous music.  The Youth makes a strong debut here as a serious deejay artist with timely and timeless Rasta infused messages.  Although the title track's lyrics draw heavily from Isaiah Chapter 11 of the Bible, the songs included are written and arranged by Big Youth.  Lyrics and arrangements are compelling.  A delightful collector's item of Jamaican folk music.

**D015**  Big Youth.  Some Great Big Youth.  Heartbeat, HB-03, 1981.

Published by Big Youth's Negusa Negast and produced by Heartbeat in the United States, this is one of the Youth's later albums distributed more widely in the United States.  Nine of the ten cuts here are original Big Youth pieces demonstrating the artist's unique fusion of roots reggae and deejay dub.  Lyrics range from the poignant and celebratory to timely social commentary, especially the haunting "World War III"; "Suffering," with its subtle use of echo; and "Green Bay Killing," with its classic Big Youth deejay style rap--breathless, rapid, serious.

**D016**  Black Slate.  Black Slate.  Alligator, AL-8301, 1980.

Based in England, Black Slate's first album includes their 1976 hit "Stick Man."  On this and their later work, the band creates mezmerizing rhythms which incorporate subtle, tasteful experiments with sound effects.  Generally heavy rockers, but also some particularly pretty melodies: "Freedom Time," "Live Up to Love," and "Amigo."

**D017**  Black Uhuru.  Anthem.  Island, 90180-1, 1983.

In Anthem, technology in the reggae industry caught up with the always sharp, heavy, experimental quality of Black Uhuru's innovative vocal harmonies (especially "What is Life?" and "Party Next Door").  Contains superb later hits from the Rose-Simpson-Jones era such as "Solidarity" and "Black Uhuru Anthem." Grammy award winner, 1986.

**D018** Black Uhuru. Black Sounds of Freedom. Greensleeves, CGR/GREL-23, 1981.

A re-mixed, re-titled release of Black Uhuru's original debut album of 1977 entitled Love Crisis. Both versions were mixed by Prince Jammy. Offers an early Black Uhuru already experiencing personnel changes. Here Uhuru consists of Derek "Duckie" Simpson, Michael Rose, Errol Nelson, Sly Dunbar, and Robbie Shakespeare. Songs here adhere to classic reggae of the time and represent an early period for the band prior to developing its later, distinctive formula. Very little of Rose's Eastern tinged, chant-like yoddle is present. The album includes a nicely done cover of Marley's "Natural Mystic." Also includes the popular "I Love King Selassie."

**D019** Black Uhuru. Brutal. RAS, 3015, 1986.

The group's first album after Michael Rose left the band to do solo work and was replaced by Junior Reid. The band here still consists of harmony vocalists Puma Jones and Duckie Simpson as well as Sly Dunbar and Robbie Shakespeare. Produced by Black Uhuru and Doctor Dread. Recorded in Jamaica and the United States. Includes Junior Reid's debut single with the band, "Fit You Haffe Fit," a song which led critics to remark that the personnel change created little or no change in the sound of the band. Indeed, much of the album is characteristic of the earlier Black Uhuru (for example, "Uptown Girl"). Also includes the interesting "Great Train Robbery" and the Rasta piece "Dread in the Mountain."

**D020** Black Uhuru. Red. Mango, MLPS-9625, 1981.

A solid production by Sly Dunbar and Robbie Shakespeare including the popular Black Uhuru dance song "Sponji Reggae." Also contains statements on violence in "Youth of Eglington" and "Carbine," as well as haunting narratives in "Sistren" and "Utterance."

**D021** Blue Riddim Band. Alive in Jamaica. Flying Fish, FF-325, 1984.

This Grammy nominated album was recorded live at Reggae Sunsplash, 1982. A refreshing and spirited concert album, Alive reveals this North American band's nervousness early on in the set at festival, but then highlights Blue Riddim's spectacular rockers and impeccable ska. Includes the delightful "Feeling Soul," "Smile," a dub version of the band's satirical deejay piece "Nancy Reagan," and a medley dedicated to Jamaican producer Coxsone that would convince many a Jamaican.

**D022**  Blue Riddim Band. Restless Spirit. Flying Fish, FF-255, 1981.

The debut album of the all white reggae band from Kansas City and Chicago. A marriage of Jamaican and African American musical roots. Mixes urban rhythm and blues with Jamaican roots reggae. Fine vocals and songwriting by Bob Zohn. Recorded at Curtis Mayfield's Curtom Studios in Chicago, Illinois. Engineered by Prince Jammy. Contains consummate rockers cuts like "One Love, One Heart" and "Cuss Cuss" as well as rich rhythm and blues tunes like "Come See About Me" (Holland-Dozier-Holland), "Shoo Be Do" (Ernie Smith), and "Twistin' the Night Away" (Sam Cooke).

**D023**  Bob Marley and The Wailers. The Birth of a Legend. Calla, PZ-34759, 1977.

Ten early Wailers' songs produced by Clement Dodd and Nate McCalla. Mixed by Tom Moulton. An important historical artifact preserving early Wailers' music recorded by Coxsone at Studio One. Includes classic Wailers' songs in pre-reggae arrangements which demonstrate Jamaican musical idioms of the early 1960s: ska, rock steady, and soul. Also illustrates the inexperienced but infectious vocal styles of The Wailers early on. Includes "One Love," "Let Him Go," "Simmer Down," "Maga Dog," and others. Jacket notes include historical information.

**D024**  Bob Marley and The Wailers. Catch a Fire. Island, ILPS-9241, 1973.

Arguably the most important album in reggae music. Catch a Fire brought reggae its first widespread international exposure. This is the Wailers' debut album with Island Records. Formative Wailers. The album vacillates between politically conscious lyrics which explore slavery and its effect on the African diaspora and folkish Jamaican love songs and dance tunes. Classic cuts include "Concrete Jungle," "Slave Driver," "Stop that Train," and "Stir It Up." An essential collector's item.

**D025**  Bob Marley and The Wailers. Confrontation. Island, 90085-1, 1983.

Published posthumously. Historical, political, and celebratory. Stunning cover art symbolizes conflict between good and evil. Includes a number of previously unreleased Marley tracks. Consummate Marley. Includes "Buffalo Soldier," "Mix Up, Mix Up," "Trenchtown," "I Know," and "Chant Down Babylon."

**D026**  Bob Marley and The Wailers. Exodus. Island, ILPS-9498, 1977.

Marley's best selling album, with good reason. Both the music and language signal a certain sophistication and wisdom born of self reflection and maturity. See Hussey's review connecting the album's material with the then recent attempt on Marley's life. (B359) Mysticism ("Natural Mystic"), unity and social change ("Exodus," "One Love," and "Jammin'"), and romantic love ("Waiting in Vain" and "Turn Your Lights Down Low") are addressed within the framework of Marley's life at the time. Precise and compelling in its expression.

**D027** Bob Marley and The Wailers. Kaya. Island, ILPS-9517, 1978.

Criticized for sentimentality and commercialism. Such reviews demonstrate the incredibly difficult catch-22 faced by international artists who at the outset demonstrate any degree of public commitment to political and cultural consciousness. Indeed, the sound here is in someways lighthearted and certainly infectious in the tradition of Western pop music. On the surface, lyrical themes of romantic love, dance, and herb seem frivolous. It was not received by critics as serious reggae. Yet, the album contains some of Marley's more haunting songs such as "Sun is Shining," "Misty Morning," and "Time Will Tell." Tinged in the ethereal, vivid metaphors from nature are created. Lessons of life unfold. In the jazz influenced "Running Away," Marley's blues scat singing shows the artist in reflection.

**D028** Bob Marley and The Wailers. Natty Dread. Island, ILPS-9281, 1974.

A monumental album introducing Marley's own band without Tosh and Wailer. Tyrone Downie is keyboardist and Al Anderson's blues rock influenced lead guitar is a welcome addition to Marley's band. The album also introduces The I-Threes as Marley's background vocalists. Each cut is musically tight and professionally executed. Lyrics function to describe ghetto life, to praise Jah, and to proclaim a revolution in consciousness. All selections have become classic Marley tunes. For example, included are the following: "No Woman, No Cry," "Rebel Music," "So Jah Seh," "Natty Dread," and the incendiary "Revolution." (B357:268)

**D029** Bob Marley and The Wailers. Survival. Island, ILPS-9542, 1979.

This publication was clearly a response to criticisms of Kaya. (D027) The album highlights Marley's dedication to African unity and his historical as well as his spiritual bond with members of the African diaspora. The memorable cover art is of brightly colored African flags and includes the stark floor plans of a slave ship. One of Marley's most accomplished albums; a powerful rhetoric. Includes some of Marley's finest works, such as "One Drop," "Babylon System," and "Survival," as well as "Zimbabwe," which Marley sang at Zimbabwe's Independence Celebration in 1980.

**D030**   Boothe, Ken.   The Ken Boothe Collection: Eighteen Classic Songs.
Trojan, TRLS-249, 1987.

A Trojan compilation of songs by this veteran Jamaican vocalist.   It traces
Boothe's recordings from the early to late 1970s.   Includes pop songs ("Ain't
No Sunshine") and classic reggae ("No Woman, No Cry").   Primarily of
historical interest.

**D031**   Brigadier Jerry.   Jamaica Jamaica.   RAS, 3012, 1985.

Brigadier Jerry's first studio LP.   Recorded at Channel One and engineered by
Scientist.   Produced by the popular Jah Love soundsystem, for which Brigadier
Jerry has long been a top deejay.   Contains popular hits such as the title track
and "Three Blind Mice" as well as trendy, conventional deejay rhythms as in
"Jah Jah Move."   Lyrics are generally worthwhile.   Includes folk themes
("Jamaica Jamaica"), unification themes ("Everyman a Me Brethren"), and
borrows from classic roots rockers for background to "Armagiddeon Style" --
elements of the introduction and bass line mimic Bunny Wailer's classic
"Amagidion." (D186)

**D032**   Broggs, Peter.   Rise and Shine.   RAS, 3011, 1985.

A sincere roots reggae singer, Peter Broggs presents ten relatively simple but
endearing cuts in this 1985 album produced by Doctor Dread of RAS Records.
Instrumentation is by members of The Roots Radics, The Wailers, and Ras
Brass.   Includes "International Farmer."

**D033**   Brown, Dennis.   No Man Is An Island.   Studio One, SOL-01112, n.d.

This debut album introduces a young Dennis Brown performing a mix of
original songs and pop tunes like "Rain Drops Deep Falling."   The
arrangements are simple--a combination of ska, rock steady, and early reggae.
Although none of the cuts are particularly exciting, Brown early on
demonstrates his compelling vocal style.

**D034**   Brown, Dennis.   The Prophet Rides Again.   A&M, SP-4964, 1983.

Dedicated to Prophet Gad of the Twelve Tribes of Israel.   A clean pressing by
A&M, this album is a mixed bag.   Here, as in some of his other albums, Brown
works to broaden his audience.   Side one is composed of funk and disco tunes
including "Save a Little Love for Me."   Side two begins with the title track and
moves on to infectious lighthearted reggae tunes like "Historical Places" and
"Shashamane Living."   Produced by Joe Gibbs and backed by The Professionals.
Consummate Dennis Brown vocals.

**D035** Brown, Dennis. Satisfaction Feeling. Yvonne's Special, YSLP-011, n.d.

This album, backed by The Roots Radics as well as Sly and Robbie and The Agrovators, offers ten cuts which affirm Brown's title as "King of Lovers Rock." Includes popular Dennis Brown tunes like "If This World Were Mine" and "Satisfaction Feeling."

**D036** Brown, Dennis. Yesterday, Today, Tomorrow. Joe Gibbs, JGML-6057, 1982.

Like others from this time period, this Dennis Brown album showcases well the sweet, sensual mix of Brown's vocals and reggae rhythms to create lasting love and folk songs. Includes popular Dennis Brown songs such as "A Little Bit More," "Rocking Time," "Hold on to What You've Got," and "Have You Ever Been In Love?" Produced by Joe Gibbs, Sly Dunbar, and Robbie Shakespeare. Backed by The Roots Radics and others. A fine collection.

**D037** Burning Spear. Garvey's Ghost. Mango, MLPS-9382, 1975.

A delightful early dub album. Consists of dub versions of Spear's Marcus Garvey album (D040), containing some of his earliest hits such as "The Ghost (Marcus Garvey)" and "I and I Survive (Slavery Days)." Simple versions by today's dub standards, but compelling throughout. Produced by Jack Ruby. A collector's item.

**D038** Burning Spear. HAILE HIM. Tuff Gong, n.n., 1981.

Represents well Spear's commitment to Rasta spirituality. The album offers a critical re-examination of European historical myths and demonstrates a desire to rebuild indigenous African knowledge. "Cry Blood Africans" laments the rape of Africa and her peoples. "Jah a Guh Raid" is a revolutionary's discourse graphically describing the murder of African ancestors at the hands of European imperialists. "Columbus," while musically playful, clearly debunks the Western interpretation of Columbus' "discovery" of Jamaica. "African Teacher" constructs a classroom scenario with Spear as a student attentive to his Amharic mentor. A Tuff Gong production.

**D039** Burning Spear. Man in the Hills. Mango, MLPS-9412, 1976.

A fine production of Spear's early work. Rich, heavy roots reggae. Good representation of Spear's distinctive blues reggae. Lyrically advocates independent thinking, peace, and Rasta. The title cut, now a well known tune, describes the virtues of rural life replete with sound effects of the Jamaican hills. Produced by Jack Ruby.

**D040** Burning Spear. <u>Marcus Garvey</u>. Mango, MLPS-9377, 1975.

An important reggae classic. Rich and resonant. Filled with Burning Spear classics: "Marcus Garvey," "Slavery Days," "Jordan River," etc. Horns, flute, and fine harmonies by early Burning Spear vocalists Delroy Hines and Rupert Wilmington. Anyone who appreciates jazz and blues will enjoy this, Winston Rodney's most classic production. Backed by Robbie Shakespeare, Aston "Family Man" Barrett, Earl "Chinna" Smith, Tony Chin, Leroy "Horsemouth" Wallace, Tyrone Downie, and others. Produced by Jack Ruby. An essential collector's item. Its dub counterpart, <u>Garvey's Ghost</u> (D037), is a fine companion piece to this classic.

**D041** Burning Spear. <u>Mistress Music</u>. Slash, 25734-1, 1988.

This, Spear's second album with Slash records, is generally filled with richly weaved arrangements--complex matrixes and patterns. Precision and sophistication mark this album of world class world beat music. Includes an unusual amount of romantic tunes compared to Spear's early productions. Recorded at Tuff Gong. It is slick and upbeat, but the heightened international tempo leaves little room for Spear's charismatic blues vocals.

**D042** Burning Spear. <u>Resistance</u>. Heartbeat, HB-33, 1985.

Superb mix of roots reggae with contemporary musical technology. Rich, full arrangements using synthesizers, call-and-response lead guitars, a solid horn section, and a crisp, precise reggae foundation. Spear embraces electronic contributions to music and uses them expertly to enrich his own allegiance to history and roots music. Memorable cuts provide history lessons about Nanny the Maroon in "Queen of the Mountain" and about Marcus Garvey in "Resistance." Spear incorporates instrumental phrases from Marley's chorus in "So Jah Seh" (D028) successfully into his own rich and original tune "Jah Say."

**D043** Byles, Junior. <u>Beat Down Babylon</u>. Trojan, TRL-52, n.d.

A representative album by this well known soul and blues influenced Jamaican singer. A pleasant album including "I've Got a Feeling," "A Place Called Africa," "Joshua's Desire," "A Matter of Time," and others. Produced by Lee Perry and Barry Lambert.

**D044** Campbell, Al. <u>The Other Side of Love</u>. Greensleeves, GREL-30, 1981.

Campbell blends elements of African American soul, dancehall, and lovers rock on this pleasant compilation of nine original songs and a cover of Smokey

Robinson's "Being With You." Recorded at Channel One. Harmonies by The Tamlins. Backed by The Roots Radics. Pretty music. Imminently danceable.

**D045** Carlos, Don. Just a Passing Glance. RAS, 3008, 1984.

A good roots reggae vocalist, Carlos incorporates elements of the deejay style successfully, particularly in the deejay version of the title track. The ten cuts included are generally smooth, resonant, enjoyable roots reggae songs (in particular the title track, "Front Line," and the jazzy "Springheel Skanking"). Produced by Doctor Dread, recorded at Tuff Gong, and engineered by Errol Brown. All songs written by Don Carlos. Backed by some of the best musicians in reggae: Sly Dunbar, the Barrett Brothers, The Roots Radics, Augustus Pablo, David Madden, Glen DaCosta, and others.

**D046** Cedric Myton and The Congos. Best of The Congos, Vol. I. Congos Ashanti Productions, n.n., 1983.

Generally compelling, high energy arrangements and the soprano, nearly falsetto vocals of Cedric Myton. Influenced by Nyabinghi drumming, especially "Congoman." Arrangements by Cedric Myton. Includes a formidable list of reggae musicians including Sly Dunbar, Carlton "Santa" Davis, Joseph Hill, Sticky Thompson, Willie Lindo, Earl "Chinna" Smith, Ernest Ranglin, Rico Rodriquez, Geoffrey Chung, and others. Recorded at Harry J's, Aquarius, Dynamic, and Black Ark.

**D047** Chalice. Live at Sunsplash. Sunsplash, RS-8902, 1983.

Recorded at Jarrett Park in 1982, this album showcases Chalice's high energy live performance style which combines roots reggae with a contagious theatrical style. While other of Chalice's works cross genres into funk, Live centers on straightforward reggae rock (in particular, "Road Block" and "Praise Him").

**D048** Churchical Chants of the Nyabingi. Heartbeat, HB-20, 1983.

Field recordings of a seven day Nyabinghi at Freeman's Hall, Trelawney, convened in response to Ronald Reagan's Jamaican visit, April, 1982. Includes print material (a primer on Rastafari and Nyabinghi). Anthropological and ethnographic. Produced by Elliot Leib. Copyrighted in 1983 by the Church Triumphant of Jah Rastafari and Haile Selassie I Theocracy Government.

**D049** The Clarendonians. The Best of Clarendonians. Studio One, SOL-1122, n.d.

A representative collection of this legendary Jamaican vocal duo (Ernest Wilson and Peter Austin). Contains eleven songs including Clarendonians' hits "Rudie Bam Bam," "He Who Laughs Last," "Sho Be Do Be," and others. Includes short biographical jacket notes by Vin Dunning.

**D050** Clarke, Johnny. Johnny Clarke. Heartbeat, HB-01, 1978.

A short album by this popular Jamaican vocalist. Contains traditional reggae rhythms and socio-spiritual oriented lyrics. Includes the traditional "Keep on Movin,'" "Judgment Day," and others.

**D051** Cliff, Jimmy. Give The People What They Want. MCA-5217, 1981.

One of Cliff's better early message oriented albums. Dominated by upbeat reggae rhythms with some sweet ballad style songs, this album includes a number of infectious and memorable tunes such as "Let's Turn the Tables," "Majority Rule," "What Are You Doing With Your Life," the title track, and others. Backed by an impressive list of musicians: Earl "Chinna" Smith, Sly and Robbie, Ansel Collins, Augustus Pablo, Sticky Thompson, Dean Frazer, Deadly Headly Bennett, David Madden, Nambo Robinson, Bobby Ellis, The Tamlins, Pam Hall, Michael Rose, Duckie Simpson, and others. Produced by Jimmy Cliff and Oneness for Sunpower Productions. Recorded at Dynamic and mixed at Compass Point Studios, Nassau. Engineered by Anthony Graham.

**D052** Cliff, Jimmy. Give Thankx. Warner, BSK-3240, 1978.

Recorded at Aquarius, backed by The Oneness Band, and produced by Cliff and Bob Johnston. Arrangements by Cliff, Earl "Chinna" Smith, Ernest Ranglin, and others. The album's opening piece is a lengthy Nyabinghi chant ("Bongo Man") with percussive foundation by Ras Michael and The Sons of Negus and backing vocals by The Meditations. From this the album moves to Cliff's sweet, sentimental soul tunes such as "Footprints," and to his upbeat socio-political themes in "Meeting in Afrika" and "Stand Up and Fight Back."

**D053** Cliff, Jimmy. I Am The Living. MCA, 5153, 1980.

A classic album by the international superstar Jimmy Cliff. Includes classic Cliff songs like the title track, "Love Again," "All The Strength We Got," "Satan's Kingdom," and others. Backing vocals by Denice Williams. Backed by Earl "Chinna" Smith (guitar), Phil Ramacon (keyboards), Deadly Headly Bennett (alto sax), Carlton "Santa" Davis (drums), Zoot "Skully" Simms (percussion), and others. Produced by Jimmy Cliff and The Oneness Band. A collector's item.

**D054** Cliff, Jimmy. The Power and The Glory. Columbia, FC-38986, 1983.

Slick pop reggae pieces grace this mid 1980s Jimmy Cliff album. Includes the popular title track and "Journey," Cliff's response to being blacklisted for playing Sun City, South Africa.

Congos. See D046.

**D055** Congo Ashanti Roy. Level Vibes. Sonic Boom, SBLP-2001, 1984.

Ashanti Roy's extensive work with Ras Michael and The Sons of Negus is evident in this enjoyable roots album. The foundation in Nyabinghi rhythms is ever present in the Rasta oriented pieces. Also includes melodious lovers rock style songs like "Yes, I Know" and "Give Me Some Love." Includes two historically interesting dub tracks and biographical jacket notes by Roger Steffens.

Count Ossie. See D127.

**D056** Culture. The International Herb. Virgin, n.n., 1979.

In these songs, Culture persistently invokes the presence of Jah within the framework of a relatively sparse but steady roots reggae that is bass heavy and punctuated with horn and percussion sections. Yet, while the narratives are religiously and culturally somber, the straightforward rhythms lend themselves to dance. "The International Herb" in particular, is, for Culture, a uniquely playful and almost "pop" sounding song.

**D057** Culture. Two Sevens Clash. Joe Gibbs, n.n., n.d.

Led by Joseph Hill's resonant, almost reverberating vocals, Culture's first album blends the fine Jamaican tradition of vocal harmony groups with pure roots reggae lyrics and rhythms. The prophetic lyrics of the popular title cut are said to have magnified an already politically tense period in Jamaica when four sevens "clashed" on July 7, 1977. (B091:212)

**D058** Desmond Dekker and The Aces. The Original Reggae Hitsound of Desmond Dekker and The Aces. Trojan, ZCTRL-226, 1985.

A Leslie Kong production of nineteen Desmond Dekker hits from 1965-1971. Includes songs like "007 (Shanty Town)," "Israelites" (which helped pave the way for an international reggae audience), and "You Can Get It If You Really

Want It." Classic ska, rock steady, and rude boy music. Compiled by Patrick Meads. Biographical notes by Meads.

**D059** Dibango, Manu. Gone Clear. Mango, MLPS-9539, 1980.

Dibango, from the Cameroon, is a saxophonist, pianist, and vocalist. Recorded at Dynamic Studios in Kingston and backed by Sly Dunbar, Robbie Shakespeare, Sticky Thompson, and others, Gone Clear offers a slick horn section and an instrumentally heavy style of reggae African music. His sassy sax and smooth arrangements are illustrated well in "Reggae Makossa," one of the six jazz influenced cuts offered on this world beat album.

**D060** Donovan. Banzani. Mango, MLPS-9838, 1989.

A fair sampling of the currently popular Jamaican roots and dancehall style vocalist, Donovan. The "Rebel Side" includes five cuts in a vocal style similar to singers like Sugar Minott and Edi Fitzroy ("I'm Not Afraid," "Banzani"). The "Soul Side" includes five cuts generally of pleasant, lilting reggae rhythms and sensible roots lyrics ("Plantation," "Serious Man"). Background vocals by Daisy Brewster, Carol "Passion" Nelson, and Belva Honey. Backed by Sly and Robbie, Handel Tucker, Stanley Ricketts, and others. Produced by Jack Ruby. Recorded and mixed at Grove Music Studio.

**D061** Dunbar, Sly. Sly-Go-Ville. Mango, MLPS-9673, 1982.

A popular production by drummer Sly Dunbar with Robbie Shakespeare on bass. Includes classic cuts like "Slippin' Into Darkness," "Hot You're Hot," "Unmetered Taxi," and others. A collector's item.

**D062** Ellis, Alton. "The Earth Needs Love"/"Diverse Doctrine." Sonic Boom, SBMS-1001, 1984.

This twelve inch single offers but two fine samples of this legendary Jamaican vocalist's work. Both songs offer beautiful vocals and worthwhile compositions. Written and produced by Alton Ellis. Recorded at Channel One.

**D063** Fitzroy, Edi. Youthman Penitentiary. Alligator, AL-8304, 1982.

A representative album of sufferer, dancehall style singing by Jamaican vocalist Edi Fitzroy. Includes some of his earliest hits such as the title track, "Check For You Once," and "African Queen." Backed by The Roots Radics. Recorded at Channel One.

**D064** Foundation. <u>Flames</u>. Mango, MLPS-9807, 1988.

Debut album by the harmony trio Foundation. Produced by Jack Ruby and Stephen "Cat" Coore, the <u>Flames</u> album contains ten original cuts backed by Cat Coore, Richard Daley, Sly Dunbar, and others. Includes a poignant ballad about the struggle of leaders like Garvey, Mandela, King, and others called "Just to See Love." Interesting and sometimes sweet vocal harmonies and upbeat arrangements ("Dance If You Dancin'" and "Pride").

**D065** The Gladiators. <u>Country Living</u>. Heartbeat, HB-36, 1985.

A recent album from one of the foundational groups in reggae. <u>Country Living</u> includes ten solid cuts of traditional roots reggae. Illustrates the sharp edged tenor of lead vocalist Albert Griffiths and his rootsy, sometimes Marley-like scatting.

**D066** Gladiators. <u>Sweet So Till</u>. Virgin, VIFL-1048, 1979.

A fine roots album by this foundational reggae group. Traditional roots reggae recorded at Channel One and Harry J's. Includes, among others, "Let Jah Be Praised," "Backyard Meditation," and "Merrily." Backed by Ernest Ranglin, Leroy "Horsemouth" Wallace, Earl Bagga, Ansell Collins, Pablov Black, Tommy McCook, and others. Produced and arranged by The Gladiators.

**D067** Griffiths, Marcia. <u>Marcia Griffiths at Studio One</u>. Studio One, SOL-1126, n.d.

Ten early recordings from Studio One by internationally known Jamaican vocalist Marcia Griffiths. Illustrates well her clean, soulful, jazzy vocal style early on. Includes early Griffiths' hits "Truly," "Melody Life," and "Tell Me Now." Also includes "Always Together," a beautiful duet with Bob Andy. Recorded, engineered, and produced by Clement Dodd. Includes brief biographical jacket notes.

**D068** Hammond, Beres. <u>Beres Hammond</u>. WKS Records, WKS LP-055, 1986.

Includes ten love songs by popular Jamaican vocalist Beres Hammond. Includes "Teeny Weeny Little Loving," "What One Dance Can Do," "Someone Phoned," "Groovy Little Thing," and others. Backing vocals by Pam Hall, The Tamlins, and others. Recorded at Dynamic Sounds and Aquarius Studios.

**D069**  The Heptones. <u>Night Food</u>. Island, ILPS-9381, 1976.

One of the great harmony trios of Jamaica, The Heptones offer a good sampling of their earlier work here, during the time when Leroy Sibbles' smooth lead vocals and composing talents heavily influenced the band. Song lyrics range from trivial romance to somber ghetto narratives to the reflective, melodic, and highly popular cut "Book of Rules." Beautiful harmonies by Earl Morgan and Barry LLewellyn.

**D070**  The Heptones. <u>Party Time</u>. Mango, MLPS-9456, 1977.

A fine late 1970s album by The Heptones. Includes "Now Generation," "Mr. President," "Serious Time," "Sufferer's Time," and others.

**D071**  Higgs, Joe. <u>Family</u>. Shanachie, 43053, 1988.

From the simple, clean reggae cuts to the more complex arrangement in "African-Can" to the reworking of "Day-O" into a dance tune, this album highlights well the rich, soulful vocals of the great Jamaican songwriter and singer, Joe Higgs. "African-Can," dedicated to United States astronaut Colonel Guion Poluford, is a marvelous fusion of musical idioms creating a kind of rhythm and blues style world beat song. Higgs' own "Free Africa" is an exceptional chant-like ballad with Ras Michael's drums, snatches of jazz piano, and Higgs' exceptional voice. Produced by Edgy Lee and Lee Jaffe.

**D072**  Higgs, Joe. <u>Triumph</u>. Alligator, AL-8313, 1985.

This album, recorded at Tuff Gong, highlights Higgs' rich, soulful voice, guitar playing, and talent for fine arrangements. Includes examples of Higgs' songwriting in cuts like "So It Go," a poignant ghetto narrative, and the haunting "Creation," a spiritual celebration.

**D073**  Holt, John. <u>Police in Helicopter</u>. Greensleeves, CGR/GREL-58, 1983.

Paragons singer John Holt offers typical dancehall style tunes with lyrics sometimes expressing ghetto concerns ("Police in Helicopter" and "Last Train") and other times expressing inane sexism ("Beach Party" and "Private Doctor"). Backed by the Roots Radics, Dean Frazer, Nambo Robinson, Al Campbell, The Tamlins, and Tony Tuff. Recorded at Channel One.

**D074**  House of Assembly. <u>Confusion</u>. Meadowlark, 409, 1987.

A fine debut album from this Philadelphia based reggae band together since the 1970s. The band plays solid rockers sometimes with the stepped up tempo of urban North America. Louis Putmon's lead vocals are rich, resonant, and consistent. His jazz blues keyboards, particularly on "One Heart, One Love," are compelling.

**D075** Identity. Identity. Mango, MLPS-9806, 1988.

A sophisticated, precisely executed debut album by a band which works out of the Midwestern states and is composed of St. Lucians and North Americans. Produced by Dennis Thompson. All songs written and arranged by lead vocalist Deighton Charlemagne. Guest musicians include Dean Frazer, Nambo Robinson, Junior "Chico" Chin, and Tyrone Downie. Includes eight original songs: six rockers songs which are upbeat and international sounding as well as two dancehall songs. The album generally is interesting both instrumentally and lyrically.

**D076** I Jahman Levi. Are We A Warrior. Mango, MLPS-9557, 1979.

Stephen Davis and Peter Simon have called British Jamaican Trevor Sutherland's (I Jahman Levi) music "atmospheric," "orchestral," "New Age." (B092:147) European influences are evident here in songs like "Two Sides of Love" and the title track.

**D077** Inner Circle. Everything is Great. Island, ILPS-9558, 1979.

A late 1970s example of both Inner Circle and the late Jacob Miller's musical styles at the time. Although rooted in a straightforward reggae foundation, the songs and arrangements are stepped up in tempo and tinged with pop, rock, and disco characteristics, especially "Music Machine," "Playing It," and the title track. Also includes the rockers piece "We A Rockers" and the ballad style "I Learned My Lesson." At this recording, Inner Circle was composed of Jacob "Killer" Miller (lead vocals), Ian "Munty" Lewis (bass), Roger "Fat Man" Lewis (rhythm guitar), Bernard "Touter" Harvey and Charles Farguharson (keyboards), Calvin "Rasheed" McKenzie (drums), David "Black Sky" Jahson (percussion), and Joe "Gitzy" Ortiz (lead guitar). Recorded at Dynamic Sounds. Produced by Inner Circle and Youth Sound.

**D078** Inner Circle. One Way. RAS, 3030, 1987.

A fine recent production by a reorganized Inner Circle subsequent to the Jacob Miller era. The title cut is yet another infectious rockers piece which devotes itself to the praise of reggae music. Includes generally enjoyable, classic-style rockers, particularly the heavy rockers piece "Champions," the Wailers-style "Front and Center," and the lighthearted arrangement in "Life." Closes with a musical dedication to the people of South Africa entitled "Keep the Faith."

**D079** Ipso Facto. <u>Communication</u>. Pendulum Productions, n.n., 1986.

A sampling of the successful Minneapolis based reggae band Ipso Facto. Includes the band's popular songs: "Communication," "Soldren," and "System." Recorded at Creation Studios in Minneapolis.  Engineered by Steve Raitt. produced by Steve Raitt and Wain McFarlane.

**D080** I-Roy. <u>African Herbsman</u>. Joe Gibbs, JGML-6045, n.d.

Ten cuts by this well known deejay who followed closely in the footsteps of U-Roy.  Generally enjoyable deejay and dub versions of stock and popular reggae rhythms.  Includes a deejay version of "Satta Massagana" entitled "Sata-Jah-Liveth."   Produced by Bunny Lee and Errol Thompson for Joe Gibbs Productions.

**D081** Isaacs, Gregory.  <u>Cool Ruler</u>.  Virgin's Front Line Records, FL-1020, 1978.

With a title reflecting Isaacs' nickname in Jamaica, this relatively early album in Isaacs' long list of records includes eight original cuts as well as one song written by Dennis Brown and one by John Holt.  Low key, but typical of Isaacs' enchanting vocals and arrangements.

**D082** Isaacs, Gregory.  <u>In Person</u>.  Trojan, TRLS-102, 1975.

Isaacs first established his distinctive, seductive lovers rock vocals in this debut album.   Recorded at Treasure Isle and backed by The Soul Syndicate.   All songs written by Isaacs.   Includes "Love Overdue," one of Isaacs' early international hits.

**D083** Isaacs, Gregory.  <u>Night Nurse</u>.  Mango, MLPS-9721, 1982.

This album codifies Isaacs' simple, but enjoyable formulaic style.  Includes the lyrically inane, but immensely popular title cut as well as the fine dancehall piece "Cool Down the Pace."   Most impressive is the mystically-tinged arrangement and the pointed questions asked in "Material Man."   Overall a good production of representative Isaacs; it showcases his distinctive mezmerizing quality--a combination of sultry vocals and sweet rhythms which has earned him his "Cool Ruler" title.

**D084** Isaacs, Gregory. <u>Soon Forward</u>. Virgin's Front Line Records, FL-1044, 1979.

One of Isaacs' better early albums. Energetic and thoughtful, the cuts here are a mix of love songs and political-spiritual commentary, but they always reflect Isaacs' sensual, smooth, resonant vocals. Includes some of the artist's finest songs, such as "Black Liberation Struggle" and the title cut written by Sly Dunbar and Robbie Shakespeare. Background vocals by Dennis Brown and Leroy Sibbles.

**D085** Israel Vibration. <u>Why You So Craven</u>. Surrey Records, AR-0001, n.d.

Recorded and mixed by Scientist at Channel One Studios and backed by The High Times Players. Produced sometime subsequent to the group's first album (1979). <u>Why You So Craven</u> illustrates the harmony trio's Rasta influenced reggae. Some interesting vocal harmonies and instrumental arrangements.

**D086** The Itals. <u>Brutal Out Deh</u>. Nighthawk, NH-303, 1981.

A beautiful debut album from this endearing roots harmony trio. Backed by The Radics and recorded at Channel One, this album showcases well the rich, rootsy harmonies of this vocal trio in a collection of fine cuts including "Herbs Pirate," "Action," and "Brutal." The arrangements generally frame meaningful narratives of social and spiritual commentary and day to day struggles.

**D087** The Itals. <u>Give Me Power</u>. Nighthawk, NH-307, 1983.

Precise and sophisticated in its execution, this album presents a "slick" Itals, but without loss of their roots framework--both instrumentally and lyrically. While the tunes lope along in true roots rockers fashion, they are quicker in tempo, higher in energy, and grace the album with more catchy hits than in their first album. Includes the title track as well as "In Deh," "Roll River Jordan," and "Make Merry." Compelling lead vocals by Alvin Keith Porter.

**D088** The Itals. <u>Rasta Philosophy</u>. Nighthawk, NH-7491, 1985.

A recent mini album confirming The Itals' allegiance to traditional Rasta infused roots reggae. Contains five fairly infectious songs.

**D089** I-Threes. "Music for the World"/"Many are Called." Shanachie, 5007, 1983.

A twelve inch single which is a good example of The I-Threes' consummate harmonies. "Many are Called" is a popular and memorable piece, but the beat on "Music of the World" gets monotonous, and moving vocal solos are anticipated but not forthcoming. Recorded at Tuff Gong.

**D090** Jah Malla. Jah Malla. Modern Records, MR38-135, 1981.

A generally fine production of this New York based reggae band composed of Cleon Douglas, Noel Alphonso, Michael Ranglin, and Ronald "Boogsie" Morris. The horn section here is headed by Noel's father, Roland Alphonso. Background vocals are by The Immortals. A mixed bag of influences. Band leader Cleon Douglas' Rasta messages in songs such as "Wisdom," "Africa," "Jah Love," and "Oh Jah" offer the most exciting moments of the album. Other cuts are generally fine versions of North American tunes, from an interesting reggae arrangement of Bob Dylan's "Ain't No Man Righteous, No Not One," to an uninteresting cover of John Fogerty's "Bad Moon Rising."

**D091** Jazzbo, Prince. Ital Corner. RAS, LPCT-0103, n.d.

Ten cuts of deejay Prince Jazzbo produced by Lee Perry and recorded at Black Ark. Songs move from typical commercial sounding deejay music ("Ital Corner"), to pieces influenced by deejay greats like Big Youth and by classic Rasta rhythms ("Prophet Live" and "Prophet Dub Satta"), to interesting jazz blues style deejay tunes ("Live Good Today").

**D092** Johnson, Linton Kwesi. Dread Beat An' Blood. Heartbeat, HB-01, 1981.

Produced by LKJ, recorded at Gooseberry, and engineered by Dennis Blackbeard. This album, backed partly by some members of Matumbi, draws material from two books by LKJ, Dread Beat An' Blood and Inglan Is a Bitch. A classic by LKJ, Dread Beat An' Blood presents precise dub rockers, but clearly centers on LKJ's dead serious dub poetry. It is confrontational in its graphic descriptions and frank narratives characterizing race and class based tensions. It includes "Five Nights of Bleeding" for Leroy Harris, "It Dread Inna Inglan" for George Lindo, and "Man Free" for Darcus Howe. See B164.

**D093** Johnson, Linton Kwesi. Making History. Mango, MLPS-9770, 1984.

Insightful/inciteful critiques of the political left and right from a working class perspective. LKJ's dub poetry here offers compelling personal narratives, especially in the bitter "Reggae Fi Dada." Instrumentally more interesting than some of his earlier albums. See B167.

**D094** Jones, Frankie, and Michael Palmer. Show-Down, Vol. 4. Empire Records, JJ-161, 1984.

A sampling of dancehall songs by two popular Jamaican vocalists. Includes "Don't Smoke the Seed," "Youth-Man Take It Easy," "In This Time," and others. Backed by The Roots Radics. Recorded and mixed at Channel One. Produced by Kenneth Hoo Kim.

**D095** Kamose, Ini. Ini Kamose. Island, MMA-101, 1983.

Produced by Sly Dunbar and Robbie Shakespeare for Taxi Productions, Kamose's first album is his most interesting to date. Includes six original songs with expert foundation laid by Sly and Robbie. The cuts are enriched with compelling dub effects, especially using bass and keyboard. Melody and harmony are not primary here. Indeed, Kamose has a rather sharp edged, staccato vocal style. His lyrics often give praise to reggae itself ("World-a-Music"). While many reggae lyricists use military symbolism to describe the potency of reggae and the power of Rasta, Kamose, in "General," also places combat in dialectical opposition to nonviolence. Thus, reggae as a powerful persuasion is rendered superior to physical combat.

**D096** Kamose, Ini. Shocking Out. RAS, 3036, 1988.

A precise and professional production, but it lacks the creative spark in Kamose's debut album. The deejay rhythmic conventions used in the title track seem worn out and overused. Some of the ten songs included contain interesting lyrical messages: "Clown Talking" takes a perceptive jab at political rhetoric, "Revolution" offers typical protest song lyrics with a background by Mutabaruka, and "Come Now" is dedicated to U.S. fighter Mike Tyson. Backed by Tyrone Downie, Danny Downie, Danny Thompson, Steelie, and Clevie Brownie. Recorded and mixed at Music Mountain.

**D097** The Killer Bees. Scratch The Surface. Beehive, n.n., 1986.

Debut album of this Texas based reggae band. A popular club band to Southern and Midwestern audiences, The Bees are generally successful at blending reggae, North American Rock, and South American sounds. Here they introduce to a wider audience some of their rockers such as "Yard Style Home" as well as the pretty and idealistic "In My Wildest Dream" and the heavily rock influenced "Rastaman Go No Vietnam."

**D098** Levy, Barrington. Englishman. Greensleeves, GREL-9, 1979.

Ten songs by this dancehall and sufferer style Jamaican vocalist. Includes enjoyable dub dancehall style rhythms in songs like "If You Give To Me,"

"Don't Fuss Nor Fight," "Look Youth Man," and "Black Heart Man." Backed by The Roots Radics. Recorded at Channel One. Mixed by Scientist and Prince Jammy at King Tubby's. Produced by Henry "Junjo" Lawes.

LKJ. See D092-093.

Marley, Bob. See D023-029, D194.

**D099** Marley, Rita. <u>Harambe</u>. Shanachie, 43010, 1982.

Includes the upbeat and popular title cut, Rita Marley's own jazzy "King Street," and Ricky Walters' sweeping, anthem-like tribute "There'll Always Be Music." "Love Iyah," by Rita Marley and A. Cooper, successfully frames advisory lyrics with a Nyabinghi-like rhythmic foundation. Interesting moments, but some cuts seem to drag by uninspired. Published in Jamaica by Rita Marley Music. Produced by Ricky Walters, Grub Cooper, and Steve Golding. Recorded at Tuff Gong.

**D100** Marley, Rita. <u>Who Feels It Knows It</u>. Shanachie, 43003, 1981.

Originally published in Jamaica by Tuff Gong, 1980. Includes songs written by Rita Marley, Bob Marley, Bunny Wailer, Grub Cooper, and Ricky Walters. Backed by a host of fine reggae musicians. This, Rita Marley's debut solo album, highlights the depths of Marley's clear, strong voice--here so well suited to soul in complement with straightforward reggae rhythms. Includes the popular original single by Rita Marley, "One Draw," and a creative arrangement of Bunny Wailer's "Who Feels It Knows It." Rita's rendition of Bob's "Thank You Jah" is a thoroughly enjoyable reminder of Bob Marley's brilliant songwriting. Rita jazzes up Bob's "I'm Still Waiting" with some captivating scat singing. Curiously, Bob and Rita's "A Jah Jah" is the least interesting cut offered here: the arrangement is drab and monotonous. The album was produced by Rita Marley and Grub Cooper. Recorded at Tuff Gong.

**D101** Marvin, Junior. <u>Apartheid</u>. Greensleeves, GREL-95, 1986.

Ten cuts with roots reggae lyrical themes and Marvin's near falsetto vocals. The charm here is in creative, catchy, and jazzy arrangements with interesting lyrics (for example, "Too Much Division"). Some monotonous cuts, but generally high energy tunes. Produced by Prince Jammy and recorded at Channel One.

**D102** Matumbi. <u>The Best of Matumbi</u>. Trojan, TRLS-145, 1977.

This album offers interesting representative pieces by this popular 1970s British band. Songs included illustrate Matumbi's versatility, ranging from smooth and classic style roots rockers ("Can't Satisfy") to pieces influenced by urban jazz, rock, and soul ("Reggae Stuff").

**D103** McGregor, Freddie. <u>All in The Same Boat</u>. RAS, 3014, 1986.

McGregor's third album published by his friend and colleague, Doctor Dread of RAS Records. This album represents a continuation of McGregor's international musical style and lyrical concerns. Here McGregor offers his band members the opportunity to showcase their own compositions as well as including four strong McGregor originals. Backed by the Studio One musicians, this is one of McGregor's finest albums. Indeed, it is a consistently excellent reggae album overall. Includes consummate McGregor vocals and personality on the popular "Push Come to Shove" and poignant social commentary on "Hungry Belly Pickney," "Mama, Mama," and Danny Browne's ballad "Somewhere."

**D104** McGregor, Freddie. <u>Big Ship</u>. Greensleeves, GREL-39, 1982.

McGregor's first album on a U.S. label, published by Greensleeves and manufactured and distributed by Shanachie. His first internationally known album. The popular title track sets the stage for a continuation of McGregor's smooth and melodic vocals. Many people consider this his best album to date. A collector's item.

**D105** McGregor, Freddie. <u>Freddy McGregor</u>. Jackal, JALP-000, 1979.

Released in England, this is McGregor's debut album. Produced by McGregor and Niney the Observer. Distributed by Tuff Gong. A mix of fine Rasta style roots reggae and naseant lovers rock, this album illustrates why McGregor has become so successful. Although some of the ten cuts included are covers of other artists' songs, McGregor wrote all the Rasta oriented numbers. Note, for example, the popular "Zion Chant" and "Rasta Have Faith," which uses the "Satta Massagana" rhythm. (D001) The opening song, "We Got Love" by Earl "Chinna" Smith, is delightful. McGregor's style is infectious here, as in his later albums.

**D106** McKay, Freddie. <u>Creation</u>. Joe Gibbs Music, JGML-6028, 1980.

Probably best known for his early hit song "Picture on The Wall," McKay, in Creation, presents an enjoyable selection of roots and blues vocals backed by classic reggae rhythms. Contains "Creation Rebel," "Rock A Bye Woman," "Jah Man," "The Rainbow," "Yesterday," and others. The album cover lists cuts included deceptively, suggesting full dub versions where there are none (except for the "Version" of "Yesterday").

**D107**  The Melodians. Irie Feeling. RAS, 3003, 1983.

In the tradition of Jamaican harmony trios, The Melodians here offer a bubbly, lighthearted, sometimes rough-edged sound framed in simple but strong reggae rhythms. The title cut is a fine example of this sound. Backed by Flabba Holt, Style Scott, Ansel Collins, Earl "Chinna" Smith, and a host of Jamaica's superb horn players. Recorded at Channel One.

**D108**  Melody Makers. Play The Game Right. EMI America, ST-17165, 1985.

A satisfying debut album by the four Marley children: David (Ziggy), Cedella, Sharon, and Stephen. Backed by The Wailers and recorded at Tuff Gong. Ziggy wrote all but one cut (the haunting "Children Playing in the Street" by Bob Marley), and a significant number of them--"What a Plot," "Unuh Nuh Listen Yet," and "Naah Leggo"--are catchy, memorable tunes. Here Ziggy walks a thin line between sounding like his father and establishing his own identity as a musician. Here he succeeds.

**D109**  Messenjah. Cool Operator. Shanachie, 43056, 1988.

A welcome addition to any reggae collection. This Canadian based band offers a strong album of lilting smooth rockers reminiscent of Steel Pulse in vocals and in some song patterns, but sweeter and generally more joyful. Particularly memorable are "Summer in Winter," "Emmanuelle Road," and the bittersweet tribute to the South African stuggle in "Glory Trail." Produced by band members Rupert "Ojiji" Harvey, Charles "Tower" Sinclair, and Carl Harvey.

**D110**  Mighty Diamonds. If You Looking for Trouble. Live & Learn, LL LP-022, 1986.

A fine mid 1980s production by this legendary harmony trio. Note especially the title track, "Where Is Garvey," "Fight, Fight, Fight," and "Cartoon Living." Harmony vocals by Al Campbell. Backed by Lloyd Parkes, Dwight Pinkney, Dean Frazer, and others. Produced and arranged by Delroy Wright. Recorded at Dynamic and Music Mountain.

**D111**  Mighty Diamonds. Reggae Street. Shanachie, 43004, 1981.

A collection of ten original songs backed by Sly Dunbar, Robbie Shakespeare, Earl "Chinna" Smith, and others plus a superb horn section composed of Dean Frazer, Nambo Robinson, and Junior "Chico" Chin. An excellent publication of the Diamonds' sweet, dreamy harmonies blended smoothly with serious social commentary. The beautiful title cut is a Diamonds' classic. An exceptional production.

**D112** Mighty Diamonds. <u>Right Time</u>. Shanachie, 43014, 1983.

A Virgin Records production, this collection of early Diamonds' music includes the 1975 hit "Right Time," which helped the band gain a North American following. Recorded at Channel One. Includes ten Diamonds' cuts which represent well this important Jamaican harmony trio's sweet, soul influenced vocals paradoxically juxtaposed with socially and politically challenging messages.

**D113** Miller, Jacob. <u>Dread, Dread</u>. Liberty, LT-5162, 1978, 1985.

This album offers a sampling of Jacob Miller's most popular reggae rockers songs like "Tenement Yard," "Suzie Wong," and "Tired fe Lick Weed in Bush." Produced by the Lewis Brothers. Engineered by Tom Moulton. Includes biographical jacket notes by Roger Steffens.

**D114** Minott, Sugar. <u>Sufferer's Choice</u>. Heartbeat, HB-21, 1983.

An enjoyable production of Minott's resonant vocals and hypnotic rhythms which cross lines between dancehall and roots rockers. Side one offers five fine sufferer's songs including the title track, "Rough Ole Life," and "Uptown Ghetto." Side two contains four loves songs (of sorts) and closes with a jazzy roots tune "The Youth Dem Gettin' Bad." Recorded and mixed at Channel One. Rhythm tracks by Sly and Robbie as well as the Roots Radics.

**D115** Misty In Roots. <u>Earth</u>. People Unite Publications Ltd., PU-102-ALB, 1983.

Eight original cuts recorded in West Germany by this creative, self-contained, international group of three good vocalists and seven fine instrumentalists. Misty here offers a sophisticated and powerful roots reggae with international themes. Strong, competent reggae rhythms, playful keyboards, and blues horns. Highly recommended as an exceptional example of international roots reggae.

**D116** Misty In Roots. <u>Musi-O-Tunya</u>. People Unite Publications, Ltd., PU-105, 1985.

A compilation of eight original songs by Misty In Roots. Here the band affirms its competence in composition and arrangement. Fine roots reggae with intelligent and critical lyrics in songs like "West Livity" and "Economical Slavery." The title track is a pretty, sentimental song dedicated to the waterfall on the Zambeze River between Zimbabwe and Zambia.

**D117**   Moses, Pablo.   <u>A Song</u>.   Mango, MLPS-9541, 1980.

This, Pablo Moses' second album, contains his first hit, "A Song." The album illustrates Moses' unique vocals, a voice with a recognizable edge that flirts with the notion of a falsetto. Backed by fine reggae musicians and vocalists, the tracks reflect Moses' typical themes of music and spiritual consciousness.

**D118**   Moses, Pablo.   <u>Pave The Way</u>.   Mango, MLPS-9633, 1981.

While in the tradition and style of Moses' earlier productions, arrangements, vocals, and lyrics here work more consistently to create memorable songs. His best collection to date. Lyrically strong and musically interesting. Cuts include the calls to action in "Pave The Way" and "Dig On," as well as the somewhat sentimental narrative in "Africa is for Me."

**D119**   Moses, Pablo.   <u>Tension</u>.   Alligator, AL-8311, 1985.

One of several electronically infused albums by Moses on the Alligator label. Moses' unique vocals are strong throughout, but are here embellished by electronic sound effects as well as an even more crisp edge and a somewhat faster tempo than in his earlier work. Generally interesting lyrics and arrangements, yet some of his earlier roots quality is sacrificed in adopting a faster tempo.

**D120**   Mowatt, Judy.   <u>Black Woman</u>.   Ashandan, GEN-3014, 1979.

A superb debut solo album. Gained wide international exposure and acclaim. Certainly significant as the first reggae production which represents a serious attitude toward sisterhood. The first of a series of fine albums which helped to build Mowatt's reputation as reggae's queen. Includes a number of Mowatt's hits such as "Slave Queen," "Black Woman," and "Joseph," which was written for and about Bob Marley. A collector's item.

**D121**   Mowatt, Judy.   <u>Love is Overdue</u>.   Shanachie, 43044, 1986.

Mowatt at her most sophisticated. While there are only three originals here, Mowatt's versions of "Love is Overdue" and UB40's "Sing Our Own Song" are outstanding. And, the sheer power and beauty of Mowatt's spiritual ballads are once again affirmed in the original cut "Who is He," which uses traditional Nyabinghi drumming for its foundation. The arrangements by Tyrone Downie are particularly interesting. Stan Harrison's tenor saxophone in "Rock Me" is exceptionally rich. Generally a fine production.

**D122**   Mowatt, Judy.   Working Wonders.   Shanachie, 43028, 1985.

Chosen as Best Album of 1985 by CMJ New Music Awards in New York and by Rockers magazine in Kingston.   Although Mowatt covers Taj Mahal's "Black Man, Brown Man" quite well, the most vibrant and sincere cuts included are the originals on Side B, especially "Mother Africa" and "Hush Baby Mother."

**D123**   Mundell, Hugh.   Africa Must Be Free By 1983.   RAS, 3201, n.d.

Reissued by RAS Records as part of its Classic Reggae Series, this is the best known album from Mundell's short career before his death in 1983.   Produced and arranged by Augustus Pablo.   Backed by Leroy "Horsemouth" Wallace, Jacob Miller, Robbie Shakespeare, Earl "Chinna" Smith, Leroy Sibbles, Geoffrey Chung, Augustus Pablo, and others.   A viable combination of Mundell's high, sometimes brittle vocals with Augustus Pablo's keyboards.   Includes the popular title track and "Why Do Black Men Fuss and Fight" with Sibbles' fine percussion, as well as seven more cuts, all written by Mundell.

**D124**   Musical Youth.   The Youth of Today.   MCA, 5389, 1982.

Trendy and popular album by the British youth group.   Includes Musical Youth's popular "Pass the Dutchie," a version of the original "Pass the Kotchie" by The Mighty Diamonds.   Includes many infectious songs and nice vocals and arrangements.   Some enjoyable touches of deejay rap.

**D125**   Mutabaruka.   Check It!   Alligator, AL-8306, 1983.

In this, his first album, Mutabaruka clearly establishes his brilliance as a dub poet.   Backed by the tight rockers of The High Times Players, this album contains some of the finest examples of the interrelationship between the spoken word and the reggae rhythm--a combination which literally defines dub poetry (especially "Everytime A Ear de Soun'").   The album's triumph is "Whey Mi Belang?"--an eerie lesson in the personal consequences of colonial history and the subsequent African diaspora.   Mutabaruka's poetry is persistently revolutionary in its scathing political and cultural criticism.   Even the most light hearted cut included, the delightful rockers piece "Hard Time Loving," bemoans the lack of privacy which is a constant companion of ghetto life.

**D126**   Mutabaruka.   The Mystery Unfolds.   Shanachie, 43037, 1986.

Divided into two "chapters" rather than "sides," this album is strong from the first to the last cut.   Here Mutabaruka finds more complex and international expression for his political concerns than in his earlier albums.   Note particularly "Revolutionary Words" and "Dis Poem."

**D127** Mystic Revelation of Rastafari. <u>Grounation</u>. MRR Records, n.n., n.d.

Circa 1960s. An historic three record set of Nyabinghi music. Performed by Count Ossie and his many drummers as well as Cedric Brook's band, the set is an audio collage of a grounation including a few traditional jazz pieces. The set was recorded non-commercially as part of a project on Rasta culture. As such, it includes poems, chants, reasonings, ritual drumming, and traditional tunes such as "Oh Carolina." One of the first recordings of Rasta music. An essential collector's item. (B014:161-162,B078:53-65)

**D128** Oku + AK7. <u>Pressure Drop</u>. Heartbeat, HB-26, 1984.

Dub poet Oku Onuora's first album. Heavy roots reggae and dead serious poetry reflect Onuora's seven year prison experience. A rich, complex tapestry of the spoken word; roots rockers; Nyabinghi drumming; dub effects; and jazz horns, sax, and flute.

**D129** The Original Wailers. "Music Lesson"/"Nice Time." Tuff Gong, 12-001, 1985.

Despite conflicts between Bunny Wailer and Rita Marley over Wailer's use of old Wailers' session tapes in this twelve inch single, Wailers' fans will appreciate the tapestry of Wailers' sounds Bunny has woven into these two cuts. Wailer combines some powerful Wailers' lyrics with his own gleeful dancehall rhythms and incomparable dub arrangements. "Music Lesson" offers pointed thoughts about the repression of African history mixed with a classic vocal interchange between Bob Marley and Bunny Wailer. The infectious harmonies in "Nice Time" clinch the success of this musical reunion. The full ensemble of Marley, Wailer, Tosh, Braithwaite, and Walker celebrates the precision and fullness of the Wailers' original sound.

**D130** Osbourne, Johnny. <u>Water Pumping</u>. Greensleeves, CGR/GREL-61, 1983.

Contains classic and catchy dancehall tunes like "Water Pumping" and "Fire Down Below." Side one contains upbeat, sometimes playful dancehall songs, successfully blending stock material--lyrically and instrumentally--with Osbourne and Prince Jammy's own creative talents and personal moods. Side two is a combination of dancehall and roots reggae, sometimes interesting, but contains an out-of-tune Osbourne in the introduction to "Love Ya Tonight" and uninspired rhythms in "Rolling Reggae" and "Na Look Nobody." Backed by Sly Dunbar, Robbie Shakespeare, Asher and Tarzan, Earl "Chinna" Smith, Black Crucials, and others.

**D131**  Pablo, Augustus.  <u>East of the River Nile</u>.  Shanachie, 1003, 1981.

The title track was originally recorded for Aquarius Records and was voted top instrumental of 1969.  The melodica here exudes an ethereal, almost mystical Eastern sound reminiscent of Africa.  The album is a fine representation of Pablo's distinctive style. (B078:134)

**D132**  Pablo, Augustus.  <u>King Tubby's Meets Rockers Uptown</u>.  Shanachie, 1007, 1984.

A classic dub album replete with all the modern dubbing techniques as well as Pablo's melodica.  The title cut, which refers to "Sound Man" King Tubby and Pablo's own early soundsystem, "Rockers," was tremendously popular and received critical acclaim. (B078:134)

Palmer, Michael.  See D094.

**D133**  The Paragons.  <u>Riding High</u>.  Treasure Isle, n.n, n.d.

Although The Paragons most clearly exemplify the rock steady genre, precursors to reggae rhythms and to excellence in vocal harmony are illustrated here, as in any Paragons' production.  Led by John Holt and backed by Tommy McCook and The Supersonics, the songs are pop music staples like "Unforgettable You," yet the style offers a worthwhile history lesson in Jamaican music.

**D134**  Perry, Lee "Scratch" (and The Majestics).  <u>Mystic Miracle Star</u>. Heartbeat, HB-06, 1982.

Best known as a producer and brilliant engineer, the legendary Lee Perry presents here his own work as vocalist and musical artist.  Some rough vocals, but the album illustrates Lee's character and style.  Includes "Holy Moses," "Radication Squad," "Chalice Afire," and others.  Backed by Ron Stackman, Jim Schwartz, Louis LaVilla, Don Grant, and "Gladdy" Anderson.  Recorded at Dynamic Sounds and Aquarius.  Produced, arranged, and mixed by Lee Perry.

**D135**  Priest, Maxi.  <u>Maxi Priest</u>.  Virgin, 7-90957-1, 1988.

Nine cuts of vocalist Maxi Priest's slick pop and soul influenced reggae.  Nice instrumental arrangements.  Includes "Wild World," "Marcus," "It Ain't Easy," "Some Guys Have All the Luck," and others.  Produced by Willie Lindo and Sly and Robbie.  Backing vocals by J.C. Lodge, Pam Hall, Beres Hammond, Dean Frazer, and Robbie Shakespeare.

**D136**  Ras Michael and The Sons of Negus.  <u>Dadawah: Peace and Love</u>. Trojan, TRLS-103, 1975.

Four lengthy cuts of Ras Michael and The Sons of Negus at their best.  Fine professional blend of Nyabinghi chants and drumming with echo and other electronic devices.  Ethereal and dream-like in its expression.  Biblically inspired lyrics here later found expression in popular reggae songs.  A collector's item. (B078:55)

**D137**  Ras Michael and The Sons of Negus.  <u>Movements</u>. Dynamic, n.n., 1978.

Good representative album of Nyabinghi chants in general and Ras Michael's work in particular.  The sound finds its foundation in Rasta drumming and is complemented by roots reggae.  Lyrically runs the gamut of Rasta political concerns: solidarity with African struggles against imperialism, criticism of materialism, and affinity with Pan-Africanism.  Some beautiful psalms to Rastafari and glimpses of eloquent poetry.

**D138**  Ras Michael and The Sons of Negus.  <u>Tribute to The Emperor</u>. Trojan, TRLS-132, 1976.

Typical Nyabinghi numbers interspersed with rhythm and blues type melodies and female harmonies.  Some noteable moments of traditional blues guitar and keyboards in conversation with the Nyabinghi repeater.  Some cuts feature Jazzboe Abukaka's jazz trombone.

**D139**  Ras Tesfa and Jafrica.  <u>The Voice of The Rastaman</u>. Meadowlark, 401, 1985.

A cultural album by Rastafarian writer, poet, actor, and singer Ras Tesfa.  His work here defies categorization as simply dub poetry, Rasta music, or straightforward reggae, but rather incorporates elements from all three.  The focus is on Tesfa's poems and they are backed nicely with fine reggae and jazz arrangements.  Includes "Children of All Beliefs," "Rasta Philosophy," "Black Lady-Love," "These Things in Life," and four more poems.  Produced by Larry McDonald for Jafrica Music.  See B325.

**D140**  The Reggae Philharmonic Orchestra.  <u>The Reggae Philharmonic Orchestra</u>. Mango, MLPS-9828, 1988.

A surprising treat which demonstrates reggae's ability to function as a rhythmic foundation for a variety of musics.  The Orchestra incorporates excellent classic reggae drumming and rhythms with jazz, progressive jazz, and classical string instruments (violin, cello, violas, double bass).  A sophisticated, fast moving, and precise album.  Includes both instrumental and lyrical songs.  Includes an arrangement of Cab Calloway's "Minnie the Moocher," an exciting mix of reggae and progressive jazz in "Working Class," bluegrass fiddle work in "Work, Eat, and Sleep," and compelling instrumental pieces like "Sharpesville" and "Scrounger." Produced and arranged by Mykaell S. Riley. Recorded at Greenwood Studios, London.

**D141** Rodriquez, Rico. <u>Jama Rico</u>. Chrysalis Records, n.n., 1982.

Rodriguez's work with Nyabinghi drummer Count Ossie in the Wareika Hills is reflected on this album which combines traditional Nya drumming with Rico's trombone playing. A mix of reggae and other internationally flavored musical motifs, the album offers nine interesting, primarily instrumental cuts.

**D142** Romeo, Max (with The Upsetters). <u>War Ina Babylon</u>. Mango, MLPS-9392, 1976.

Although Romeo has recorded both before and since this album, <u>War Ina Babylon</u> is a representative collection of some of Romeo's more conscious and interesting songs. The title track, written by Romeo and producer/musician Lee Perry, as well as the striking emotion depicted within the cover art quickly became classic moments of early reggae. "Uptown Babies" adeptly contrasts the everyday childhood experiences of wealthy and poor children. Musically, the album reflects simple, rootsy, early reggae, here influenced by Perry's input.

**D143** Sibbles, Leroy. <u>Strictly Roots</u>. Micron, 0038, 1980.

Includes six songs and four dub versions by this classic Jamaican vocalist. Generally comprised of slow, mellow roots reggae rhythms and ghetto lyrics (for example, "Life in the Ghetto" and "Love and Happiness"). Produced by Sibbles and recorded at Channel One.

**D144** Skatalites. <u>Scattered Lights</u>. Alligator, AL-8309, n.d.

Includes twelve songs by the legendary and historically important Jamaican band, The Skatalites. Showcases classic ska and some of Jamaica's finest musicians. Includes "Marcus Jr.," "Re-Burial," "Ska-Ta-Shot," "Lawless Street," and others. Recorded at Federal and Studio One. Historical and biographical notes by Dermott Hussey.

**D145** Sly and The Revolutionaries (With Jah Thomas). <u>Black Ash Dub</u>. Trojan, TRLS-186, 1980.

A classic Channel One dub recording by Sly and Robbie and The Revolutionaries (drums: Sly and Carlton "Santa" Davis, organ: Ansel Collins, Bass: Robbie and Errol "Flabba" Holt, percussion: Sticky and Skully, Rhythm guitar: Bo Peep and Bingy Bunny, piano: Gladstone Anderson, Horns: Bobby Ellis and Deadly Headly Bennett). Mixed at King Tubby's by Prince Jammy and Scientist. Opens with the proclamation "Strictly yard music!" A fine showcase for Sly and for the hypnotic but playful work of legendary dub engineers Prince Jammy and Scientist. Produced by Nkrumah "Jah" Thomas.

**D146** Sly and Robbie. <u>Language Barrier</u>. Island, 90286-1, 1985.

Ironically titled, this mid 1980s Sly and Robbie album illustrates clearly the duo's universal appeal and secure position as a major international rhythmic force in reggae, pop, rock, funk, and world beat music. Composed of six precise, electronically sophisticated, high energy instrumental pieces intertwining elements of jazz, funk, rock, and African rhythms. Among others, backing artists include Herbie Hancock, Manu Dibango, Bob Dylan, Afrika Bambaataa, Mike Hampton, and Mikey Chung. Produced by Bill Laswell. Recorded at RPM in New York and Dynamic and Channel One in Kingston.

**D147** Smith, Michael. <u>Mi C-Yaan beLieVe iT</u>. Mango, MLPS-9717, 1982.

Smith's only album before his tragic death includes nine superb dub poems in heavy patois. Topics focus on racism, African Jamaican identity, and the hard realities of emigrants' lives. The title track offers a vivid description of poverty and oppression in Jamaican folk life. Smith's poetry readings are dynamic and dramatic in style. Record jacket includes lyrics--a must for the ear unattuned to Jamaican patois. A collector's item. See B310.

**D148** Steel Pulse. <u>Earth Crisis</u>. Elektra, 60315-1, 1984.

A fine Steel Pulse production from the mid 1980s. One of the band's best albums. Scattered with enough exceptional cuts ("Steppin' Out," "Roller Skates," "Bodyguard," and "Earth Crisis") to make the album consistently interesting.

**D149** Steel Pulse. <u>Handsworth Revolution</u>. Mango, MLPS-9502, 1978.

In Steel Pulse's debut album, the British based band first establishes its fusion of rockers with Western urban sounds, especially rock and blues. Yet, unlike later Pulse albums with internationally commercial and catchy tunes, <u>Handsworth Revolution</u> delivers a subtle, hypnotic rockers--less impatient and self-conscious and more rootsy and imbued with a blues sensitivity. Includes "Ku Klux Klan" and the playful "Macka Spliff." Produced by Karl Pitterson and dedicated to the people of Handsworth, England.

**D150** Steel Pulse. <u>True Democracy</u>. Elektra, E1-60113, 1982.

Steel Pulse's fourth album illustrates well the band's continued musicial precision and catchy songwriting/arranging via ten worthwhile cuts. Side one ends with "Rally Round"--now a well known tune in praise of Marcus Garvey. Similarly, the album closes with a superb dub version of that song entitled "Dub Marcus Say." Also includes Pulse's popular dance song "Ravers."

**D151** The Tamlins. <u>I'll Be Waiting</u>. Live & Learn, LL-LP027, 1987.

Ten sweet, soul influenced reggae tunes by one of several historically important Jamaican harmony trios. Mainly lilting, lighthearted love songs. Includes "Weeny Teeny Bit," "Play on Reggae Music," "Never Gonna Leave You," and "People Makes The World Go Round." Produced and arranged by Delroy Wright and Al Campbell. Recorded at Music Mountain and Dynamic.

**D152** Third World. <u>All The Way Strong</u>. Columbia, FC-38687, 1983.

The band's second album with Columbia Records includes a variety of musical styles. The title track is a romantic Ballad. "Swing Low" and "Seasons When" are pretty reggae tunes. "Love is Out To Get You" and "Rock and Rave" are influenced heavily by rock, and "Lagos Jump" showcases Carrot's exhilerating percussive work which embellishes the song's lyrical narrative about the band's trip to Africa.

**D153** Third World. <u>Hold on to Love</u>. Columbia, FC-40400, 1987.

Technically precise and musically sophisticated, this recent album illustrates a competence and expertise Third World has developed from many years of working together. The production includes strong rockers pieces such as "We Could Be Jammin' Reggae" and "Reggae Radio Station," a poignant ballad called "Peace Flags," and too little of Bunny Ruggs' compelling scat singing in the jazz influenced "Manners."

**D154** Third World. <u>Journey to Addis</u>. Island, ILPS-9554, 1978.

This production includes the popular disco oriented piece "Now That We Found Love." The title track, an instrumental piece, as well as "Cool Meditation" and "African Woman" contain some of the finest early examples of instrumental conversations among Third World's musicians--especially in the playful "dances" between Ibo's (Michael Cooper) keyboards and Cat's (Stephen Coore) lead guitar.

**D155** Third World. 96 Degrees in the Shade. Island, ILPS-9443, 1977.

Includes a beautiful arrangement--both lyrically and instrumentally--of Bunny Wailer's classic ballad, "Dreamland." (D186)  Also contains fine cuts which address colonialism ("Tribal War") and slavery ("96 Degrees in the Shade").

**D156** Third World. The Story's Been Told. Island, ILPS-9569, 1979.

Although the general ambiance of the album is that of low key dance music, the relatively small number of cuts included (seven) allow for rich instrumental development and a fine opportunity to study the excellence of the individual and collective musicianship of Third World.  "Irie Ites" and "Always Around" are both beautiful lyrical and instrumental sentiments.  "Having a Party" and "The Story's Been Told" are fine pop dance tunes.  Recorded at Crystal Studios in Los Angeles.

**D157** Third World. Third World. Island, ILPS-9369, 1976.

A brilliant debut album.  Although Third World is known best for its fusion of reggae and pop funk music, this first album firmly establishes the band's roots in Rasta and traditional Jamaican music.  It also establishes Third World's reputation for rich, well executed arrangements.  Memorable cuts include the band's extraordinary version of the Abyssinians' "Satta Massagana" (D001) and Burning Spear's "Slavery Days." (D040)  The production utilizes natural sound effects from the hills of Jamaica for continuity between cuts.  The album also includes two short and interesting transitional pieces: "Kumina," a brief taste of traditional Jamaican religious music, and "Cross Reference," a superb blend of traditional African drumming and Jimi Hendrix-like lead guitar riffs.  A collector's item.

**D158** Toots and The Maytals. Funky Kingston. Mango, MLPS-9330, 1975.

A good album of mid 1970s Toots and The Maytals.  Includes fine and popular soul reggae songs like "Louie Louie," "Pressure Drop," and "Sailin' On." Recorded at Dynamic and at Island Studios, London.  Produced by Warrick Lyn, Chris Blackwell, and Dave Bloxham.

**D159** Toots and The Maytals. Knock Out. Mango, MLPS-9670, 1981.

This sampling of the historically important soul reggae singer Toots Hibbert includes, among others, the moving songs "Never Get Weary" and "Missing You."

**D160** Tosh, Peter. <u>Equal Rights</u>. Columbia, BL-34670, 1977.

Includes eight strong and memorable cuts, and is one of Tosh's most consistently fine productions. A popular album which indicates the early development of Tosh's individual musical style as an arranger and composer, and offers a clear definition of Tosh as philosopher and revolutionary. "Equal Rights," "Down Presser Man," "Apartheid," and the delightful "African" offer sharp political statements while "I Am That I Am" and "Jah Guide" address metaphysics. A collector's item.

**D161** Tosh, Peter. <u>Legalize It</u>. Columbia, BL-34253, 1976.

Tosh's first solo album after leaving The Wailers in 1975. Includes nine songs written by Tosh, some in partnership with Marley and Wailer. The popular title track first established Tosh's lifelong advocacy for the legalization of marijuana due to its importance as an aspect of Rastafari as well as of Jamaican traditional folk culture and medicine. This is a theme echoed in many of Tosh's later albums. Some cuts, such as "Ketchy Shuby" and "Watcha Gonna Do" employ Jamaican folk idioms. "Igziabeher"--"Let Jah Be Praised" establishes Tosh's own reverent style of praising Jah musically. Generally the album follows the style of early and classic Wailers' reggae.

**D162** Tosh, Peter. <u>Mystic Man</u>. Rolling Stones, COC-39111, 1979.

One of the albums Tosh produced while working and recording with Mick Jagger. A memorable album of philosophical and political songs. Includes the infectious, well known dance tune and satire "Buk-in-Hamm Palace"--a song whose lyrics have been censored on Jamaican radio, even during radio tributes to Tosh following his death.

**D163** Tosh, Peter. <u>No Nuclear War</u>. EMI, ELT-46700, 1987.

Significant primarily as Tosh's last album before he was murdered in September, 1987. Essentially mirrors the musical style Tosh had already established. Lyrically signifies a more mature resolve in his ideas. Includes eight original cuts. "Fight Apartheid" is a new and more interesting arrangement of the 1977 "Apartheid" on <u>Equal Rights</u>. (D160)

**D164** Trinity. <u>Side Kiks</u>. Vista Sounds, VSLP-4009, 1983.

Ten cuts by the deejay Trinity, whose style closely follows that of Big Youth and U-Roy. Includes "Side Kiks," "Bye, Bye," "In The Ghetto," and others. Produced by Bunny Lee.

**D165** Twinkle Brothers. <u>Live at Reggae Sunsplash</u>. Sunsplash Records, RS-8907, 1984.

This is the first compilation of Twinkle Brothers music produced in the United States. The cuts included here were recorded live at the 1982 Reggae Sunsplash Festival in Montego Bay, Jamaica, as part of Synergy's Sunsplash series. The compilation adeptly reflects the band's characteristic scathing lyrical diatribes against "Babylon" in pieces like "Babylon Falling" and "Jah Kingdom Come." Also includes popular classics by the band: "Jah Jahovia," "It Dread All Over," and "Since I Throw the Comb Away"--a narrative which accurately recounts societal reactions to dreadlocked Rastas. A fine example of Twinkle Brothers rough-around-the-edges heavy roots reggae and Norman Grant's compelling lead vocals.

**D166** Twinkle Brothers. <u>Praise Jah</u>. Virgin, FL-1041, 1979.

The second of several albums the Twinkle Brothers published with Virgin Records. A self-contained band with noteable vocal harmonies, original songs, and serious Rasta influenced lyrics, Twinkle Brothers offers a good representation of their recognizable roots style here in songs such as "Praise Jah" and "Africa."

**D167** UB40. <u>The Earth Dies Screaming</u>. Graduate Records, AW-25006, 1980.

In this, one of the band's earlier albums, the British reggae group UB40 presents some of its most brilliant songs--both lyrically and instrumentally. The title cut, for example, utilizes an almost sinister rhythm embellished by tasteful horns and exciting dub effects to frame lyrics which lament current international situations. The band chooses similar thought provoking narratives in cuts like "Madam Medussa" and in the haunting version of "Strange Fruit," which recounts racial violence in the Southern United States.

**D168** UB40. <u>Labour of Love</u>. A&M, SP-4980, 1983.

UB40 gained a wider audience by releasing this album as well as <u>Jeffery Morgan</u>, A&M, CS-5033, 1984. A very popular album, <u>Labour of Love</u> uses versions of North American pop songs and old reggae ("Cherry Oh Baby," "Red, Red Wine," "Keep On Moving," "Many Rivers To Cross," etc.) to create a slick, pop rock reggae music.

**D169** UB40. <u>Rat in the Kitchen</u>. A&M, CS-5137, 1986.

This more recent UB40 production reflects a marriage between the band's older style with their new, slick, more commercial sound. The majority of cuts here are not as memorable as some of the band's earlier work. Yet, "Tell It Like

It Is" offers an infectious, fast-paced reggae dance tune with UB40's recently more frequent use of deejay style vocals. The rich instrumental version of the title track with its superb jazz horns and heavy bass and drum foundation offers the most powerful moments of the album. "Sing Our Own Song" contains fine lyrics and an interesting arrangement, but Judy Mowatt's recent cover of this tune is more powerful vocally. (D121)

**D170** UB40. The Singles Album. Graduate Records, GRADLSP-3, 1980.

A 1980 production by UB40, this album contains many of the band's sweet melodies, rich rhythmic arrangements, and haunting lyrics. See, for example, the superb "King" and the sweet, sultry instrumental piece, "Adella." In "Key," the generally European sounding vocals of UB40, here used in the chorus, are juxtaposed with resonant deejay style lead vocals which recount the history of reggae music and reverently recall some of its great names.

**D171** U-Roy. Dread In A Babylon. Virgin, VX-1007, 1975.

A classic album by the master of roots deejay music. A distinctive and endearing album which includes "Chalice in The Palace," "Dub It with Her Majesty," "Dread Locks Dread," "Silver Bird," "Trench Town Rock," and others. Produced and arranged by Tony Robinson. Engineered by Errol Thompson at Joe Gibbs. A collector's item.

**D172** Various Artists. African Dub All-Mighty, Chapter 3. Joe Gibbs, JGML-3735, 1981.

The third album in a series of Gibbs' dub productions, Chapter 3 has been considered one of the most successful dub albums ever. (B078:136) Produced and arranged by Gibbs and Errol Thompson, the cuts utilize a wealth of sound effects including bells, running water, growling dogs, as well as phasers and echo units to create delightful and innovative dub versions of popular tunes such as The Wailers' "Hypocrites." A collector's item.

**D173** Various Artists. Black Star Liner: Reggae From Africa. Heartbeat, HB-16, 1983.

In this album, the first of a proposed series, producers Ken Bilby and Bill Nowlin chose selections of African reggae which are sung in English and adhere to classic Jamaican reggae. Artists include Sonny Okosun (Nigeria), Sabanoh 75 (Sierra Leone), Cloud 7 (Nigeria), Bongos Ikwue and The Groovies (Nigeria), Sir Victor Uwaifo and his Titibitis (Nigeria), and Miatta Fahnbulleh (Liberia). While these artists work within a number of musical genres, the classic reggae rhythms and lyrical messages offered here illustrate a cross cultural exchange between African citizens and West Indian members of the

African diaspora.  The eight cuts offered are generally interesting and well executed.  Includes cover notes and an informational leaflet which discusses the emergence of Rasta and reggae throughout the African continent and provides short biographies of the artists included here.

**D174**  Various Artists.  <u>Blow Mr. Hornsman:  Instrumental Reggae 1968-1975</u>. Trojan, TRLS-257, 1988.

A fine historical compilation which illustrates relationships among jazz, soul, and reggae music.  Traces the development of Jamaican music from the traditional jazz influenced genre of ska through rock steady to mature reggae. The list of artists featured is a litany of Jamaica's best and legendary musicians. Indeed, the album essentially is a dedication to a group of immensely talented musicians who have--on the whole--been given little credit for their significant contributions to the development of Jamaican music.   Included are Carl "Cannonball" Bryan; Lester Stirling; The Hippy Boys; The Soul Mates; The Crystalites; Roland Alphonso and The Upsetters; Joe Gibb's Allstars; Jo Jo Bennett with Muddie's Allstars; Herman's Allstars; Val Bennett; Augustus Pablo; Tommy McCook and Impact Allstars; Carl Masters; Zap Pow; Skin, Flesh and Bones; and Vin Gordon.   An historical overview and information about specific tracks are included in Steve Barrow's jacket notes.  A collector's item.

**D175**  Various Artists.   <u>Jimmy Cliff in The Harder They Come</u>.   Original Soundtrack Recording.  Island, ILPS-9202, 1972.

The popular soundtrack album of the movie by the same name includes many classic reggae songs and served to introduce Jamaican music to many people. The following artists are included: Jimmy Cliff, Derrick Harriot, The Melodians, Toots and The Maytals, The Slickers, and Desmond Dekker.  Includes classics like The Melodians' "Rivers of Babylon," Toots' "Pressure Drop," Desmond Dekker's "Shantytown," Cliff's "Many Rivers To Cross," and others.  See B046, V13.

**D176**  Various Artists.   <u>King Tubby's Presents Soundclash: Dub Plate Style</u>. Taurus/King Tubby's Music, FHLP-005, 1988.

This album offers a sampling of the work of veteran record producer King Tubby.  It also illustrates the character of the dancehall or soundsystem clashes. The ten cuts included are "specials," recorded solely for soundsystem competitions.  Cuts open with dancehall introducer Fuzzy Jones.  Includes the following artists: King Everald, Johnny Osbourne, Trevor "Pan Bird" Levy, Banana Man, Michael Bitas, Gregory Isaacs, Little John, Sugar Minott, Conroy Smith, and Pad Anthony.  Mixed by Carl "Fitzie Banton" Nelson.  Produced by and recorded at King Tubby's.

**D177** Various Artists. "Land of Africa." RAS, 5001A, Disco 45, 1985.

In the mid 1980s, at a time when all manner of musicians from their respective nations and musical genres gathered to record music in the name of the Ethiopian famine, Ibo Cooper's production and arrangement for Music Is Life shined bright. Written by Ibo Cooper and Willie Stewart from Third World and Grizzly Nesbitt of Steel Pulse, "Land of Africa" is backed by members of Third World, Steel Pulse, and Ras Brass. The piece was engineered by Errol Brown, Scientist, and David Rowe and was recorded at Tuff Gong. Poignant cover art by Neville Garrick. Lead singers take turns with the verses to create a significant song in terms of both politics and music. Like other similar compilations, proceeds went in aid of Ethiopian famine victims. But unlike recordings such as the insipid U.S. production "We Are The World," "Land of Africa" offers substantive lyrics which observe the interdependence of political and social conditions throughout the African continent and argue a relationship to the situation of African Jamaicans as part of the larger African diaspora. Furthermore, a tribute to the African experience is clearly re-presented via use of African vocal effects by Amaniyea Payne, an Amharic message by Addis Gessesse, and the choice of the reggae genre itself. Side one includes some of the best lead vocalists in reggae music: David Hinds, Freddie McGregor, Bunny "Rugs" Clarke, and The I-Threes. Side two offers a different fare with verses led first by Mutabaruka, and then by Tristan Palma, Edi Fitzroy, and Gregory Isaacs. A fine production.

**D178** Various Artists. МИР: Reggae From Around The World. RAS, 3050, 1988.

The title, pronounced "mir," is Russian for peace, community, and world. This album certainly demonstrates the universal appeal and spread of reggae music. A commendable production by Alan Kirk, it illustrates the ease with which musical artists from Poland, Israel, Uruguay, and other countries have articulated their own cultural concerns and musical traditions within the foundation of the reggae rhythm. Includes Peter Broggs (Jamaica), Aotearoa (New Zealand), Gedeon Jerubbaal (Poland), Sandii and The Sunsetz (Japan), Reggae Team (Sweden), Dallol (Ethiopia), The Naturalites (England), Alpha Blondy (Ivory Coast), Avi Matos (Israel), Ruina De Moda (Uruguay), Different Stylee (Italy), Kino (U.S.S.R.), and Stingray (U.S.). Recorded and mixed at Lion and Fox Studios, Washington, D.C.

**D179** Various Artists. Reggae Sunsplash 81': A Tribute to Bob Marley. Elektra, EL-60035-G, 1982.

Recorded live at Reggae Sunsplash 1981, this two record set is the original soundtrack album from the film/video by the same name. This popular festival compilation offers a good cross section of reggae at the beginning of its second decade and shortly after the loss of its international representative, Bob Marley. Side one is composed entirely of early Steel Pulse songs. Side two is backed mainly by The Wailers and moves from The I-Threes' performance of "Dem Belly Full" through the Melody Makers, Eek-A-Mouse, to Dennis Brown. Side three opens with two classic Black Uhuru songs ("Plastic Smile" and "Guess Who's Coming To Dinner"). Uhuru is followed by Sheila Hylton and then Gregory Isaacs' "Soon Forward." The closing side includes Carlene Davis, The Mighty Diamonds, and Third World's "1865 (96 Degrees In The Shade)" and "Rock The World." Produced by Jay Steinberg. A collector's item. See V24.

**D180** Various Artists. <u>Rock Steady: Coxsone Style</u>. Coxsone Records, CSL-8013, n.d.

Twelve songs from the studios of Clement Dodd illustrating the rock steady genre (circa mid 1960s). Artists include the Soul Vendors, The Termites, The Sultans, Jacob Milner, Winston Holness, Winston and Robin, Bennett and Dennis, Eric Frater, Bumps Oakley, and Marshall Williams.

**D181** Various Artists. <u>Rockers</u>. Mango, MLPS-9587, 1979.

Soundtrack from the film <u>Rockers</u>. The album, compiled by Chris Blackwell, includes Inner Circle, The Maytones, Junior Murvin, The Heptones, Peter Tosh, Jacob Miller, Junior Byles, Bunny Wailer, Gregory Isaacs, Rockers All Stars, Kiddus I, Burning Spear, Third World, and Justin Hinds and The Dominoes. A smooth, well executed compilation which offers a cross section of fine reggae. While all cuts included are strong, some of the most memorable moments include Bunny Wailer's "Rockers," Winston Rodney's a capella performance of "Jah No Dead," Third World's rich arrangement of the classic "Satta Massagana," and Jacob Miller's popular "Tenement Yard." A collector's item. See V25.

**D182** Various Artists. <u>Tidal Wave</u>. Unicorn Records, UNIC-9510, 1983.

An early 1980s compilation album of deejay artists including Bobby Culture, Brimestone and Fire, Nicodemus, and Louie Rankin. Among the ten cuts are "The Dreadlocks Man," "Vibes In Me," "Nice It Up," and "Valley of Decision." Produced by White Buffalo Multimedia, Nathan Koenig, and Eric Greenberg.

**D183** Various Artists. <u>Woman Talk: Caribbean Dub Poetry</u>. Heartbeat, HB-25, 1986.

One of the few published works focusing on women artists in the Caribbean. Mutabaruka, whom Heartbeat solicited to produce this follow-up to the compilation album <u>Word Soun 'Ave Power</u> (D184), chose to focus on women dub poets from a number of countries. Included are Afua, Louise Bennett,

Breeze, Cheryl Byron, Anita Stewart, and Elaine Thomas. Consistently professional arrangements by Mutabaruka and The High Times Players show sensitivity to the individual styles of the women writers. Among other political and cultural topics, the lyrics elaborate indignation over the continued degradation of women in Jamaican deejay lyrics, jokes, and day to day life. A fine production and a collector's item.

**D184** Various Artists. Word Soun' 'Ave Power. Heartbeat, HB-15, 1983.

Produced by Mutabaruka, arranged by Mutabaruka and The High Times Players, and recorded at Tuff Gong (except Mutabaruka's "Out of Many One," which was recorded at Music Mountain). This compilation of dub poetry provides a representative cross section of Jamaican poets working within the genre. The album includes cuts by Breeze, Mutabaruka, Malachi Smith, Tomlin Ellis, Glenville Bryan, Navvie Nabbie, and Oliver Smith. Generally interesting artistry and strong political and social statements. See, in particular, the sardonic juxtaposition in Mutabaruka's "Out of Many One," "Aid Travels with a Bomb" by Breeze, and the brief, straightforward anti-heroin dub poem by Tomlin Ellis, "Drop It." Cover notes are written by Dr. Ginger Beer, who situates dub poetry as a response to the persistence of lyrically frivolous and musically monotonous Jamaican deejay songs. Pertinent quotes by Mutabaruka and Malachi Smith are included.

**D185** The Viceroys. Chancery Lane. Greensleeves, GREL-67, 1984.

An enjoyable, steady compilation of this harmony group's solid roots rockers tunes. Strong arrangements and social-spiritual messages grace cuts such as "Take Care of the Youths" and "Voice Like Thunder."

**D186** Wailer, Bunny. Black Heart Man. Mango, MLPS-9415, 1976.

Bunny Wailer's first solo album after leaving The Wailers in 1975. Wailer delivers quintessential Rasta reggae in what is called "The Ten Messages"--ten songs which have all become classic reggae hits. The album is backed by the best in reggae: The Wailers, Bob Marley, Peter Tosh, Earl "Chinna" Smith, Robbie Shakespeare, and Tommy McCook. Backing vocals in all but three cuts (which use Marley and Tosh for harmonies) are dubbed by Wailer himself--a strategy which has since consistently been successful for Wailer due to his own distinctive vocal style. Here Wailer first established the excellence of his own artistic expression by introducing classics like "Black Heart Man," "Dreamland," "Rasta Man," and "Amagideon." The acclaim this album still continues to receive is well supported by Wailer's vocals, percussion, and guitar; the somewhat ethereal effect of McCook's flute and Tosh's melodica; and the prayer like quality of Wailer's lyrics. An essential collector's item.

**D187** Wailer, Bunny. <u>In I Father's House</u>. Solomonic, n.n., 1980.

Rich and heavy rockers album containing six superb original cuts. Includes the theme from the reggae movie, <u>Rockers</u> (V25), and a dynamic tribute to Jah in "Love Fire." This album was repackaged and retitled <u>Roots, Rockers, Radicals, Reggae</u> (Shanachie, 43013, 1983) for distribution in the United States. The Shanachie production offers a better pressing and two strong, additional cuts: "Cease Fire" and "Conqueror," but loses the personal touch of Wailer's own jacket designs.

**D188** Wailer, Bunny. <u>Liberation</u>. Shanachie, 43059, 1988.

Many critics are comparing this album to Wailer's classic debut album, <u>Black Heart Man</u>. (D186) Indeed, this album will most likely become a reggae and Bunny Wailer classic. Here Wailer finds a comfortable blend between his recent, more international pop sound and his earlier and classic Rasta messages. The album contains ten message oriented songs with a perceptive international consciousness and expressions of the charm and sincerity of Rasta logic (see especially "Baldhead Jesus"). Includes two popular and exceptional Jamaican singles: "Rise and Shine" and "Botha The Mosquito." The list of backing musicians is typically impressive, including Cat Coore, Earl "Chinna" Smith, Carlton Davis, Sly Dunbar, Sticky Thompson, and others. Recorded at Dynamic. Produced by Bunny Wailer for Solomonic Productions.

**D189** Wailer, Bunny. <u>Rock 'n' Groove</u>. Solomonic, n.n., 1981.

Albums like this and Bunny Wailer's collection of old Wailers' tunes, <u>Sings the Wailers</u> (D191) illustrate the relationship between dancehall music and rockers reggae. A true classic. Seven cuts of mezmerizing dancehall music in Wailer's own traditional style. Produced, performed, arranged, and directed by Bunny Wailer. All songs by Bunny Wailer except "Another Dance," by Curtis Mayfield. Backed by The Radics, Sly Dunbar, and Robbie Shakespeare. Includes exemplar dancehall classics such as "Rock 'n' Groove," "Cool Runnings," and "Dance Rock."

**D190** Wailer, Bunny. <u>Rule Dancehall</u>. Shanachie, 43050, 1987.

Published by Solomonic Music. More than any other reggae artist, Bunny Wailer has worked persistently to explain that the roots of reggae music lie in the soundsystem dances, and that the best dancehall music advocates not only conscious lyrics, but musical creativity and originality. This album is clearly intended as a strong message aimed at the plethora of meaningless lyrics, monotone vocals, and overworked old rhythms churned out daily by the various deejay and dancehall artists in Jamaica. A current focal point of conflict in reggae music, dancehall is here shown as a vital, creative, original form of reggae music. Backed by The Radics. Includes nine Wailer originals, two Bob Marley songs, and a delightful arrangement of Sam Cooke's "Saturday Night."

**D191**   Wailer, Bunny. <u>Sings The Wailers</u>. Mango, MLPS-9629, 1980.

Backed by Sly Dunbar and Robbie Shakespeare. Bunny Wailer devotes this album to early Wailers' tunes.  Like freeze frames, the cuts act as markers capturing moments of The Wailers' early history: the rude boy days in Trench Town and the emerging Rasta consciousness shared personally and expressed musically by the three most legendary names in reggae music.

**D192**   Wailer, Bunny. <u>Struggle</u>. Solomonic, n.n., 1978.

This album as well as Wailer's preceding album, <u>Protest</u> (Solomonic, n.n., 1977), are often discounted by critics.  Yet <u>Struggle</u> offers one of the purest examples of Rasta consciousness expressed via the musical idiom of reggae. Lyrically the cuts interrelate spiritual, moral, and political issues to create powerful psalms and parables laced with traditional Jamaican folk lyrics.  See particularly "The Old Dragon" and "Bright Soul." Musically, the album offers a very danceable roots reggae embellished by Bunny Wailer's own percussive work on the talking drum and repeater.

**D193**   Wailer, Bunny. <u>Tribute</u>. Solomonic, n.n., 1981.

Since Marley's death, a plethora of songs have been written in memory of him, and many productions have been dedicated to his life and work.  Yet, Bunny Wailer's performance of eight Bob Marley songs (chosen according to popular opinion) is in some ways the most appropriate of all dedications.  Wailer, after all, was Marley's close lifelong friend and is one of the three original Wailers. Wailer brings to these international classics his personal sense of timing, his distinctive arrangements, the superb resonance of his own harmony vocal overlays, and his small, yet significant changes in lyrics.  Backed by Sly Dunbar, Robbie Shakespeare, Flabba Holt, Style Scott, Dean Frazer, Nambo Robinson, Sticky Thompson, and others.  All eight cuts are exceptional.  See particularly Wailer's  dance rock arrangement of "No Woman, No Cry" and the piano and bass accompaniment on "Redemption Song."  Cover notes by Dermott Hussey.

**D194**   The Wailers. <u>Burnin'</u>. Island, ILPS-9256, 1973.

Released the same year as <u>Catch a Fire</u> (D024), but without the "Bob Marley and" attribution to the band's name.  Much more roots oriented than <u>Catch a Fire</u>.  Combines the language of revolution with Rasta metaphysics.  Includes Wailers' classics such as "Get Up, Stand Up," "Small Axe," the traditional "Rasta Man Chant," and the beautiful psalm-like "Pass It On," written by Jean Watt.

**D195**  The Wailers Band.  I.D.  Atlantic, 81960-1, 1989.

A recent production composed mostly of veteran Wailers' musicians. Technically excellent reggae, but much of the album has a runaway tempo that sounds more pop than roots.  Resistance messages traditional to reggae lyrics are often reduced here to sentimental ballads.  Includes the pretty ballad "Children of The World," a dedication to Nelson and Winnie Mandela in "Love is Forever," the calypso/mento influenced "Love One Another," and the more roots oriented "Life Goes On."  The band is composed of Aston "Family Man" Barrett (bass), Junior Marvin (lead vocals), Al Anderson (lead, rhythm, slide guitars), Irvin "Carrot" Jarrett and Alvin "Seeco" Patterson (percussion), Martin Batista (keyboards), Michael "Boo" Richards (drums), and others.  Recorded at Marathon Studios, New York and Dynamic, Kingston.  Produced by The Wailers Band.

**D196**  The Wailing Souls.  Inchpinchers.  Greensleeves, CGR-47, 1982.

A roots album by this veteran Jamaican harmony group which ambles along brightly but subtly.  Includes the catchy "Tom Sprang," the philosophical "Things and Time," and the popular "Modern Slavery" and "Ghettos of Kingston Town."  Recorded at Channel One.  Engineered by Errol Thompson.  Mixed at Joe Gibbs.  Backed by The Roots Radics.

**D197**  The Wailing Souls.  Kingston 14.  Live & Learn, LL-LP028, 1987.

The epitome of light, bubbly roots reggae with sweet vocal harmonies. Eminently danceable with proud lyrics.  Much of the album is composed of enjoyable roots rockers such as in "Dem Coming" and "Pity The Poor," yet some cuts are not memorable.  The title track is excellent.  Produced by Delroy Wright and recorded at Music Mountain and Dynamic.  Backed by Robbie Shakespeare, Lloyd Parkes, Sly Dunbar, Style Scott, Flabba Holt, Dwight Pinkney, Glen DaCosta, and others.

**D198**  Yabby You.  One Love, One Heart.  Shanachie, 43016, 1983.

Rasta roots singer Yabby You offers ten Rasta messages in traditional roots style.  Somewhat similar to groups like Culture and Ras Michael and The Sons of Negus.  Includes the traditional Rasta chant "Run Come Rally" as well as "Babylon Gone Down," "Chant Down Babylon," "Conquoring Lion," and others. Backed by Leroy "Horsemouth" Wallace, Sly Dunbar, Aston "Family Man" Barrett, Earl "Chinna" Smith, Augustus Pablo, Tommy McCook, and others. Recorded at Channel One.  Overdubs mixed at King Tubby's.  Good cultural roots music.

**D199** Yellowman. <u>Rides Again</u>. RAS, 3034, 1988.

A recent album by this internationally popular Jamaican deejay of the 1980s. Includes advisory messages ("Aids," "Girl You're Too Hot"); sex, sexist and homophobic songs ('I'm Ready," "Pretty Girl," "Want A Virgin"); the political "Ease Up President Botha"; a good humored satire of military life ("In The Army"); and a dedication to deceased musicians ("In Memory Of"). Backed by The Roots Radics and Augustus Pablo. Recorded at Lion and Fox Studios in Washington, D.C. Engineered by Jim Fox. Produced by Doctor Dread.

**D200** Ziggy Marley and The Melody Makers. <u>Conscious Party</u>. Virgin, 90878-1, 1988.

In the historical pattern of his father, Ziggy Marley establishes his lead in the band by name here for the first time. Despite the album title, the lyrics function less as a form of protest or confrontation than in his earlier work. Likewise, the arrangements, while crisp and precise, seem more slick than imbued with a sense of roots or mission. While Ziggy's tenor still has an uncanny resemblance to his father's, most cuts are consistently unexciting. For example, "Dream Home" is interesting lyrically and percussively, but Ziggy's vocals are uninspired.

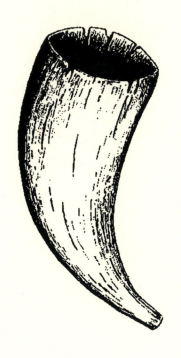

**ABENG**

# Annotated Videography

**V01**  <u>Aswad Live</u>. Videocassette. Dir. Geoff Sax. Tasty Productions, 1985. Approx. 60 min.

An enjoyable and engaging concert tape with good sound quality and effective, unobtrusive video effects and editing. Includes "Dub Fire," "I Asked the Question," "Roots Rocking," "In My Father's House," "Rebel," "African Children," and more. Visual focus is on the stage, yet there are a few camera shots of the audience. Recorded live at Limehouse Studios in London. Produced by Dave Cash and Alistair Rae. Edited by Phil Moss and Gayle A. Hall.

**V02**  <u>The Best of Reggae Sunsplash, Vol. I</u>. Videocassette. Dir. Annie Rowe. KSR Group. A Sony Video, 1983. 60 min.

This video compilation of Sunsplash performances contains eleven songs divided into three sets. It also uses shots of Montego Bay, Jarrett Park, and the beach to set moods and indicate transitions. Included are Chalice, Steel Pulse, Eek-A-Mouse, Aswad, Burning Spear, Mutabaruka, Big Youth, Lloyd Parkes and We the People, Mighty Diamonds, and Blue Riddim Band. Nearly all cuts included are strong, the sound engineering is generally clear, and the video editing is rarely distracting. See in particular the sequence of performances by Burning Spear, Mutabaruka, and then Big Youth. Produced by Stuart Reid in association with Synergy Productions, Les Souci, and Channel Four.

**V03**  <u>Best of Reggae Sunsplash, Vol. II</u>. Videocassette. A Sony Video, n.d. 60 min.

(Not Viewed)  The companion piece to V02, this video offers Sunsplash footage which includes Chalice, Byron Lee and The Dragonaires, Big Youth, Toots and The Maytals, Home T Four, Taj Mahal, Eek-A-Mouse, Mutabaruka, Yellowman, Lloyd Parkes, Denice Williams, and The Twinkle Brothers.

**V04** <u>The Best of Sunsplash, Vol. I</u>. Videocassette. A Synergy Production, n.d. Approx. 90 min.

Although the copy of this video I reviewed was marked "Volume I," the footage was filmed at Reggae Sunsplash 10 and 11 (1987 and 1988), long after Synergy produced another video of Sunsplash also titled "Volume I" (V02). This tape offers a very fine cross section of live reggae music in the late 1980s. It includes Chalice; the Japanese reggae vocalist Sandii and her band The Sunsetz; a brief appearance by Japanese deejay Ranking Taxi; Bloodfire Posse; Dennis Brown; Coco Tea; a fine example of various deejay styles in the combined performance of Charlie Chaplin, Brigadier Jerry, and Yellowman; Gregory Isaacs; a fine performance with Isaacs, Dennis Brown, Freddie McGregor, John Holt, and Josey Wales; and an energetic closing with three songs by Bunny Wailer ("Rule Dance Hall," "Jolly Session," and "Camoflauge"). Recorded live at the Bob Marley Performing Centre in Montego Bay. Edited by Hopeton Fullwood. Produced by Junior Lincoln in association with Synergy Productions.

**V05** <u>Best of the Rootsman: The Music</u>. Videocassette. Rootsman Productions, 1987. 59 min.

There is little continuity between video sequences in this tape, and the quality of the production is rather poor, but the musicians and songs included speak for themselves. Contains songs and performances by Bob Marley, Gregory Isaacs, The Meditations, Leroy Sibbles, Jacob Miller, Ras Michael and The Sons of Negus, and Roman Stewart. Produced by Earl "The Rootsman" Chin.

**V06** <u>Bob Marley and The Wailers</u>. Videocassette. Dir. Jo Merell and Charles Chabot. An Arena Presentation, 1986. Approx. 60 min.

A fine documentary tracing Marley's career from his childhood days in Trench Town to his state funeral in 1981. Discusses the evolution of singing groups in Jamaica, the rude boy phenomenon, the effect of Selassie's coronation on Jamaicans, Rastafari and Marley's perception of Rastafari, Blackwell's packaging of Marley as a rock star, Bunny Wailer and Peter Tosh's split from The Wailers, Marley's Island House, the politics of the Smile Jamaica and the One Love Peace concerts, and Marley's illness and eventual death. The tape includes music and still photographs, concert, practice, and studio footage as well as interviews with Marley, Cedella Booker, Bunny Wailer, Joe Higgs, Peter Tosh, Rita Marley, Chris Blackwell, Neville Garrick, and Judy Mowatt. An historically valuable documentary including excellent sequences from The Wailers' Old Graywhistle test recordings with the BBC. Commentary by Darcus Howe. Produced by Anthony Wall and Nigel Finch. Executive producer, Chris Blackwell. A collector's item.

**V07**   Bob Marley and The Wailers: Legend.   Film/Videocassette.   Island Records, 1984.  RCA/Columbia Pictures Home Video, 1985.  55 min.

While little in this audio-visual collage of Marley memorabilia is new to Marley fans, the video is generally well composed and is a good addition to any Bob Marley collection.   It consists of twelve songs separated by brief interview segments with Marley.  Included are "Is This Love," "Jammin,'" "Could You Be Loved," "No Woman, No Cry," "Stir It Up," "Get Up, Stand Up," "Satisfy My Soul," "I Shot the Sheriff," "Buffalo Soldier," "Exodus," "Redemption Song," and "One Love."  Video aspects range from concert and studio footage to Jamaican urban and rural scenes.  There are few attempts at gearing visual segments explicitly to song messages, although dramatic enactments occur with "Buffalo Soldier" and "Exodus."  Segments are taken from different periods of Marley's career.  For instance, "Stir It Up" features a young Marley-Wailer-Tosh looking a bit stiff and uncomfortable on stage.  Particularly moving are the ballad style version of "No Woman," the studio solo of "Redemption Song," and the exhilarating concert footage of "I Shot the Sheriff."  The video sequence of Marley singing at a children's birthday party is delightful.

**V08**   Bob Marley and The Wailers Live at The Rainbow.  Film/Videocassette. Dir. Keef.  Blue Mountain Films, 1978.  RCA/Columbia Pictures Home Video, 1986.  40 min.

A rather dry concert tape.  The visual focus is entirely on the stage, creating concert footage devoid of audience participation or presence except on "Get Up, Stand Up."  Includes thirteen songs: "Trench Town Rock," "Them Belly Full," "I Shot the Sheriff," "Rebel Music," "Lively Up Yourself," "Crazy Baldhead," "War," "No More Trouble," "The Heathen," "No Woman, No Cry," "Jammin,'" "Get Up, Stand Up," and "Exodus."  Musicians include Tyrone Downie on keyboards, Junior Marvin on lead guitar, Carlton Barrett on drums, Aston "Family Man" Barrett on bass, and Alvin "Seeco" Patterson on percussion.  Filmed live at the Rainbow Theatre in London, 1977.  Produced by Scott Millaney.

**V09**   Bongo Man.  Film/Videocassette.  Dir. Stefan Paul.  A Stefan Paul Film Production, 1981.  Approx. 90 min.

A ponderous documentary/music video containing a collage of footage and discussion concerning Jimmy Cliff's life and musical career.  The first segment centers on Cliff's African Oneness concert in his home town of Somerton, St. James.  Other sequences include footage from Cliff's concert in Soweto, South Africa (May 1980) and from his Hamburg concert the same year, reasonings with Preacher Brown and later with Mortimer Planno, a Maroon celebration, Cliff's participation in a small Nyabinghi, and a discussion of Cliff's starring role in The Harder They Come. (V13)  The video attempts to explain Cliff's personal philosophy and personality as well as to illustrate his musical talents. Musical segments are sometimes frustrating, as they are short, incomplete, and repetitive. For example, we see Cliff performing "Bongo Man" at least three times, but never are allowed to watch his entire performance of the song. Includes "Fundamental Reggae," "Stand Up and Fight Back," "Many Rivers To Cross," "She is a Woman," "The Harder They Come," "Turn the Tables," "I Am The Living," and more. Recorded in 1981 in Somerton, Kingston, Montego Bay, Hamburg, Montreux, and Soweto. Edited by Hildegard Schroder. Narrated by Lister Hewan-Lowe. Written by Stefan Paul. Produced by Gerd Unger and Edgar Deplewski.

**V10**  Classic Reggae '86. Videocassette. Dir. Paul Campbell. Bareback Productions, 1986. 120 min.

Footage from a deejay dancehall concert in Miami, Florida. Includes songs by Beres Hammond, Delroy Wilson, Tonto Irie, Little John, Anthony Red Rose, Robert Ffrench, Echo Minott, and Johnny Osbourne. Edited by Geno Tulchin. Produced by Bareback Productions.

**V11**  Cool Runnings. Videocassette. Dir. Andy McConnell. Island Visual Arts, n.d. 52 min.

This video is composed of footage from a variety of documentary, concert, and narrative fiction films/videos directed by Keef, Paul Alessandrini and Jean Pierre Janssen, Bruno Tilley, Jeff Walker, Derek Burbidge, Don Letts and Mick Calvert, Theodoros Bafaloukos, and Jerome Lapersousaz. Many of the sequences, therefore, may seem familiar. The video features several songs by Bob Marley and The Wailers, Toots and The Maytals, Black Uhuru, Burning Spear, and Third World. Edited by Torquil Dearden and Kelvin Duckett. Produced by Andy McConnell.

**V12**  Countryman. Film/Videocassette. Dir. Dickie Jobson. Island Pictures. Media Home Entertainment, 1984. 103 min.

Adapted by Dickie Jobson and Michael Thomas from the original Jobson story. This feature film is dedicated to Bob Marley and includes music by Bob Marley and The Wailers, Dennis Brown, Aswad, Toots and The Maytals, Steel Pulse and others. The story features a wiry dreadlocked fisherman from Hellshire with mystical powers who protects a wide-eyed North American woman and her partner from becoming victims of a deadly political game. The film generally handles implications of Countryman's mystical powers with tact and a wry sense of humor. It also contains some visual accounts of Rasta lifestyles and cultural traditions (an ital feast, a Nyabinghi session, etc.). In general, Countryman is an interesting and coherent story with a twist of karmic justice in the conclusion.

**V13**   The Harder They Come.   Film/Videocassette.   Dir. Perry Henzell.
International Films Limited, 1972.   A Thorn EMI Video.   93 min.

This film starring internationally known reggae musician Jimmy Cliff has
become a cult classic.   The story is of the legendary Jamaican outlaw Rhygin-
-a country boy who hopes to become a successful musician, only to be
exploited by his producer and his employer.   Rhygin turns to dealing ganja and
to violence to survive, and meets his demise.   Offers insight into the rude boy
phenomenon.   Includes classic reggae music.   (D175)   Screenplay by Perry
Henzell and Trevor D. Rhone.   Produced by Perry Henzell.   A collector's item.
See B046, B326.

**V14**   Heartland Reggae.   Videocassette.   Dir. Jim Lewis.   Continental Video,
1984.   90 min.

A good documentary/music video which combines a cultural and historical
narrative about both Rastafari and reggae music with footage from the historic
One Love Peace Concert.   Includes live concert performances by Bob Marley
and The Wailers, The I-Threes, Peter Tosh, Jacob Miller and Inner Circle, Judy
Mowatt and Light of Love, Dennis Brown, U-Roy, Junior Tucker, Althea and
Donna, and Lloyd Parkes and We The People.   Includes a memorable set by
the frenetic Jacob Miller and historically valuable footage of Marley bringing
political opponents Michael Manley and Edward Seaga on stage for a symbolic
handshake of peace.   A collector's item.

**V15**   Island Reggae Greats.   RCA/Island Records, 1985.   28 min.

A brief compilation of short promotional videos produced by Island Records.
The tape begins with Winston Rodney singing "Jah is My Driver" a capella and
is followed by Third World's "Now That We Found Love," Black Uhuru's
"Solidarity," Aswad's "Chasing For the Breeze," Bob Marley's "War," LKJ's "Di
great insoh reckshan," and Toots Hibbert's "Reggae Got Soul."

**V16**   Land of The Look Behind.   Film.   Dir. Alan Greenberg.   1982.   88 min.

(Not viewed)   A documentary on the funeral of Bob Marley which also
functions as a dramatic piece illustrating relationships among poverty,
oppression, and spirituality in Jamaica.   See B288.

**V17**   The Mighty Quinn.   Film/Videocassette.   Dir. Carl Schenkel.   An A&M
Films Production, 1989.   98 min.

This feature length narrative fiction offers a seemingly simple murder mystery
plot with a Caribbean isle location.   The unnamed island obviously is Jamaica,
and the story is of two old friends who appear to find themselves on opposite

sides of the law.  Police chief Quinn (Denzel Washington) unearths a foul political deal gone bad and clears his childhood friend Maubee (Robert Townsend) of murder in the process.  Interesting cultural themes are addressed: Maubee is a benevolent trickster, clearly a manifestation of anancy, and Quinn must work out tensions between his upwardly mobile live style and his loyalty to his own people.  Includes music by Michael Rose, UB40, Gregory Isaacs, Yellowman, Sister Carol, The Neville Brothers, and others.  Appearances by Michael Rose, Rita Marley, Cedella Marley, and Bob Andy.  Densell Washington provides a fine performance of Taj Mahal's "Catwalk into Town." Screenplay by Hampton Fancher.  Produced by Sandy Lieberson, Marion Hunt, and Ed Elbert.

**V18**  Mutabaruka Live.  Videocassette.  Dir. Ashani.  A Step Lively Production, 1986.  49 min.

Concert footage from a nightclub performance at the Lone Star Cafe in New York.  Despite some rather awkward camera work and editing, this somewhat low key session includes some memorable performances by dub poet Mutabaruka.  Always frank, dramatic, and compelling, Mutabaruka excells in his performance of "Cannan Land" and "Every Time I Hear the Sound." Includes a sequence devoted to women; reasonings about drugs, racism, and religion; and other fine dub poems by Mutabaruka.  Edited by Diane Gurwitz.

**V19**  Peter Tosh Live.  Videocassette.  Dir. Michael C. Collins.  A Picture Music International Presentation.  EMI Records, 1984.  55 min.

Peter Tosh always put on a good concert, and this footage shows that his concert at the Greek Theater in Los Angeles, August 23, 1983, was no exception.  The highlight of the video is Tosh's performance of "Rastafari Is." Not only are the arrangement and instrumental sequences excellent, but Tosh also joins his percussionists (Vision Walker and Winston Morgan) on the stage floor for Nyabinghi drumming and Rasta chants and reasonings in Amharic. Also included are performances of "African," "Comin' in Hot," "Glass House," "Equal Rights," Downpressor Man," "Get Up, Stand Up," and others.  Backed by Word Sound and Power.  Edited by Susan Crutcher.  Produced by Michael C. Collins.  A collector's item.

**V20**  Rastafari: Conversations Concerning Women.  Videocassette.  Dir. Renee Romano.  Eye in I Filmworks, 1983.  60 min.

(Not viewed)  Documentary on the role of women in Rastafari.  The video offers a primer on Rastafari; a variety of interviews representing a cross section of Jamaican and Rastafarian women and men; songs, chants, and poems; and discussion of taboos associated with women.  Clearly states the patriarchal character of Rastafari and its subsequent poor treatment of women. See Sister Ikeda's review in Reggae and African Beat, 4, 6 (December 1985): 29.

**V21** Rastafari Vocies. Videocassette. Eye in I Filmworks, 1979. 60 min.

(Not viewed) A documentary on Rastafari which offers a series of interviews with both urban and rural Rastas, Rasta reasonings and Nyabinghis, and traditional chants and drumming. Produced by Elliot Leib and Renee Romano. See Tony Thompson's review in Reggae and African Beat, 4, 4 (August 1985): 35.

**V22** A Reggae Session. Film/Videocassette. Dir. Stephanie Bennett and Thomas Adelman. A Delilah Films Production, 1988. Approx. 60 min.

An interesting selection of artists and performances filmed live in Jamaica. Offers a fine cross section of late 1980s reggae (both Jamaican and international). Includes performances by the I-Threes, Bunny Wailer, Ziggy Marley and The Melody Makers, Chrissie Hyndes (of The Pretenders), Toots Hibbert, Grace Jones, The Neville Brothers, and Jimmy Cliff. Also features Carlos Santana, Sly and Robbie, Coati Mundi, Tyrone Downie, and Stephen "Cat" Coore. Introduced by Neville Garrick. Backed by the 809 Band, The Solomonic All Stars, Dallol, and Oneness. Edited by Paul Justman. Produced by Stephanie Bennett and Albert Spevak.

**V23** Reggae Sunsplash II. Film/Videocassette. Dir. Stefan Paul. A Stefan Paul Film Production. Columbia Video, n.d. Approx. 100 min.

Live footage from the 1979 Reggae Sunsplash festival in Montego Bay. Includes performances and festival scenes interspersed with street scenes of Jamaica. Sound quality and mixing as well as continuity in editing are rather poor, but many good performances are included (Winston Rodney, Peter Tosh, Third World, and Bob Marley). Narrated discussions and scenes cover Jamaica and herb; Peter Tosh and his views on music and spirituality; Winston Rodney and his celebration of Marcus Garvey; Nyabinghi drummers and a reasoning about Africa, drums, and reggae music; and Bob Marley and his views on Rastafari and reggae music. Edited by Hildegard Schroder.

**V24** Reggae Sunsplash: A Tribute to Bob Marley. Film/Videocassette. Dir. Karen Baxter and Robert H. Peitscher. A Reggae Tribute Corporation Film. Sony Video LP, 1985. Approx. 100 min.

A competent video counterpart to the classic two album set. (D179) Recorded live at Reggae Sunsplash 1981 in Jarrett Park, Montego Bay. Includes performances by Third World, Steel Pulse, The Mighty Diamonds, Black Uhuru, Gregory Isaacs, Sheila Hylton, Eek-A-Mouse, Carlene Davis, Dennis

Brown, Marcia Griffiths, Louie Lepke, Judy Mowatt, Dean Frazer, The Melody Makers, and The I-Threes. There is a particularly moving finale performance of "One Drop" with lead vocals by Bob Marley's son Ziggy. Edited by David Collins. Produced by Michael Butler and Robert H. Peitscher. Filmed from a live concert production by the Jamaica Cultural Development Commission in association with Synergy Productions and the Reggae Tribute Corporation. A collector's item.

**V25** Rockers. Film. Dir. Theodoros Bafaloukos. A Rockers Film Corporation Production, 1979?

The popular, nearly cultish reggae movie starring drummer Leroy "Horsemouth" Wallace. This feature length narrative film chronicles the problems and frustrations musicians face in their association with the Jamaican music industry. Includes a number of well known musicians such as Big Youth, Jacob Miller, Gregory Isaacs, etc. Excellent cross section of popular and classic reggae music. Produced by Patrick Hulsey. Edited by Susan Steinberg. (D181) See B079, B289.

**V26** Roots, Rock, Reggae: Inside the Jamaican Music Scene. Videocassette. Dir. Jeremy Marre. A Harcourt Films Production. Shanachie, 1202, 1988. Approx. 55 min.

The finest reggae documentary I have had the opportunity to view. This is one part of Beats of the Heart, a series by Jeremy Marre which examines different forms of music from a street level perspective. Offers a no nonsense view of Jamaican producers' control of and role in developing reggae music. We see Jack Ruby auditioning young singers. At Black Ark Studio the overlay of bass and drum, rhythm, and vocal tracks is demonstrated clearly. The video presents memorable acoustic practice sessions, a visit to Joe Gibbs pressing factory and Randy's Records, a discussion of the relationship between reggae music and Jamaican politics, and a sequence on the role of radio and soundsystems in Jamaican music. Includes performances by the following artists: Toots and The Maytals, Jimmy Cliff, The Upsetters, Joe Higgs, The Gladiators, The Mighty Diamonds, Ras Michael and The Sons of Negus, The Abyssinians, Third World, U-Roy, Inner Circle, and Jacob Miller. Produced by Jeremy Marre. Historically valuable footage. An essential primer describing reggae as a recorded music which functions both as a cultural commodity and as a rhetorical process. A collector's item.

**V27** Splashin' The Palace '84. Videocassette. Dir. Don Coutts. Capital Records, 1984. 59 min.

A good, clean concert video which preserves the energy of a live performance and the interaction between performers and audience. Includes performances by Prince Buster, The Skatalites, Leroy Sibbles, King Sunny Ade and The African Beats, Musical Youth, Black Uhuru, and Aswad. The last two sequences are composed of a long set by Dennis Brown backed by members of Aswad and a moving performance of "Redemption Song" by Dean Frazer backed by We The People. Recorded at the Capital Music festival in England, 1984. Edited by Robert Parsons. Produced by Tony Johnson.

**V28** Ziggy Marley and The Melody Makers: Conscious Party. Videocassette. Dir. Leslie Libman and Larry Williams. Virgin Records America, 1988. Approx. 60 min.

Taped live at the Palladium, this video primarily promotes Ziggy Marley's Conscious Party album. (D200) Includes engaging concert performances of "Conscious Party," "Tomorrow People," "What's True," "We Propose," "Time Will Tell," "Lee and Molly," and others. Clean video editing and effects. Backing vocals by Stephen and Cedella Marley, Sharon Marley Pendergast, and Errica Newell. Backed by Earl "Chinna" Smith, Dallol, and others. Edited by Keva Rosenfeld. Produced by David Naylor.

**CHALICE**

# Annotated Bibliography

**B001**  Abebe, Helen.  "Bob Marley High Priest of Reggae."  <u>AFRICA WOMAN</u> 16 (July /August 1978): [n.p.]

Sketches the development and growth of reggae music and its impact internationally.

**B002**  Alleyne, Mervyn C.  <u>Roots of Jamaican Culture</u>.  London: Pluto Press; Bridgetown, Barbados: Karia, 1988.  "Rastafarianism," 103-105, 146-147, 150, 157; "Art," 104; "Dreadlocks," 104; "Language," 105, 146, 150, 171.

Suggests that the Rastafarian language flows from its beliefs and there is a basic link between human kind and nature.

**B003**  Allsopp, R.  <u>Theoretical Orientation in Creole Studies</u>.  New York: Academic Press, 1980. "Dread Talk," 102-103, 401.

Sketches the morphological, lexical, and semantic characterization aspects of "Dread Talk."

**B004**  Alvaranga, Filmore, Douglas Mack and Mortimo Planno.  "Minority Report of Mission to Africa."  In <u>Report of the Mission To Africa</u>, 15-23. Kingston, Jamaica: Government Printer, 1961.

Gives evidence for the need and the feasibility of expeditious repatriation of Rastafarians from Jamaica to Africa.  See B269.

**B005**  Amoa-Fong, D.  "Forward Africa."  YARD ROOTS JOURNAL 1 & 2 (Summer 1984): 59.

A poem by a Rastafarian who states the hard times he is having in Ghana with the school authorities for wearing his locks.

**B006**  Amoaku, William.  Review of Reggae Bloodlines: In Search of the Music and Culture of Jamaica, by Stephen Davis. (B091)  BLACK PERSPECTIVE IN MUSIC 7, 2 (Fall 1979): 260-262.

Views the relationship between the Rastafarian movement and reggae music as a significant aspect of the Jamaican religion and cultural milieu.

**B007**  Attridge, A.  Review of The Rastafarians: The Dreadlocks of Jamaica, by Leonard Barrett. (B015)  AFRICAN SOCIAL RESEARCH 27 (1979): 605-606.

Concludes that: "Its great value is an account rather than an analysis, and despite its patchiness it does leave the reader with a vivid sense of the historical and social reasons for the Rasta's existence and of their present beliefs and direction."

**B008**  Austin, Diane J.  Urban Life in Kingston, Jamaica: The Culture and Class Ideology of Two Neighborhoods.  New York: Gordon/Breach, 1984. "Rastafarians," xx, 69, 73, 125-129, 215.

Focuses on the activities of a group of dreadlocks living in a particular neighborhood of Kingston, Jamaica, with special emphasis on their participation in the sports and other leisure aspects of the community.

**B009**  Backus III, Leroy M.  "An Annotated Bibliography of Selected Sources on Jamaican Music."  BLACK PERSPECTIVE IN MUSIC 8 (1980): 35-53.

Includes sources on both the Rastafarian movement and reggae music.

**B010**  Backus III, Leroy M.  "Stylistic Development of Reggae Music in Jamaica, West Indies."  M.A. thesis, University of Washington, 1976.

Traces the origin, growth, and development of reggae music in Jamaica.

**B011** Barkun, Michael. Disaster and the Millennium. New Haven and London: Yale University Press, 1974. "Rastafarians," 174-175.

Suggests that millenarianism can develop in an urban environment like that of the Rastafarians in West Kingston, Jamaica.

**B012** Barrett, Leonard E. "Rastafarianism as a Life Style." In Black Presence in Multi-Ethnic Canada, ed. Vincent D'Oyley, 149-165. Vancouver, Canada: Center for the Study of Curriculum and Instruction, University of British Columbia, 1979.

Treats the Rastafarian movement as an alternative for social change.

**B013** Barrett, Leonard E. "The Rastafarians: A Study in Messianic Cultism in Jamaica, West Indies." Ph.D. diss., Temple University, 1967.

Claims that the Rastafarian movement is one which has both political and religious characteristics. See B013(a).

**B013(a)** Barrett, Leonard E. The Rastafarians: A Study in Messianic Cultism in Jamaica. Rio Piedras, Puerto Rico: Institute of Caribbean Studies, University of Puerto Rico, 1968. (B013) See review B038.

**B014** Barrett, Leonard E. The Rastafarians: Sounds of Cultural Dissonance. Boston: Beacon Press, 1977.

Demonstrates the ways in which Rastafarianism is rooted in various Jamaican revivalist traditions. See item B200 and reviews B217, B371.

**B015** Barrett, Leonard E. The Rastafarians: The Dreadlocks of Jamaica. Kingston, Jamaica: Sangster's Book Stores, Ltd., 1977.

Exploration of certain truths and untruths of the Rastafarian movement as well as its significant contributions made in the Jamaican society. See reviews B007, B064, B245, B337.

**B016** Barrett, Leonard E. Soul-Force: African Heritage in Afro-American Religion. Garden City, New York: Anchor Press/Doubleday, 1974. "Rastafarians," 9, 10, 153-202.

Comments on the Rastafarians, which includes their origin, development, beliefs, practices, and function.

**B017** Barrett, Leonard E. Review of Mirror, Mirror: Identity, Race and Protest in Jamaica, by Rex Nettleford. (B234) CARIBBEAN STUDIES 2, 3 (October 1971): 101-104.

States that Mirror, Mirror is a very unsettling book because it unearths some disturbing truths about Jamaican society.

**B018** Bender, Wolfgang. Rastafari-Kunst aus Jamaica. Bremen: Edition Con, 1984. [German]

Collection of essays and poetry by and about Rastafarians.

**B019** Benn, D. M. "Historical and Contemporary Expressions of Black Consciousness in the Caribbean." M.Sc. thesis, University of West Indies, 1972.

Claims that the Rastafarian movement is both a partial and secular ideological expression of African consciousness.

**B020** Bilby, Kenneth and Elliot Leib. "Kumina, The Howellite Church and the Emergence of Rastafarian Traditional Music in Jamaica." JAMAICA JOURNAL 19, 3 (August-October 1986): 22-25.

Examines factors relating to the "connection between the Rastafari Nyabingi tradition and the musical practices of the religious cult known as Kumina."

**B021** Birhan, Iyawata Farika. Haile Selassie: A Collection of Theocratic Rastafari Poetry. San Jose, California: Queen Omega Communication, 1983.

Poetry which expresses the basic and fundamental tenets of the Rastafarian movement. There is also a glossary of Rastafarian terms.

**B022** Birhan, Iyawata Farika. Jah is I Shepherd. San Jose, California: Rastafari Roots Redemption Repatriation Unlimited, c1983.

Poems which describe the influence and significance of Haile Selassie on the Rastafarian movement.

**B023** Birhan, Iyawata Farika. Sing I a Song of Black Freedom: A Collection of Rastafarian Poetry. Pal Alto, California: Penny Press/Zikawuna Books, 1979.

Poems which address the contents of Pan Africa and Jamaica in general, as well as Pan Africa and Rastafari in particular.

**B024** Bishton, Derek. Black Heart Man: A Journey into Rastafari. London: Chatto & Windus, 1986.

Elaborates on the genesis, growth, and aesthetics of the Rastafarian movement in Jamaica, Great Britain, the United States, and Africa. See review B063.

**B025** Bones, Jah. "Rastafari Literature and Authorship: A Critique." WEST INDIAN DIGEST 9, 90 (December 1982): 28-29, 31-32, 34.

Explains the methodologies used by the Marxist-socialists, liberal-functionalists, and theologians in their interpretations of the Rastafarian movement.

**B026** Boot, Adrian and Vivien Goldman. Bob Marley--Soul Rebel--Natural Mystic. London: Eel Pie Publishing/Hutchinson, 1981.

Photographs and text tracing the genesis, growth, and demise of Bob Marley.

**B027** Boot, Adrian and Michael Thomas. Jah Revenge: Babylon Revisited. London: El Pie, 1982.

Photographs and sketches of certain contours of the Jamaican society which form the context of Rastafarian life.

**B028** Boot, Adrian and Michael Thomas. Jamaica: Babylon on a Thin Wire. London: Thames and Hudson, 1976.

Photographs and text portraying the contradictions and inconsistencies of Rastafarian relations with other Rastafarians and non-Rastafarians in the Jamaican society.

**B029** Bowen, W. Erol. "Rastafarianism and the New Society." SAVACOU 5 (June 1971): 41-50.

Describes the political, social, and economic conditions which form the basis for Rastafarianism and suggests that "the future and real promise of the Rastafari is that some of their offsprings will become the dynamic standard bearers of a new Jamaican society."

**B030** Boyne, Ian. "Jamaica: Breaking Barriers Between Churches and Rastafarians." ONE WORLD 86 (May 1983): 3-4.

Discusses the changes being made in the Rastafarian movement and its implications for the Jamaican churches.

**B031** Bramwell, Osula. "Redemption Song: Protest Reggae and the Jamaican Search for Identity." Ph.D. diss., University of Waterloo (Canada), 1984.

Studies the use of reggae music in transfusing a cultural void with profound African-West Indian (identity) uniqueness.

**B032** Brathwaite, Edward Kamau. "The Love Axe/1: Developing a Caribbean Aesthetic 1962-1964." <u>BIM</u> 16, 61 (1977): 53-65.

Focuses on Rastafari poets and poetry with their contributions to the growth of a Caribbean aesthetic.

**B033** Brathwaite, Edward Kamau. "Nametracks." In <u>Mother Poem</u>, 56-64. London: Oxford University Press, 1977.

Describes a Rastafarian who sees himself as a particular African brother.

**B034** Brathwaite, Edward Kamau. "Wings of a Dove." In <u>The Arrivants: A New World Trilogy</u>, 42-45. Oxford, London: Oxford University Press, 1973.

Contains the attitude of rebelliousness by the Rastafarians, namely "Brother Man."

**B035** Breeveld, Hans. [<u>The Rastafarian Movement in Jamaica</u>]: <u>Tussen Kulturele Overheering en Emanciparie</u>. Amstelveen: The Author, 1980. [German]

Shows the Rastafarian movement to be a continuation of the earlier struggles of the Arawaks, the Maroons, and the participants in the Morant Bay rebellion.

**B036** Breiner, Laurence A. "The English Bible in Jamaican Rastafarianism." <u>JOURNAL OF RELIGIOUS THOUGHT</u> 42, 2 (Fall-Winter 1985-1986): 30-43.

Discusses the Bible as the main source for Rastafarians' identity, authority, doctrine, and language.

**B037** Breitwieser, Thomas and Hermann Moter. [<u>Made in Kingston, Ja.</u>]: <u>Babylon in der Karibik ein Buch uber die Rastafari Bewegung und die Reggae-Musik</u>. Darmstadt: ms edition, 1981. [German]

Describes the origin and evolution of the Rastafarian movement and traces its connection with reggae music.

**B038**   Brice-Laporte, Roy S.   "The Rastas." Review of The Rastafarians: A Study in Messianic Cultism in Jamaica, by Leonard E. Barrett. (B013(a)) CARIBBEAN REVIEW 7, 2 (Summer): 3-4.

Suggests that "this is a very instructive book on a persistent political-religious movement of Black people in Black Jamaica."

**B039**   Brodber, Erna and Edward J. Greene.   Reggae and Cultural Identity in Jamaica.   Kingston, Jamaica: Institute of Social and Economic Research, University of the West Indies (Mona), 1981.

Examines the transmitters of reggae music and their Rastafarian connection. See B039(a).

**B039(a)**   Brodber, Erna and Edward J. Greene.   "Roots and Reggae-Ideological Tendencies in the Recent History of Afro-Jamaica." (B039)   Paper presented at the Conference on Human Development in Action; Fanon Research Center; Mogadishu, Somalia, June 1979.

**B040**   Brooks, Cedric.   "Cedric Brooks."   Interview by editor.   JAMAICA JOURNAL 11 (August 1977): 14-17.

Highlights the origin, growth, and development of Rastafarian music.

**B041**   Brown, Jennifer.   "Dread."   CARIBBEAN QUARTERLY 23, 4 (December 1977): 133.

Portrays the fears and hopes, visible as well as invisible elements of Rastafarians in the Jamaica society.

**B042**   Brown, Sam.   "Sam Brown."   Interview with Valerie Harris. (Toronto, July 1982) FUSE (November/December 1982): 177-180.

Brown discusses Rastas in relation to the press, the international community, politics, theology, and their places of exile.

**B043**   Brown, Samuel Elisha.   "Treatise on the Rastafarian Movement." CARIBBEAN STUDIES 6, 1 (April 1966): 39-40.

A major leader in the Rastafarian movement outlines its ten basic tenets.

**B044** Burnett, Michael. <u>Jamaican Music</u>. London: Oxford University Press, 1982.

Summarizes the origin, growth, and development of Jamaican music as a whole with special case examples: Rastafarian and reggae music (lyrics, melody, and musicians).

**B045** Burt, Arthur E. "Three Resistance Movements in Jamaica: The Maroons, Garveyism and the Rastafarians." <u>JOURNAL OF THE AFRO-AMERICAN HISTORICAL AND GENEALOGICAL SOCIETY</u> 3, 1 (1982): 33-39.

Identifies the social, economic, and political milieu from which three movements (Maroons, Garveyism, and Rastafarianism) emerged.

**B046** Burton, Julianne. Review of <u>The Harder They Come</u>, directed by Perry Henzell. (V13) <u>CARIBBEAN REVIEW</u> 7, 2 (April/May/June 1978): 33-37.

Declares the themes of "self-righteous," "pompous," and "hypocrisy" in characterizing Ivan, a youth from the rural areas determined to make it in the city, who seeks stardom by way of the pop culture. See D175.

**B047** Byfield, Bevis B. "Transformation and the Jamaican Society." <u>CARIBBEAN JOURNAL OF RELIGIOUS STUDIES</u> 5 (April 1983): 29-38.

Examines the role of the Rastafarian movement as a change-agent in the Jamaican society.

**B048** Callam, Neville G. "Invitation to Docility: Defusing the Rastafarian Challenge." <u>CARIBBEAN JOURNAL OF RELIGIOUS STUDIES</u> 3 (September 1980): 28-48.

Discusses factors relating to the evolution of the internal and external dynamics of Rastafarian religious beliefs.

**B049** Campbell, Festus Amtac. "Dread Thoughts-Excerpts from Amtac's Unpublished Manuscript, Natty Dread Chant on Reggae Mountain." [S.I., s.n.] 1978.

Includes poems and other writings emphasizing the ideas and beliefs of Rastafari.

**B050** Campbell, Horace. <u>Bob Marley and the Development of Reggae as a Distinctive Caribbean Musical Force</u>. [S.I., s.n., n.d.]

Suggests that reggae is both a reflection of the past and present struggles of the masses of Jamaican people, and shows its connection with the music of Rastafarians.

**B051** Campbell, Horace. <u>Bob Marley Lives: Reggae, Rasta and Resistance</u>. Dar es Salaam, Tanzania: Tackey, [1981].

Sketches the life, times, and work of Bob Marley and suggests that he "was clearly the cultural spokesperson for this generation of the oppressed."

**B052** Campbell Horace. "Jamaica: The Myth of Economic Development and Racial Tranquility." <u>BLACK SCHOLAR</u> 4, 5 (1973): 16-23.

Contains an historical account of Rastafarianism in Jamaica between 1938 and 1973.

**B053** Campbell, Horace. <u>Rasta and Resistance: From Marcus Garvey to Walter Rodney</u>. London: Hansib Publishing Limited, 1985.

A cultural pluralistic approach to the Rastafarian movement in Jamaica, Great Britain, and the Eastern Caribbean.

**B054** Campbell, Horace. "Rastafari: A Culture of Resistance." <u>RACE AND CLASS</u> 22 (Summer 1980): 1-22.

Explores the relationship between "the resistance of the Maroons, the Pan Africanist appeal of Marcus Garvey, the materialist and historical analysis of Walter Rodney and the defiance of Reggae."

**B055** Campbell, Horace. "The Rastafarians in the Eastern Caribbean." <u>CARIBBEAN QUARTERLY</u> 26, 4 (1980): 42-61.

Traces the history of the Rastafarian movement in the Eastern Caribbean, which includes St. Lucia, Dominica, Grenada, St. Vincent, and Trinidad/Tobago.

**B056** Campbell, Horace. Review of <u>Rastaman: The Rastafarian Movement in Britain</u>, by Ernest Cashmore. (B062) <u>CARIBBEAN QUARTERLY</u> 26, 4 (December 1980): 86-91.

Suggests that "the kind of disparaging stereotypes being highlighted by Cashmore is a hand-me-down from colonial Jamaica which has been retailored to the conditions of the British crisis."

**B057** Case, Charles G. "Ras Tafari and the Religion of Anthropology: An Epistemological Study." Ph.D. diss., McGill University (Canada), 1981.

Explores the relationship between the author's concepts of Rastafarian beliefs and those of anthropologists and anthropological theory.

**B058** Cashmore, Ernest. "After the Rastas." NEW COMMUNITY 9 (Autumn 1981): 173-181.

Argues that the Rastafarian movement is within the metaphysical-idealistic mode.

**B059** Cashmore, Ernest. "More than a Version: A Study of Reality Creation." BRITISH JOURNAL OF SOCIOLOGY 30, 3 (September 1979): 307-321.

Describes West Indian youths during the late 1970s in Great Britain and their immersion in the movement known as Rastafari.

**B060** Cashmore, Ernest. The Rastafarians. London: Minority Rights Group, 1984.

Sketches the evolution of Rasta from its earliest posture in Jamaica to the ghettos of the United Kingdom.

**B061** Cashmore, Ernest. "The Rastaman Cometh." NEW SOCIETY 25 (August 1977): 382-384.

Examines both the theoretical and practical aspects of Rastafarianism and shows its impact on some of the West Indian immigrants living in England.

**B062** Cashmore, Ernest. Rastaman: The Rastafarian Movement in England. London: Unwin Paperbacks, 1979.

Argues that "the importance of Rasta was that blacks in the 1970's seized the initiative and in an upsurge of religious zeal, plunged themselves into a quest for culture; and it was a quest which took place in England." See reviews B056, B108, B110, B131, B171, B255, B264.

**B063** Cashmore, Ernest. Review of Black Heart Man: A Journey Into Rasta, by Derek Bishton. (B024) NEW SOCIETY 22 (April 1986): 24-25.

Reviewer suggests that the author could have thrown more light by "offering new evidence on the Rasta experience in Ethiopia: how the land was used, how its population was maintained or discarded, its beliefs, what kind of social structure was built, and what kind of condition it's in now."

**B064** Cashmore, Ernest. "Jah People." Review of The Rastafarians: The Dreadlocks of Jamaica, by Leonard Barrett. (B015) NEW SOCIETY (1977): 479-480.

Reviewer cites the main weakness of the book to be: "insufficient attention is paid to the critical role of Marcus Garvey" and "the omission of Alexander Bedward's movement."

**B065** Chambers, Iain. Urban Rhythms: Pop Music and Popular Culture. London: Macmillan, 1985. "Reggae," 18, 139, 141, 150-174, 190-191, 206, 210, 222-226, 229, 235; "Reggae and Rastafarianism," 153-154, 159, 160, 164-165, 167-171, 190, 198, 247.

Shows the distinctiveness of both the Rastafarian movement and reggae as well as their interdependence.

**B066** Chevannes, Barry A. Drug Use in Jamaica: Report Prepared for UNESCO. [S.I., s.n.], 1976.

Discusses the uses of legitimate and illegitimate drugs in the Jamaican society, with special reference to the manner of treatment meted out to Rastafarians.

**B067** Chevannes, Barry A. "Era of Dreadlocks." Paper presented at the Conference on the African Diaspora. Hampton Institute, Virginia, 1977.

Explains the origin, development, and practices of the organization known as the House of Dreadlocks.

**B068** Chevannes, Barry A. "The Impact of the Ethiopian Revolution on the Rastafari Movement." SOCIALISM 2, 3 (March 1978): 23-33.

Suggests that the more progressive elements of Rastafari will be drawn into the working class trend and the more conservative "will become religious, looking for redemption, no longer by the revolutionary overthrow of the oppressors, but by inner, spiritual renewal."

**B069** Chevannes, Barry A. "Jamaica Lower Class Religion: Struggles against Oppression." M.Sc. thesis, University of the West Indies (Mona), 1971.

Compares and contrasts the genesis, growth, and development of two organic religions within the Jamaican society, namely revivalism and Rastafarianism.

**B070** Chevannes, Barry A. "The Literature of Rastafari." SOCIAL AND ECONOMIC STUDIES 26 (June 1977): 239-262.

Lists selected and major publications on the Rastafarian movement.

**B071** Chevannes, Barry A. "The Rastafari and the Urban Youth." In Perspectives on Jamaica in the Seventies, ed. Carl Stone and Aggrey Brown, 392-422. Kingston, Jamaica: Jamaica Publishing House, 1981.

Suggests that the Rastafarian doctrine has a marginal effect on the various youth gangs in certain areas of urban Kingston.

**B072** Chevannes, Barry A. "The Repairer of the Breach: Reverend Claudius Henry and Jamaican Society." In Ethnicity in the Americas, ed. Frances Henry, 262-289. Hague: Mouton Publishers, 1976.

Identifies the varied groupings within the Rastafarian movement, but focuses on one particular group led by Claudius Henry.

**B073** Chevannes, Barry A. Social Origins of the Rastafari Movement. Mona, Kingston: Institute of Social and Economic Research, University of the West Indies, c1978.

Concentrates on the rural aspects of the early Rastafarians and their class position in the Jamaican society.

**B074** Chevannes, Barry A. Review of Black Religions in the New World, by George Eaton Simpson. (B298) CARIBBEAN QUARTERLY 26 (1980): 91-92.

Contends that the approach used by the bringing together in this monograph of both European based religions and those traceable to Africa "is a refreshing one."

**B075** Chevannes, Barry. Review of Dread, The Rastafarians of Jamaica, by Joseph Owens. (B247) In CARIBBEAN QUARTERLY 24 (1978): 61-69.

Claims that the book's major weakness was not recognizing the importance of class struggle.

**B076** Clark, David. "The Roots and Soul of Reggae." RECORDS AND RECORDING 16, 11 (August 1973): 26-29.

Argues that reggae music is the syncretic result of these influences: African, European (English and Spanish), and American.

**B077** Clarke, Peter B. (Peter Bernard). <u>Black Paradise: The Rastafarian Movement</u>. Wellingborough, Northamptonshire, England: The Aquarian Press, 1986.

Elaborates on various aspects of the Rastafarian corpus, such as rituals, language, concept of God, use of ganja, and the wearing of dreadlocks.

**B078** Clarke, Sebastian. <u>Jah Music: The Evolution of the Popular Jamaican Song</u>. London: Heinemann Educational Books Ltd., 1980.

Shows the primary offering of Rastafarians to the chronological development of both Jamaican popular music and society.

**B079** Collum, Danny. "Jubilee, Rastafarian Style: A Vibrantly Human Film of Reggae and Justice." Review of <u>Rockers</u>, written and directed by Theodoros Bafaloukos. (V25) <u>SOJOURNERS</u> 9 (November 1980): 35-36.

Discusses the struggles encountered by a Rastafarian musician as he attempts to "make a living" by his craft. See D181.

**B080** Constant, Dennis. <u>Aux Sources du Reggae</u>. Paris: Edition Parentheses, 1983. [French]

Examines the historical relationships between reggae and Rastafari within the Jamaican society.

**B081** Cooper, Carolyn. "Chanting Down Babylon: Bob Marley's Song a Literary Text." <u>JAMAICA JOURNAL</u> 19, 4 (November-January): 2-8.

Examines Marley's eight albums produced over the ten year period (1973-1983) and finds that the lyrics are based on these: biblical allusions, Rastafarian symbolism, proverbs, riddles, aphorisms, and metaphors.

**B082** Craig, Dennis R. "Language, Society and Education in the West Indies." <u>CARIBBEAN JOURNAL OF EDUCATION</u> 7, 1/2 (1980): 1-17.

Author noted, among others, that "the Rastafarians have created what can be regarded as a special in-group dialect of Creole with a distinctive vocabulary and a set of distinctive communicative mannerisms."

**B083** Criner III, Clyde. "Black Music: Three Instructional Modules and Resources for Urban Education." ED.D. diss., University of Massachusetts, 1981.

Describes various musical styles of African American music such as reggae.

**B084**  Cross, Malcolm.  "Urbanization and Urban Growth in the Caribbean: An Essay on Social Change in Dependent Societies."   London: Cambridge University Press, 1979.  "Rastafarians," 99-100, 158.

Author concludes: "Rastafarianism is a product of enforced marginality on the periphery of a major Caribbean city."

**B085**  Cruchley, Francis Anne.   "The Ras Tafari Brethren: An Analysis of Political Developments in a Black Millenarian Movement."   M.A. thesis, University of Alberta (Canada), 1971.

Examines the relationship between the political and religious aspects of the Rastafarian movement.

**B086**   Cumper, George E.   The Potential of Rastafarianism as a Modern National Religion.  New Delhi, India: Recorder Press, 1979.

Rastafarianism is covered in these main areas: "superiority of men over women;" "dispersed decision-making;" "fundamentalist avoidance of certain foods;" "the arts," "especially music and sculpture;" and "use of distinctive symbols and their ethics."

**B087**   Cumper, Gloria.   Review of Mirror, Mirror--Identity, Race and Protest in Jamaica, by Rex Nettleford. (B234)   CARIBBEAN QUARTERLY 17, 3/4 (September-December 1971): 144-145.

Claims that the Rastafarian movement "has become not only an agent of protest, but a point of departure for those, especially the young, actively seeking change."

**B088**   Dalrymple, Henderson.   Bob Marley: Music, Myth and the Rastas.  Sudbury, England: Carib-Arawak, 1976.

Traces the life and activities of Bob Marley with emphasis on his relationship with the Rastafarian movement.

**B089**   Davis, Stephen.   Bob Marley.  New York: Doubleday, 1985.

Author describes the origins and evolution of Bob Marley's outlook in Jamaica and the world.

**B090** Davis, Stephen. "The Rastas: Jamaica's Extraordinary Brotherhood." NEW AGE 11, 6 (November 1976): 18-27.

Discusses the Rastafarians as an option of metaphysical polity "for thousands of young Jamaicans stranded between their school years and an endless cycle of demeaning labor and unemployment."

**B091** Davis, Stephen. Reggae Bloodlines: In Search of the Music and Culture of Jamaica. New York: Anchor Press/Doubleday 1979, c1977.

Primarily states the development of reggae music in the Jamaican society and shows the connection between Rastafarian and reggae music. See review B006.

**B092** Davis, Stephen and Peter Simon. Reggae International. New York: Alfred A. Knopf/Rogner and Bernhard Books, 1983.

An anthology dealing with music of Jamaica which describes Bob Marley and his work and makes the claim that Rasta became the ideology of reggae in the 1970s. See review B134.

**B093** De Albuquerque, Klaus. "The Future of the Rastafarian Movement." CARIBBEAN REVIEW 8, 4 (Fall 1979): 22-25/44-46.

Argues that "the Rastafarian movement has made a positive contribution toward pointing some youths away from crimes and toward a trade or formal education."

**B094** De Albuquerque, Klaus. "Millenarian Movements and the Politics of Liberation: The Rastafarians of Jamaica." Ph.D. diss., Virginia Polytechnic Institute and State University, 1977.

Investigates the connection between millenarian movements and freedom, with special emphasis on the Rastafarians of Jamaica.

**B095** De Albuquerque, Klaus. "Rastafarianism and Cultural Identity in the Caribbean." REVISTA INTERAMERICANA 10, 2 (Summer 1980): 230-247.

Considers the spread of Rastafarianism from Jamaica to other countries of the English speaking Caribbean.

**B096** Dizzy I, Ras. "Ghost Riding Coffen in City." SAVACOU 3/4 (March 1971): 29-30.

Expressions of death by Rastafarians and non-Rastafarians.

**B097**  Dizzy I, Ras.  The Human Guide Line.  Kingston: s.n., 1969.

Collection of poems and essays which range from purely religious hymns of praise to castigations of the ways of Babylon [Jamaica] as well as comments on its political landscape.

**B098**  Dizzy I, Ras.  Jamaican Journalist Creates Imagination.  Kingston: s.n., 1974.

Demonstrates "imagination which is not owned, not contained within oneself, even though the experience of it is intensely interior."

**B099**  Dizzy I, Ras.  "A Poem by the Poet: I Wants no Part with You." CARIBBEAN QUARTERLY 13, 4 (1967): 43.

Shows the characteristics of both the oppressors and oppressed, the ruled and the rulers as well as the poor and wealthy in the Jamaican society.

**B100**  Dizzy I, Ras.  A Prince Who is a Pauper.  Kingston, Jamaica: Author, 1973.

Collection of poems by a Rastafarian adherent who describes the problems faced by persons who are marginalized by the system.

**B101**  Dizzy I, Ras.  Rastafarians Society Watchman.  [S.I., s.n., 1971?]

Contains prose and poetry by a Rastafarian who offers solutions to certain problems that plague both members of his group and others within the Jamaican society.

**B102**  Dizzy I, Ras.  "The Rastas Speak."  CARIBBEAN QUARTERLY 13 (December 1967): 41-42.

Brief description of the visit of Haile Selassie I to Jamaica on Thursday, April 21-23, 1966, and the reception he received from the Rastas.

**B103**  Dizzy I, Ras.  Run Wide Run Deep.  Kingston: The Author, 1970.

Poems which capture the essence of the Rastafarian ideology in the movement's attempt to act as a catalyst in generating hope for an embattled group in the larger society of Jamaica.

**B104** Dizzy I, Ras. [Poems]--This Baby from Heaven, Deserted Lover; A Heavenly Star is Seen. Jamaica: The Author, 1972.

Poems which consider the offspring of mother and father as separate entities, but show their unity as well.

**B105** Dizzy I, Ras. Visions of Black Slaves. Kingston, Jamaica: The Author, 1971.

Collection of poems and essays describing the fears and hopes, difficulties and solutions, as well as the sufferings and happiness of the majority of persons living in the Jamaican society.

**B106** Douglass, Lisa. Review of Race, Class and Political Symbols: Rastafari and Reggae in Jamaican Politics, by Anita M. Waters. (B346) AMERICAN JOURNAL OF SOCIOLOGY 91, 5 (March 1986): 1272-1275.

Author concludes that: "Future analyses that recognize the multivocal nature of symbolic processes may demonstrate how Rastafarianism and Reggae share, adopt, and transform symbols embedded in other aspects of Jamaican society."

**B107** Dreher, M. C. and C. M. Rogers. "Getting High: Ganja Man and his Socio-Economic Milieu." CARIBBEAN STUDIES 16 (July 1976): 219-231.

Authors compare the use of ganja [marijuana] among the Rastafarians and a rural Pentecostal group and find that "it is not the ganja itself that is considered 'bad,' but the mode of ingestion."

**B108** Durant, Constance J. Review of Rastaman: The Rastafarian Movement in England, by Ernest Cashmore. (B062) SOCIOLOGICAL ANALYSIS 45, 1 (Spring 1984): 66-67.

Argues that Cashmore failed to discuss adequately the role of women and the family in the Rastafarian movement.

**B109** Ebanks, Margaret. The Rastafari Cookbook: Ital Recipes. Kingston, Jamaica: Antilles Book Co., 1981.

Describes various types of foods and methods in the preparation of Rastafarian meals.

**B110** Elliot, Jean Leonard. Review of <u>Rastaman: The Rastafarian Movement in England</u>, by Ernest Cashmore. (B062) <u>CANADIAN JOURNAL OF SOCIOLOGY</u> 7, 1 (1982): 94-96.

Claims that the author fails to offer any predictions concerning the possible future of the Rastafarian movement.

**B111** Emtage, J. B. "The Black Man who was God." <u>PUNCH</u> (November 13, 1963): 710-711.

A sketchy biographical account of L. P. Howell (Gangunja Moraj), one of the founders of the Rastafarian movement.

**B112** Emtage, J. B. <u>Brown Sugar: A Vestigal Tale</u>. London: Collins, 1966.

States the similar and dissimilar patterns between the effects of rum (alcohol) and ganja (marijuana).

**B113** Eyre, L. Alan. "Biblical Symbolism and the Role of Fantasy Geography Among the Rastafarians of Jamaica." <u>JOURNAL OF GEOGRAPHY</u> 84, 4 (July-August 1985): 144-148.

An exposition of biblical geography in an unusual way that seems rational and furnishes a universal plan necessary for Rastafarians and their demeanor.

**B114** Eyre, L. Alan. "Questions of Fact and Interpretation." <u>JOURNAL OF GEOGRAPHY</u> 83, 2 (March-April 1984): 51.

Author contends that Rastafarian ideology and reggae music "represents one facet and not the most dominant one at that" of the Jamaican society.

**B115** Faiers, Chris. <u>White Rasta in Wintertime</u>. Toronto: Unfinished Monument Press, 1982.

Collection of poems which celebrates the Rastafari lifestyle and mentions the difficulties faced by members of the movement.

**B116** Faristzaddi, Millard and Iyawata Farika Birhan. <u>Itations of Jamaica and I Rastafari: Art and Iconographics</u>. New York: Rogner & Bernhard, distributed by Grove Press, 1982.

Contains essays, graphic arts, poetry, and photographs describing the aesthetic aspects of Rastafarian culture.

**B117** Fitz-Henley, Trevor. <u>Boy in a Landscape</u>. Gordon Town, Jamaica: Anbasa-Judah Press, 1980.

Collection of essays on various themes such as race consciousness, identity, and Rastafarianism.

**B118** Flemming, R. "Reggae: The Musical Legacy of Rastafarians." <u>ENCORE</u> 9 (January 1980): 26-32.

Traces the relationships between the music of reggae and the Rastafarian movement.

**B119** Forsythe, Dennis. <u>Rastafari: For the Healing of the Nation</u>. Kingston, Jamaica: Zaika Publications, 1983.

Views the Rastafarian movement from a metaphysical idealist framework.

**B120** Forsythe, Dennis. "West Indian Culture Through the Prism of Rastafarianism." <u>CARIBBEAN QUARTERLY</u> 26, 4 (December 1980): 62-81.

Author concludes: "Rastas have turned to an alternative means of feeling like 'Man' and 'real people' with flesh, blood and feelings deserving of full respect like other human beings."

**B121** Fraser, Flip. "Long Live the King: Tribute to Bob Marley." <u>WEST INDIAN DIGEST</u> 8, 78 (June 1981): 7-9.

Sketches the life, times, work, and funeral of Bob Marley.

**B122** Fraser, H. Aubrey. "The Law and Cannabis in the West Indies." <u>SOCIAL AND ECONOMIC STUDIES</u> 23, 3 (September 1974): 361-385.

States the various areas of beliefs held by Rastafarians concerning cannabis (ganja).

**B123** Friday, Michael. "A Comparison of 'Dharma' and 'Dread' as Determinants of Ethical Standards." <u>CARIBBEAN JOURNAL OF RELIGIOUS STUDIES</u> 5 (September 1983): 29-37.

Discusses the similarities and differences between Dharma (Hindus) and Dread (Rastafarians) as they relate to these: deportment, duty, and discipline.

**B124** Gannon, John C. "The Racial Ideology in Jamaican Politics: The People's Political Party in the Parliamentary Elections of 1962." CARIBBEAN STUDIES 16, 3-4 (1976): 85-108.

Presents the differences between the Rastafarian movement and the People's Political Party of Jamaica.

**B125** Garrison, Len. "Back to Africa: Rastafarians Protest Movement of Jamaica." AFRAS REVIEW 1 (1975): 10-13.

Discusses the positive and negative trends of the Rastafarian movement.

**B126** Garrison, Len. Back to Africa: The Idea of the Return and Structural Migration as a Response to Cultural and Economic Deprivation in the Jamaican Society. Sussex, Great Britain: University of Sussex, 1975.
Examines certain factors which tend to be overshadowed by the concept of a return to Africa.

**B127** Garrison, Len. Black Youth, Rastafarianism and the Identity Crisis in Britain. London: Afro-Caribbean Education Resource Project, 1979.

Explores the ideas and philosophies of the Rastafarian movement and its effects on the African youths residing in Great Britain.

**B128** Garrison, Len. "Out of Exile: A Study of the Historical Development of the Rastafari Movement in the Jamaican Society, 1932-1972." Dip. DS. thesis, Ruskin College, Oxford, 1973.

Discusses the Rastafarian movement as an example of a continuum of struggles waged by various groups and individuals at different times throughout the history of the Jamaican society.

**B129** Garrison, Len. "The Rastafarians: Journey out of Exile." AFRAS REVIEW 2 (Summer 1976): 43-47.

Discusses the manner in which the Rastafarian movement has become the catalyst for the creative energies of the African Caribbean people.

**B130** Gayle, Carl. "There is Nowhere I would Rather be than in Rasta Country," BLACK MUSIC 4, 38 (January 1977): 16-23.

Comments on the music of certain musicians such as Keith Hudson, Fred Locks, and Leroy Smart as well as their relationship with the Twelve Tribes of Israel.

**B131** Gerloff, Roswith. Review of <u>Rastaman: The Rastafarian Movement in England</u>, by Ernest Cashmore. (B062) <u>ETHNIC AND RACIAL STUDIES</u> 4, 3 (1981): 357-359.

Discusses the author's uncritical approach to Rastafarian ideology.

**B132** Glazier, Stephen D. "Religion and Contemporary Religious Movements in the Caribbean: A Report." <u>SOCIOLOGICAL ANALYSIS</u> 41, 2 (1980): 181-182.

Suggests that "Rasta has become church-like in its dealings with the state."

**B133** Goodison, A. <u>Dietary Survey and Eating Habits of the Rastafarians</u>. Kingston, Jamaica: Caribbean Food and Nutrition Institute, 1976.

Examines the cultural and dietary beliefs of the Rastafarians in the context of understanding their eating patterns.

**B134** Greenberg, Alan. "Reggae International, Spiritual Balm for a Trembling World." Review of <u>Reggae International,</u> by Stephen Davis and Peter Simon. (B092) <u>CARIBBEAN REVIEW</u> 12, 2 (Spring 1983): 32-33.

Reviewer claims that "Reggae has become a worldwide medium of dance and protest, and this internationalization of what began as Kingstonian slum music is the prevailing theme of the book."

**B135** Gullick, Charles. "Afro-American Identity: The Jamaican Nexus." <u>JOURNAL OF GEOGRAPHY</u> 82, 5 (September-October 1983): 205-211.

Contends "that Rastafarianism, an extremist Black nationalist movement, arose after independence. Its militancy is due to an overwhelmingly Black majority population, with few countervailing ethnic groups."

**B136** Gullick, Charles. "Rastafarianism and Arawaks." <u>JOURNAL OF GEOGRAPHY</u> 83, 3 (May-June 1984): 98-99.

Applies three theoretical models (pluralistic, class, and bicultural) to the Jamaican milieu.

**B137** Hamid, Ansley A. "A Pre-Capitalist Mode of Production: Ganja and the Rastafarians in San Fernando, Trinidad." Ph.D. diss., Columbia University, 1981.

Discusses the effects of the ganja trade and Rastafarianism on the political economy of San Fernando, Trinidad.

**B138**  Hanson, Aravita Laurel.  "The Rastafarians of Kingston, Jamaica: A Movement in Search of Social Order." M.A. thesis, Harvard University, 1975.

Considers the historical and socio-economic contexts which form the basis of the Rastafarian movement.

**B139**  Harris, Bruce Murray.  "What Go 'Round, Come Round: Dissimilation in a Caribbean Society." Ph.D. diss., University of California, San Diego, 1980.

Contains an assessment of dissimilation, with the Rastafarians as an example.

**B140**  Harris, Valerie.  "Rastafari: Issues and Aspirations of the Toronto Community." FUSE (November-December 1982): 174-185.

Report on the first International Rastafarian Conference held from July 23 to July 25, 1982, in Toronto "whose purpose was to facilitate exchange among Rastafarians in North America, the Caribbean and Britain, as well as the non-Rasta community of Toronto, about Rastafarian culture."

**B141**  Hebdige, Dick.  "Reggae, Rastas and Rudies." CULTURAL STUDIES 7 & 8 (Summer 1975): 135-154.

Explores the relationship between Rastafarianism and reggae, and the use of Rasta's ideology by Africans living in England, especially the "rude boys." See B141(a).

**B141(a)**  Hebdige, Dick.  "Reggae, Rastas & Rudies." (B141) Resistance Through Rituals: Youth Sub-Cultures In Post-War Britain, ed. Stuart Hall and Tony Jefferson, 135-155.  London: Hutchinson & Co. (Publishers), 1976.

**B142**  Hebdige, Dick.  Reggae, Rastas and Rudies: Style and Subversion of Form.  Birmingham: University of Birmingham, Center for Contemporary Cultural Studies, 1974.

Treats Rastafarianism as synonymous with the Africanization of reggae, which results in a loose connection between the African West Indian and European youth cultures in Great Britain.

**B143**  Hebdige, Dick.  Subculture: The Meaning of Style.  London: Methuen, 1979.  "Rastafarianism," 33-39.

Claims that the message of Rastafarianism is transmitted through the medium of reggae music in Great Britain.

**B144** Hellstrom, Jan A. ["Jah Live: Selassie-I Live"] "En Studie Kring Reggae-Musik och Afrikansk Messaskuit pa Jamaica." <u>SVTK</u> 53, 4 (1977): 145-155. [Swedish]

Suggests that the Rastafarian movement is a result of the struggle of some African Jamaicans to retain and or return to their African identity.

**B145** Henriques, Fernando. <u>Family and Colour in Jamaica</u>. London: MacGibbon and Kee, 1968. "Ras Tafarites," 68, 180-182.

Views the major hinderance against the spread of the Rastafarian movement as its identification with things African.

**B146** Higgins, Chester/Renelda. "Rasta." <u>CRISIS</u> 88 (July 1981): 304-306.

A brief look at the announcement of Marley's death, his Rastafarian beliefs, and his state funeral in Kingston, Jamaica.

**B147** Hill, Robert A. "Dread History: Leonard Howell and Millenarian Visions in Early Rastafari Religion in Jamaica." <u>EPOCHE</u> 9 (1981): 30-71.

Author concludes: There "is the need to appraise the study of the phenomenon of Rastafari awakening as an integral aspect of the larger matrix of black (Africa) religious nationalism, folk religious revivalism, and Jamaican peasant resistance to the plantation economy and state." See B147(a).

**B147(a)** Hill, Robert. "Leonard P. Howell and Millenarian Visions in Early Rastafari." (B147) <u>JAMAICA JOURNAL</u> 16, 1 (February 1983): 24-39.

**B148** Hogg, Donald W. "Statement of a Ras Tafari Leader: An Introduction." <u>CARIBBEAN STUDIES</u> 6, 1 (April 1966): 37-38.

Claims that "the Jamaican Rastafarian movement is one of the most misunderstood and maligned developments in the modern Caribbean."

**B149** Homiak, John P. (John Paul). "This Ancient of Days' Seated Black Eldership, Oral Traditions and Ritual in Rastafari Culture." Ph.D. diss., Brandeis University, 1985.

Explores the role of the Nyabingi Order within the Rastafarian movement.

**B150** Hurwitz, Samuel J. and Edith F. Jamaica: A Historical Portrait. New York, Washington, London: Praeger Publishers, 1971. "Ras Tafarians," 190-191.

Describes the connection between Garvey and the Rastafarian movement.

**B151** Hussey, Dermott. "Bob Marley, The Man of Music for 1975." PEPPERPOT (December 1975): 41, 43, 44-45.

Shows the connection between Bob Marley, the human being, and his music.

**B152** Hylton, Patrick. "The Politics of Caribbean Music." BLACK SCHOLAR 7, 1 (1975): 23-29.

Discusses calypso and reggae as political expressions and protests against the exploitation and oppression of Africans in both Trinidad/Tobago and Jamaica.

**B153** Hylton, Patrick. "The Role of Religion and Music in Caribbean History." [S.I., s.n., 198?] Typewritten. "Rastafari movement," 101-122; "Reggae," 280-328.

Investigates the essential interdependence between religion and music in the general areas of the political economic history of the Caribbean as well as the specific aspects of the Rastafarian movement and reggae music within the Jamaican setting.

**B154** Jackson, Michael. "Rastafarianism." THEOLOGY 83 (January 1980): 26-34.

Explores Rastafarians' theological comprehension and use of the Bible, their views of churches, concepts of Babylon, and way of life.

**B155** Jacobs, H. P. "The Ras Tafarians." In Ian Flemming Introduces Jamaica, ed. Morris Cargill, 78-92. New York: Hawthorn Books, Inc., 1965.

Shows the similarities and differences between the Quakers and Rastafarians.

**B156** Jacobs, Virginia Lee. Roots of Rastafari. San Diego, California: Avant Books, 1985.

Traces the historical relationship between Haile Selassie and the Rastafarian movement.

**B157** Jamaica Information Service. Religion In Jamaica. rev. ed. Kingston, Jamaica: Jamaica Information Service, 1972.

Describes the major tenets, similarities, and differences concerning the various interpretations of religion (inclusive of Rastafarians) and denominations in the Jamaican society.

**B158** James, C. L. R. "Rastafari of Home and Abroad." Review of The Children of Sisyphus, by Orlando Patterson. (B250) NEW LEFT REVIEW 25 (May-June 1964): 74-76.

Discusses the influence of neo-colonialism and its abhorrence by a group of people in the Jamaican society called the Rastafarians.

**B159** Jerry, Bongo. "Black Mother." SAVACOU 3/4 (March 1971): 16-17.

Portrays Africa as the home for all Africans.

**B160** Jerry, Bongo. "Mabrak." SAVACOU 3/4 (March 1971): 13-15.

Contains the condemnation of Babylon [Jamaica] and the celebration of Africa.

**B161** Jiwani, Yasmin. "The Forms of Jah: The Mystic Collectivity of the Rastafarians and its Organizational Precipitates." M.A. thesis, Simon Fraser University (Canada), 1984.

Aims of the thesis are two-fold: "to assess the utility of the concept of the mystic collectivity and to analyze the range of groups generated by the Rastafarian religious tradition."

**B162** Johnson, Howard. "Introduction." In Boy in a Landscape: A Jamaican Picture, by Trevor Fitz Henley, 4-6. Gordon Town, Jamaica: Anbasa-Judah Press, 1980.

States that the themes of Rastafarian poems and essays are concerned with the history and culture of Africa. See B117.

**B163** Johnson, Howard and Jim Pines. Reggae: Deep Roots Music. London: Proteus Publishing Group, 1982.

Suggests that revival and Rastafari have been the sources for reggae music.

**B164**  Johnson, Linton Kwesi.  <u>Dread Beat and Blood</u>.  London: Bogle 'L 'Ouverture, 1975.

Collection of poems which speaks to the experiences and struggles of the author in the British society. (D092)

**B165**  Johnson, Linton Kwesi.  "Jamaican Rebel Music."  <u>RACE AND CLASS</u> 17, 4 (1976): 397-412.

Suggests that: "The historical phenomenon called Rastafarianism which is saturating the consciousness of the oppressed Jamaica--which represents a particular stage in the development of the consciousness of the oppressed--is in fact laying the spiritual and the cultural foundation from which to launch a struggle for liberation."

**B166**  Johnson, Linton, Kwesi.  "Linton Kwesi Johnson."  Interview by Mervyn Morris.  <u>JAMAICA JOURNAL</u> 20, 1 (February-April 1987): 17-20, 22-23, 25-26.

Discusses these subjects: early life, British Panthers, Rastas, and "Race Today Collective."

**B167**  Johnson, Linton Kwesi.  "Reggae Fi Dada."  <u>JAMAICA JOURNAL</u> 20, 1 (February-April 1987): 28+

Poem which expresses the disadvantages experienced by persons living in the urban ghettos of Jamaica. (D093)

**B168**  Johnson, Linton Kwesi.  "The Reggae Rebellion."  <u>NEW SOCIETY</u> 36, 714 (10 June 1976): 589.

Gives reasons for the proliferation of the musical sound reggae and suggests that artists such as Bob Marley and others have "tried to produce a kind of sound that transcends its socio-historical conditioning, its social context."

**B169**  Johnson, Linton Kwesi.  "Roots and Rock: The Marley Enigma."  <u>RACE TODAY</u> 7, 10 (October 1975): 237-238.

Author suggests that reggae music presented by Bob Marley "lent a new style of rhetoric to his lyricism; this defiance and rebellion, [in] the language of Rastafari."

**B170** Jones, Kenneth M. "Say Brother." ESSENCE (October 1988): 8.

Claims that "Dreads serve as antennae allowing even clearer perspective on the moral deficiencies of the West. Yet dreads do not negate the reality that I am a Black American."

**B171** Jones, Peter D. "A New Black Reality." Review of Rastaman: The Rastafarian Movement in England, by Ernest Cashmore. (B062) SOCIAL ALTERNATIVES 2, 3 (1972): 71.

Author concludes: "Rastafari offers a useful sympathetic understanding of the most important development in the history of the West Indian presence in Britain."

**B172** Kallyndyr, Rolston and Henderson Dalrymple. Reggae: A Peoples Music. London: Carib-Arawak, 1973.

Describes the American and English influences on reggae music.

**B173** Kaslow, Andrew. "The Roots of Reggae." SINGOUT 23, 6 (January-February): 1975, [11]-13.

Traces the roots of Jamaica's modern music and shows the relationship between Rastafarian and reggae music.

**B174** Kaufman, Jay S. "Music and Politics in Jamaica." CARIBBEAN REVIEW 15, 3 (Winter 1987): 9.

Emphasizes the importance of the Rastafarians in the Jamaican society by suggesting that their music "was able to have such a dramatic impact on the political and cultural life."

**B175** Kelly, Ras Carlisle A. Revelation of Jah Throne. Kingston: [s.n., n.d.].

Comprehensive survey and synthesis of Rastafarian teachings.

**B176** Kerridge, Roy. "Marley in Africa." NEW SOCIETY (September 6, 1985): 343.

Shows the influence of Marley, reggae music, and Rastafarians in Africa. Also suggests that "the influence of Rastafarianism on Jamaica has been to destroy or oppose genuine African survivals."

**B177**  Kilgore, John Robert.  "Rastafarian: Theology for the African-American Church."  D.MIN. diss., School of Theology at Claremont, 1984.

Considers the Rastafarian movement as a possible source for the development of an African American theology.

**B178**  King, Audvil.  "The Awakening: A Journey into the Rastafarian Experience."  In <u>One Love</u>, ed. Audvil King, Althea Helps, Pam Wint and Frank Hasfal, 75-71.  London: Bogle-L'Ouverture Publications, 1971.

A metaphysical idealist interpretation of the political, economic, and cultural insights of the Rastafarian.  See B180.

**B179**  King, Audvil.  "Letter to a Friend."  In <u>One Love,</u> ed. Audvil King, Althea Helps, Pam Wint, and Frank Hasfal.  London: Bogle-L'Ouverture Publications, 1971.

Discusses the connection between Rasta and Black power.  See B180.

**B180**  King, Audvil, Althea Helps, Pam Wint, and Frank Hasfal.  <u>One Love</u>. London: Bogle-L'Ouverture Publications, 1971.

Collection of essays on Pan African consciousness among the dispersed Africans in Jamaica and the United States.  See review B373.

**B181**  King, Rev. Vernon.  <u>What I Think of the Rastas</u>.  Kingston, Jamaica: The Author, 1962.

Compares and contrasts Rastafarians and communists, Rastas and Black Muslims as well as Rastas and Hawaiians.

**B182**  Kitzinger, Sheila.  "Protest and Mysticism: The Rastafari Cult of Jamaica."  <u>JOURNAL FOR THE SCIENTIFIC STUDY OF RELIGION</u> 3, 2 (Fall 1969): 240-262.

Explores the Rastafarian movement based on these features: history, religion, attitude, and faith.

**B183**  Kitzinger, Sheila.  "The Rastafarian Brethren of Jamaica." <u>COMPARATIVE STUDIES IN SOCIETY AND HISTORY</u> 9, 1 (1966): 34-39.

Elaborates on Rastafari as having "within it the possibility of [a] sincere and valid religious experience."  See B183(a).

**B183(a)**   Kitzinger, Sheila.   "The Rastafarian Brethren of Jamaica."   (B183)   In Peoples and Cultures of the Caribbean, ed. Michael M. Horowitz, 580-588. Garden City, New York: Natural History Press, 1971.

**B184**   Kopkind, Andrew.   "Reggae: The Steady Rock of Black Jamaica." RAMPARTS 11, (12 June 1973): 50-51.

Views reggae music as "the only true popular--that is to say--music capable of commercial success."

**B185**   Kuper, Adam.   Changing Jamaica.   London and Boston: Routledge & Kegan Paul, 1976.   "Rastafarians," 58-59, 67, 91, 93, 94-99, 103-105, 135, 140-142.

Author suggests that: "The ideology is obviously one of retreat or rejection from Jamaican society and values, if in many central respects it simply inverts them--Africa replaces England, black replaces white, at the top of the class totem-pole.   However, it is not to be read too literally."

**B186**   Kyle, John.   "Rastaman in the Promised Land."   NEW SOCIETY (24th/31st December 1981): 535-537.

Compares and contrasts the Rastafarians associated with the Ethiopian World Federation and the Twelve Tribes of Israel living at   Shashemane, a small market town in the Rift Valley region of Ethiopia, two hundred miles South of the capital, Addis Ababa.

**B187**   Lacey, Terry.   Violence and Politics in Jamaica 1960-1970: Internal Security in a Developing Country.   Oxford Road, Manchester: Manchester University Press, 1977.   "Rastafarianism," 27, 35, 38-39, 41, 42-44, 49, 59, 78, 81-85, 94, 139, 147.

Author claims: "The principal contribution of the Rastafarian movement towards the creation of a Jamaican identity was through painting, writing and most important, through music."

**B188**   Laing, Andrew B.   Rastafarian Culture.   [S.I., s.n.] 1984.

Comments on the theoretical and practical aspects of the Rastafarian movement, as well as its use of music.

**B189** Lake, Obiagele. "A Feasibility Study on the Prevalence and Cultural Determinate of Breast Feeding Among Jamaican Rastafarians." M.Sc. thesis, Cornell University, 1985.

Examines a selected group of Rastafarian and non-Rastafarian women, as to their length of breast feeding.

**B190** Landman-Bogues, Jacqueline. "Rastafarian Food Habits." CAJANUS 94 (1976): 228-233.

Examines the dietary patterns of Rastafarians.

**B191** Lanternari, Vittorio. The Religions of the Oppressed: A Study of Modern Messianic Cults. London: MacGibbon & Kee, 1963. "Rastafarians," 160,164-165, 313. See B191(a).

Contains the view that the Rastafarian operation is "a typically escapist movement rather than a revolutionary force."

**B191(a)** Lanternari, Vittorio. "Religious Movements in Jamaica." (B191) In Black Society In The New World, by Richard Frucht, 308-372. New York: Random House, 1971.

**B192** Larsen, Egon. Strange Sects & Cults: A Study of Their Origins and Influence. London: Arthur Barker Ltd., 1971. "Rastafarian," 87-89.

Views the Rastafarian movement as essentially escapist.

**B193** Lawrence, E. Review of Dread: The Rastafarians of Jamaica, by Joseph Owens. (B247) RACE AND CLASS 22, 3 (1981): 321-322.

Contends that the glaring weakness of the treatise is the absence of any treatment of the Rasta female.

**B194** Lee, Barbara Makeda. Rastafari: The New Creation. Kingston, Jamaica: Jamaica Media Productions, 1981.

Views Rastafarianism as an alternative to both capitalism and socialism.

**B195** Lee, Mark. "Scientific Animalism. (A Report)." CARIBBEAN QUARTERLY 26, 4 (December 1980): 82.

Poem which shows the resistance theme of Rastafarians.

**B196** Leslie, L. C.; M. B. Douglas; Cecil Geo. Gordon; V. M. Blackwood; V. M. Reid and Z. Monroe Scarlett. "Majority Report of Mission to Africa." In Report of Mission to Africa, [1]-13. Kingston, Jamaica: Government Printing Office, 1961.

Describes meetings with individuals and groups during their visits to Ethiopia, Ghana, Liberia, Nigeria, and Sierra Leone. See B269.

**B197** Lewis, Rupert. "Black Nationalism in Jamaica in Recent Years." In Essays on Power and Change in Jamaica, ed. Carl Stone and Aggrey Brown, 65-71. Kingston, Jamaica: Jamaica Publishing House, 1977.

Addresses the ideals and principles of the Rastafarian movement and locates it within the overall nationalist movement of Jamaica.

**B198** Lewis, Rupert. Marcus Garvey, Anti-Colonial Champion. London: Karia Press, 1987. "Rastafari Movement," 89-91, 171.

Challenges the view that Garvey was critical of the Rastafarian movement.

**B199** Lewis, Rupert. "A Political Study of Garveyism in Jamaica and London: 1914-1940." MSc. thesis, University of West Indies, 1971. "Rastafarians," 181-183.

Expresses the differences and conflicts between middle class persons and Rastafarians in Jamaican society.

**B200** Lincoln, C. Eric. "An Introduction to the Rastafarian Movement." In The Rastafarians: Sounds of Cultural Dissonance, by Leonard E. Barrett, ix-xiii. Boston: Beacon Press, 1977.

Compares and contrasts the Black Muslims (U.S.) and Rastafarians (Jamaica). See B014.

**B201** Lockard, Craig A. "Repatriation Movement Among the Javanese in Surinam: A Comparative Analysis." CARIBBEAN STUDIES 18, 1/2 (April-July 1978): [85]-113.

Considers the connection between the movement in Surinam and the Rastafarians.

**B202** Logan, Wendell. "Conversation with . . . Marjorie Whylie: Some Aspects of Religious Cult Music in Jamaica." BLACK PERSPECTIVE IN MUSIC 10 (1982): 85-94.

Shows the similarities and differences between Rastafarian and the other types of Jamaican folk music.

**B203** A Look at the Black Struggle in Jamaica. Kingston: Black House Publishing, 1969.

Criticizes the government for its unsympathetic attitude towards those groups in the society such as the Rastafarians who are active progenitors of the African cultural identity.

**B204** Lowenthal, David. West Indian Societies. New York, London, Toronto: Oxford University Press, 1972. "Rastafari," 125, 142, 250, 280, 283-284.

Claims that the Rastafarians "fashioned a repatriation movement so militant that fear for domestic safety impelled the Jamaican government to sponsor missions to assess colonization prospects in Africa."

**B205** Lynn, Kwaku Eddie. "American Afrikan Music: A Study of Musical Change." Ph.D. diss., University of California, Los Angeles, 1987.

Discusses the relationship between contemporary African American music which includes reggae and African modern music.

**B206** McCormack, Ed. "Bob Marley With a Bullet." ROLLING STONE (August 12 1976): 37-41.

Explores Bob Marley's use of music to spread the beliefs of the Rastafarian movement.

**B207** McLeod, Joan and A. A. Jackson. "Nutrition: The Rasta Diet and Rehabilitation of a Malnourished Rastafarian Child." YARD ROOTS JOURNAL 1-2 (Summer 1984): 9-12.

Describes the results of feeding a Rastafarian child on the foods prescribed by the movement.

**B208** McPherson, E. S. P. and L. T. Semaj. "Rasta Chronology." CARIBBEAN QUARTERLY 26, 4 (December 1980): [vii-viii]/97-98.

Chronological listing of dates and events of Ethiopian Rastafarian history from fourteenth century B.C.-1980.

**B209** Mais, Roger. <u>Brother Man</u>. London: Jonathan Cape, 1954.

Describes the activities of Brother Man (a Rastafarian) and shows the overall reaction of his community toward him, in the beginning (love, respect, and adoration) and at the end (hate, disrespect, and rejection).

**B210** Mais, Roger. <u>The Hills were Joyful Together</u>. London: Heinemann, 1981.

Describes the interactions between a Rastafarian living in the same physical area with non-Rastafarians.

**B211** Malloch, Theodore R. "Rastafarianism: A Radical Caribbean Movement on Religion." <u>CENTER JOURNAL</u> 4, 4 (Fall 1985): 67-87.

Evaluates the Rastafarian movement as both an individual and collective socio-political one, with emphasis on the religious impact and political views.

**B212** Manley, Michael. "Reggae, the Revolutionary Impulse, Introduction." In <u>Reggae International</u>, ed. Stephen Davis and Peter Simon, 11-13. London: Thames and Hudson, 1983.

Contends that the significance of both Rastafarians and reggae is due to their universal appeal. See B092.

**B213** Marley, Bob. "Marley in his Own Words." Interview by Basil Wilson and Herman Hall. <u>EVERYBODY'S</u> 5, 4 (July 1981): 33-36.

Covers these subjects: "peace movement in Jamaica," "future of Reggae music," "defining the third world," "writing Reggae music outside of Jamaica," "touring North America," "soccer and the injured toe," "protest music," "politics," and "assassination attempt."

**B214** Martin, Tony. <u>Marcus Garvey, Hero: A Biography</u>. Dover, Massachusetts: Majority Press, 1983. "Rastafarians," 93, 138-140, 150.

Identifies the differences on certain issues between Marcus Garvey and some Rastafarians.

**B215** Martin, Tony. <u>The Pan-African Connection: From Slavery to Garvey and Beyond</u>. Dover, Massachusetts: Majority Press, 1984, c.1983. "Rastafarian Movement," 19-24.

Explains the connection between the early Rastafarian movement and Marcus Garvey.

**B216**  May, Chris.  <u>Bob Marley</u>.  London: Hamish Hamilton, 1985.

Discusses Marley's early childhood, education, and his development as a Rastafarian and reggae musician.

**B217**  May, Chris.  "Living is Hard in a Babylon Yard: A Party Political Broadcast on Behalf of the Rastafari Party."  <u>BLACK MUSIC</u> 4 (November 1977): 12-13.

Discusses the harassments of Rastafarians by the police in Great Britain and the beliefs of one member of the movement.

**B218**  Medrano, Rebecca Read.  "Reggae, Roots and Razzmatazz." <u>AMERICAS</u> 36, 1 (January-February 1984): [34]-39.

Relates the impact of Sunsplash and its links with the dissemination of reggae both within Jamaica and abroad.

**B219**  Michels, Peter M.  [Rastafari] Auflage.  Munchen: Trikont, 1981 [German].

Narratives and poetry presenting the beliefs and practices of Rastafarians.

**B220**  Miguel, Brother.  <u>Rastaman Chant</u>.  Castries, St. Lucia, W.I.: African Children Unlimited, 1983.

Poems describing the fears and hopes of Rastafarians who are affected negatively by the oppressive system which forms the Jamaican society.

**B221**  Miles, Donald.  <u>BOAST</u>.  New York: St. Martin's Press, 1980.

Emphasizes three techniques which include extrapolation, parody, and juxtaposition of detail as sharply contrasting points of view.  The author dramatizes several conflicts that haunted the Rastafarian character (Ras Putain) in this novel.

**B222**  Miles, Robert.  <u>Between Two Cultures: The Case of Rastafarianism</u>. Bristol, Great Britain: Scientific and Social Research Council, Research Unit on Ethnic Relations, 1978.

Describes the factors which led certain youths in Great Britain to adopt elements of the Rastafarian nomenclature.

**B223** Morrish, Ivor. <u>Obeah, Christ and Rastaman</u>. Cambridge, England: Jane Clarke & Co., 1982. "Rastafarians," 68-91, 106, 109-111.

Claims that the Rastafarian movement is a representation of sociological, psychological, and religious escapist trends.

**B224** Mulvaney, Becky Michele. "Rhythms of Resistance: On Rhetoric and Reggae Music." Ph.D. diss., University of Iowa, 1985.

Explores the relationship between Rastafari and reggae music.

**B225** Mutabaruka. <u>24 Poems</u>. Kingston: Paul Issa Publications Ltd., 1980.

Poems centered within and representative of Rastafarian thought, African awareness, and hope for the oppressed.

**B226** Review of <u>Mystic Revelation of Rastafari</u>. <u>SCOPE</u> (8 November 1971): 5.

Suggests that the religion and music of Rastafarians are inseparable.

**B227** N.Y.C.P.D. "Rasta Crime: A Confidential Report." [Excerpts] <u>CARIBBEAN REVIEW</u> 14, 1 (Winter 1985): 12-15/39-40.

Brief review "of the philosophical and religious doctrines of the Rastafarians in Jamaica and the United States." There is also a glossary of terms used by the various Rastafarian groups.

**B228** National Library of Jamaica. <u>Bob Marley: A Bibliography</u>. Kingston, Jamaica: National Library of Jamaica, 1985.

Contains a selected list of materials on Bob Marley.

**B229** Nagashima, Yoshiko S. <u>Rastafarian Music in Contemporary Jamaica: A Study of Socioreligious Music of the Rastafarian Movement in Jamaica</u>. Tokyo, Japan: Institute for the Study of Languages and Cultures of Asia-Africa, 1984.

Outlines the history, method, and function of Rastafarian music.

**B230** Naipaul, V. S. <u>The Middle Passage</u>. New York: The Macmillan Company, 1963. "Ras Tafarians," 215-222.

Discusses Rastafarian views concerning race.

**B231**  Nettleford, Rex.  "African Redemption: The Rastafari and the Wider Society, 1959-1969."  [S.I., s.n., n.d.].  Typewritten.

Contends that there is a simultaneous interaction between the Rastafarian movement and the wider society of Jamaica.

**B232**  Nettleford, Rex.  Caribbean Cultural Identity: An Essay in Cultural Dynamics.  Los Angeles, California: Center for Afro-American Studies and University of California, Los Angeles, Latin American Center Publications, 1978.  "Rastafarians," 16, 20, 33, 48-49, 71, 86, 113, 187-188, 201, 213.

Alludes to the appeal of Rastafarianism to the oppressed section of the Jamaican society.

**B233**  Nettleford, Rex.  "Introduction."  In Dread: The Rastafarians of Jamaica, by Joseph Owens, vii-xix.  Kingston, Jamaica: Sangster's Book Stores Ltd., 1976.

Author concludes: "It is clear that as long as the fundamental changes for which Jamaican society yearns remain frustrated or are slow in coming Rastafarianism (whether a mood, source of energy for rebellious action, or as theology) is bound to have a major role in the country's dynamic development process."  See B247.

**B234**  Nettleford, Rex.  Mirror Mirror: Identity, Race and Protest in Jamaica.  Kingston, Jamaica: William Collins and Sangster (Jamaica) Ltd., 1970.  "Rastafarianism," 12-14, 16, 27, 30, 33, 39-111, 120, 124-127, 150-151, 159-161, 163, 152, 184, 206, 218-224.

Discusses the Rastafarians and their relationship with the wider society of Jamaica.  Among his conclusions is that "one of the things Jamaicans have yet to accept about themselves is what the Rastafarians have long asserted--the recognition of the African connection in the national ethos."  See reviews B017, B087, B319.

**B235**  Nettleford, Rex, ed.  Norman Washington Manley and the New Jamaica.  New York: Africana Publishing Company, 1971.  "Rastafarians," lxviii, 192, 277-280.

Collection of speeches by a former Prime Minister of Jamaica (Norman Washington Manley) who in one of his addresses in the House of Representatives defended action of sending a government mission to certain African countries investigating the possibilities for the repatriation of Rastafarians.

**B236** Nettleford, Rex. <u>Rastafari in the Sixties</u>. In <u>Readings in Government and Politics of the West Indies</u>, ed. Trevor Munroe and Rupert Lewis, 41-53. Mona, Jamaica: Department of Government, University of West Indies, 1971.

Covers the Rastafarian movement in these areas: social context, Jamaicanism, and repatriation.

**B237** Nettleford, Rex. "The Rastafarians of Jamaica: A Prophetic Presence in Plantation America." Paper presented at the Second World Black and African Festival of Arts and Culture (FESTAC) 1977. Typewritten.

Argues that the Rastafarian movement "challenges the entire society on grounds of conscience, moral commitment and cultural identity."

**B238** Nicholas, Tracy and B. Sparrow. <u>Rastafari: A Way of Life</u>. New York: Anchor Books, 1979.

Text and photographs explore the basic and fundamental world view of Rastafarians.

**B239** Norris, Katrin. <u>Jamaica: The Search for an Identity</u>. London, New York, Toronto: Oxford University Press, 1962. "Rastafarians," 43-60.

Argues that "the Rastafarian mentality has many degrees, ranging from the fanatic who lives in an imaginary world to the man whose way of life outwardly conformed with orthodox society, but who has some consciousness of Black solidarity and racial dignity."

**B240** Noyes, John L. <u>The Rastafarians in Britain and Jamaica: A Bibliography</u>. Brighton, England: The Author, 1978.

A selected list of materials about Rastafarians in Britain and Jamaica.

**B241** Obadiah. <u>I Am a Rastafarian</u>. London: F. Watts, 1986.

Sketches the Rastafarian movement with statements on these aspects: beliefs, procedures at meetings, history, holy book symbols, apparel, music, festivals, arts, and crafts.

**B242** O'Gorman, Pamela. "An Approach to the Study of Jamaican Popular Music." <u>JAMAICA JOURNAL</u> 7, 1-2 (March-June 1973): 50-54.

Compares and contrasts Rastafarian and reggae music.

**B243** O'Gorman, Pamela. "On Reggae and Rastafarianism and a Garvey Prophecy." JAMAICA JOURNAL 20, 3 (August-October 1987): 85-87.

Alludes to the connection between reggae and the Rastas as well as African American popular music.

**B244** O'Gorman, Pamela. "Reggae has Achieved National Recognition." PEPPERPOT (December 1975): 33, 35.

Traces selected trends in the different areas of Jamaican music.

**B245** Ojo-Ade, Femi. Review of The Rastafarians: The Dreadlocks of Jamaica, by Leonard Barrett. (B015) THE JOURNAL OF MODERN AFRICAN STUDIES 17, 2 (June 1979): 349-357.

Reviewer chides the author for being repetitious on occasion as well as not devoting more attention to the Rasta language.

**B246** Onoura, Oku. "Thinking." YARD ROOTS JOURNAL 1-2 (Summer 1984): 59.

A poem by a Rastafarian who portrays the selfishness and unwillingness of a human being. (D128)

**B247** Owens, Joseph. Dread: The Rastafarians of Jamaica. London: Heinemann Educational Books, 1982.

Outlines the religious aspects of the Rastafarian movement. See reviews B075, B193.

**B248** Owens, J. V. "Literature on the Rastafari 1955-1974: A Review." SAVACOU 11/12 (September 1975): 86-105, 113.

Select list of writings by and about Rastafarians during the period 1955-1974. See B248(a).

**B248(a)** Owens, J.V. "Literature on the Rastafari 1955-1974." (B248) NEW COMMUNITY 6, 1/2 (Winter 77/78): 150-164.

**B249** Owens, Joseph. "The Rastafarians of Jamaica." In Troubling of the Waters. A Collection of Papers and Responses presented at Two Conferences on Creative Theological Reflections held in Jamaica on the 3rd-4th of May, and in Trinidad on the 28th-30th of May, 1973, ed. Idris Hamid, 165-170. San Fernando, Trinidad: Rahanan Printery Ltd., 1973.

Describes the similarities and differences between the early Christians of the first century A.D. and the Rastafarians.

**B250** Patterson, Orlando. The Children of Sisyphus. Kingston, Jamaica: Bolivar Press, 1971.

Explores the behavior of the Rastafarian members of the Jamaican society who are concerned about the demeaning aspects of British society which persons of the Jamaican middle class seek to place on them. See review B158.

**B251** Patterson, Orlando. "Rastafari: The Cult of the Outcasts." NEW SOCIETY (12 November 1964): 15-17.

Identifies two main groups in the Rastafarian movement and further suggests that they are not really interested in leaving Jamaica (Babylon) for Ethiopia (Zion), their promised land. See B251(a).

**B251(a)** Patterson, H. O. "Ras Tafari: Cult of Outcasts." (B251) In Readings in Government and Politics of the West Indies, comp. A. W. Singham et.al., 266-272. Kingston: [s.n.] 1968.

**B252** Patterson, Sheila. Dark Strangers. Bloomington, Indiana: Indiana University Press, 1964 c1963. "Ras Tafari movement," 225, 329-330, 352, 354, 360.

Sketches the effect of the Rastafari movement on African West Indian families in Great Britain.

**B253** Payen, Marc. [Bob Marley]: Le Rasta. Paris: Encre, 1981. [French]

Describes the life of Bob Marley.

**B254** Pearn, Julie. "Mickey Smith Dread Poet Murdered." YARD ROOTS JOURNAL 1-2 (Summer 1984): 13-16.

Sketches the life, times, and selected poems of Mickey Smith. (D147)

**B255** Pearson, G. Review of <u>Rastaman: The Rastafarian Movement in England,</u> by E. Cashmore. (B062) <u>SOCIOLOGY--THE JOURNAL OF THE BRITISH SOCIOLOGICAL ASSOCIATION</u> 14, 3 (1980): 469-471.

Claims that the author was marginal in describing the significance of the "locks, prayer sticks, Ethiopian colours, ganja and dub music for the black youths of Britain."

**B256** Plummer, Brenda Gayle. Review of <u>Race, Class and Political Symbols: Rastafari and Reggae in Jamaican Politics,</u> by Anita Waters. (B346) <u>CONTEMPORARY SOCIOLOGY</u> 15, 1 (January 1986): 140-141.

Author suggests that "the absence of a theoretical perspective to inform and verify the work, places the burden of coherence on the narrative structure itself and as the supporting body of statistical data."

**B257** Plummer, John. <u>Movement of Jah People</u>. Birmingham: Press Gang, 1978.

Contains the genesis, growth, flowering, and future of the Rastafarian movement.

**B258** Pollard, Velma. "Social History of Dread Talk." <u>CARIBBEAN QUARTERLY</u> 28, 4 (1982): 17-40.

Analyzes "Dread Talk," which reflects the religious, political, and philosophical positions of Rastafari adherents.

**B259** Pollard, Velma. "Word Sounds: The Language of Rastafari in Barbados and St. Lucia." <u>JAMAICA JOURNAL</u> 17, 1 (February 1984): 57-62.

Demonstrates the influence of the Rastafarian use of words on the speech patterns in Barbados and St. Lucia and vice versa.

**B260** Post, Ken. <u>Arise Ye Starvlings: The Jamaican Labour Rebellion of 1935 and its Aftermath</u>. The Hague, Boston: Martinus Nijhoff, 1978. "Rastafarians," 171-172, 188, 192, 205, 234, "Rastafarianism," 163-167, 187-189, 193-194, 239, 246.

Discusses the differences and similarities between the Bedward and Rastafarian movements.

**B261** Post, Ken. "The Bible as Ideology: Ethiopianism in Jamaica, 1930-38." In African Perspectives: Papers in the History, Politics and Economics of Africa, presented to Thomas Hodgkin, ed. Christopher Allen and R.N. Johnson, 155-207. London: Cambridge University Press, 1970.

Discusses the similarities and differences between Ethiopianism and Rastafarianism in Jamaica during the 1930s.

**B262** "A Preliminary Rastafari Bibliography." CARIBBEAN QUARTERLY 24, 3/4 (September-December 1978): 56-58.

List of materials on Rastafari.

**B263** Prescod, Colin. "Black Thoughts." Review of Endless Pressure: A Study of West Indian Life-Styles in Bristol, by Ken Pryce. (B265) NEW SOCIETY (3 May 1979): 280-281.

Claims that the author demonstrates very limited understanding concerning the historical context of the Rastas.

**B264** Prescod, Colin. Review of Rastaman: The Rastafarian Movement in England, by Ernest Cashmore. (B063) NEW SOCIETY 13 (December 1979): 614.

Reviewer argues that the book "tells a story of the emergence of Rasta which is exotic even if incoherent; authentic even if partial; compelling even if not original. It is impressively well-informed with detail--but replete with factual inaccuracies."

**B265** Pryce, Ken. Endless Pressure: A Study of West Indian Life-Styles in Bristol. England: Penguin Books Ltd., 1979. "Rastafarianism," 18-21, 136-171.

Examines the impact of Rastafarianism on the African West Indian youths in England. See review B263.

**B266** Rastafarian Movement Association. A Modern Antique. Kingston, Jamaica: Rastafari Movement Association, 1976.

Explains the Rastafarian movement in terms of its connection with Africa.

**B267** Reckord, V. "Rastafarian Music: An Introductory Study." JAMAICA JOURNAL 11 (August 1977): 2-13.
Demonstrates with photographs, diagrams, and texts the nature, local origins, and function of Rasta music.

**B268** Reid, H. "Bob Marley Up From Babylon." FREEDOMWAYS 21, 3 (1981): 171-179.

States Marley's Rastafarian ideology and studies its relationship with his music.

**B269** Report of Mission To Africa. Kingston, Jamaica: Government Printing Office, 1961.

Elaborates on the reception given to the mission in each of the countries visited and then gives a sketchy assessment of emigration possibilities and concludes: "Skilled persons would be welcome and agricultural ventures would be the most beneficial."

**B270** Reynolds, Julian "Jingles." "Understanding the Society in Which Peter Tosh was Murdered." EVERYBODY'S 11, 7 (November 1987): 18, 23, 36-37, 39.

Reveals the impact of the economic and social conditions of the Jamaican society on Peter Tosh.

**B271** Ricketts, Don. "Apocalypso." CARIBBEAN QUARTERLY 26, 4 (December 1980): 83-85.

Poem inspired with the objective of the ultimate victory of all Africans over their oppressors.

**B272** Ringenberg, Roger. Rastafarianism Expanding Jamaican Cult. Kingston: Jamaica Theological Seminary, 1978.

Evaluates the Rastafarian movement based on a comprehension of "its historical development, doctrines and practices" within an "evangelical" framework.

**B273** Rodney, Walter. The Groundings with my Brothers. London: Bogle-L'Ouverture Publications, 1969.

Portrays the Rastafarian movement as the progenitor of African awareness and consciousness within the Jamaican society.

**B274** Rogers, Claudia. "Comparison of Rastafarians with Pentecostal Revivalists." Paper presented at the meeting of the Society of Applied Anthropology, 1971. Typewritten.

Applies network analysis to groups of both Rastafarians and revivalists living in an area known as Western Kingston, Jamaica.

**B275** Rogers, Claudia. "Social Transformations in Jamaica: The Internal Dynamics of the Rastafarian Movement." Paper presented at the annual meeting of the Caribbean Studies Association, Fort-de-France, Martinique, 1978. Typewritten.

Author reports that "as Rastas have gained media access and have been portrayed not as dangerous to Jamaican society but as its political savior, opposition to Rastas has shifted and it has become much more difficult to recruit new members."

**B276** Rogers, Claudia. "What's a Rasta?" CARIBBEAN REVIEW 7, 1 (Jan/Feb/March 1975): 9-12.

Comments on the various aspects of the Rastafarian beliefs and lifestyles.

**B277** Rogers, Claudia. Review of The Rastafarians: Sounds of Cultural Dissonance, by Leonard Barrett. (B014) AMERICAN HISTORICAL REVIEW 83, 5 (December 1978): 1381-1382.

Reviewer claims the only significance of this book is it "furnishes solid and extensive descriptive data" about the Rastafarian movement.

**B278** Rohlehr, Gordon. "Background Music to Rights of Passage." CARIBBEAN QUARTERLY 26, 1/2 (March-June 1980): 32-40.

Among the musical works mentioned were compositions from the Rastafarian genre.

**B279** Rohlehr, Gordon. "Jamaica Music: A Select Bibliography." In Caribe: West Indians at Home and Abroad, ed. Cliff Lashley, 11-12. New York: Visual Arts Research and Resource Center Relating to the Caribbean, 1980.

Contains not only works on music, but ancillary materials, as well as general monographs on the social and political background of Jamaican music.

**B280** Rohlehr, Gordon. "Some Problems of Assessment: A Look at New Expressions in the Arts of the Contemporary Caribbean." CARIBBEAN QUARTERLY 17, 3/4 (September/December 1971): 92-113.

Enlarges the dialogue on dialect, but includes the more current representation of "Dread," reggae, Rastafarianism, etc.

**B281** Rose, Terence B. "Emerging Social Problems in Jamaica and Their Pastoral Implications." CARIBBEAN JOURNAL OF RELIGIOUS STUDIES 6 (April 1985): 29-45.

Describes the relationship between the church and Rastafarianism.

**B282** Rowe, Maureen. "The Woman in Rastafari." CARIBBEAN QUARTERLY 26, 4 (December 1980): 21-31.

Describes the evolution, growth, and development of the female role and contribution to the Rastafarian movement.

**B283** Rubin, Vera. Cannabis and Culture. Hague: Mouton, 1975. "Rastafarians," 363, 487-488.

Describes the genesis and diffusion of ganja among the Rastafarians.

**B284** Rubin, Vera and Lambros Comitas. Ganja in Jamaica: The Effects of Marijuana Use. Garden City, New York: Anchor Press, 1976.

Detailed analysis of ganja in Jamaica and its use by the Rastafarians.

**B285** Rycenssa, Seretha. "The Rastafarian Legacy: A Rich Cultural Gift." ECONOMIC REPORT JAMAICA 4, 1 (August 1978): 22-24.

Discusses the legacies of Rastafarians which include dress, language, religion, a way of life, and music.

**B286** Saakana, Amon Sahar. "Ijahman: A Vision of Rastafari: A Quality of Roodness." FRONTLINE (Mid August-October 1962): 105-108.

Considers certain factors which seem to be creating an unhealthy state for reggae music and cites an example by summarizing the life and activities of Ijahman.

**B287** Salkey, Andrew. "Introduction." In One Love, ed. Audvil King, Althea Helps, Pam Wint, and Frank Hasfal, 5-9. London: Bogle-L'Ouverture Publications, 1971.

Author concludes: "with the assurance of its compelling narrative and its moral example, and with its definition of our new Caribbean alternatives in language and life-style, will I think, be remembered as the very first work of its kind." See B180.

**B288** Segal, Aaron. "The Land of Look Behind: A Film about Reggae and Rastafarianism." Review of Land of Look Behind, directed and produced by Alan Greenberg. (V16) CARIBBEAN REVIEW 12, 2 (Spring 1983): 36-37.

Asserts that Land of Look Behind "fails as a film about Rastafarians although it tries much harder than its predecessors."

**B289** Segal, Aaron. "Rockers: A Different Image." Review of Rockers, written and directed by Theodoros Bafaloukos. (V25) CARIBBEAN REVIEW 10, 2 (Spring 1981): 38-39.

Claims that "Rockers shows Rastas as part of the vital mainstream of Jamaican society, contributing to a national culture and economy, while foreswearing some of the materialism." See D181.

**B290** Semaj, Leahcim Tufani. "Inside Rasta: the Future of a Religious Movement." CARIBBEAN REVIEW 14, 1 (Winter 1985): 8-11/37-38.

Focuses on the Rastafarian movement as it "questions the alien values that black people have adopted and has been working towards articulating and implementing corrective measures." Lists the major aspects of an evolving Rastafarian social theory.

**B291** Semaj, Leahcim Tufani. "Race and Identity and Children of the African Diaspora: Contributions of Rastafari." In Caribe: West Indians at Home and Abroad, ed. Cliff Lashley, 13-18. New York: Visual Arts Research and Resource Center Relating to the Caribbean, 1980.

Shows the Rastafarian movement as one model for the building of movements which could enhance dispersed Africans positively in group organization. See B291(a).

**B291(a)** Semaj, Leahcim Tufani. "Race and Identity and Children of the African Diaspora: Contributions of Rastafari." (B291) STUDIA AFRICANA 1, 4 (Fall 1981): 412-419.

**B292** Semaj, Leahcim Tufani. "Rastafari: From Religion to Social Theory." CARIBBEAN QUARTERLY 26, 4 (December 1980): 22-30.

Examines the positive aspects of Rastafarian religion, and shows how it could be used as strategy in the liberation of the dispersed Africans.

**B293** Service, L. V. "The Rastafarian Cult." JAMAICA CONSTABULARY FORCE MAGAZINE 19, 1 (December 1974): 12-14.

Places the Rastafarian movement in the forefront of urging African Jamaicans to remember their African heritage and that its "influence is all pervasive in all sections of Jamaican society."

**B294** Sewell, Tony. Garvey's Children: The Legacy of Marcus Garvey. London: Voice Communication, 1987. "Rastafarians," 94-127.

Describes the Rastafarian interpretations of Garvey's "Black God" and "Back to Africa" concepts.

**B295** Shibata, Yoshiko S. Development of Rastafarian Music--Its Growth and Diversification. Kingston, Jamaica: Department of History, University of West Indies, 1980.

Identifies the differences between the early and current stages of Rastafarian music.

**B296** Shibata, Yoshiko S. "Rastafarian Music in Jamaica: Its Historical and Cultural Significance as a Study of Socio-Religious Music in Culturology of Area Studies." M.A., thesis, University of Tsukuba, Japan, 1981.

Covers Rastafarian music from its ancestral heritages; local origins; development, growth and diversification; influences and responses; and finally its relationship with reggae.

**B297** Silvera, Makeda. "An Open Letter to Rastafarian Sistrens: Dear Sisters." FIREWEED 16 (Spring 1983): 114-120.

Describes both the theoretical and practical problems of inequality faced by women in the Rastafarian movement.

**B298** Simpson, George Eaton. Black Religions in the New World. New York: Columbia University Press, 1978. "Rastafarian," 124-130.

Sketches of the history, method, and "mystique" of the Rastafari movement in Jamaica and Dominica, as well as their evolution. See review B074.

**B299** Simpson, George Eaton. "Culture Change and Reintegration found in the Cults of West Kingston, Jamaica." PROCEEDINGS OF THE AMERICAN PHILOSOPHICAL SOCIETY 99 (April 1955): 89-92.

Shows the similarities and differences between the revivalist and Rastafarian movements.

**B300** Simpson, George Eaton. Jamaican Cult Music. [Introduction Notes] New York: Folkways Records and Service, 1954.

Shows the similarities and dissimilarities between the music of revivalists and that of the Rastafarians.

**B301** Simpson, George Eaton. "Political Cultism in West Kingston, Jamaica." SOCIAL AND ECONOMIC STUDIES 4, 2 (June 1955): 133-149.

Author concludes: "This cult has some aspects of the nativistic movement, that is a return to native life, to the good old days. All members insist that they are ready and eager to leave for Africa even though they are rather far removed from African ways of life and are almost completely uninformed about African cultures."

**B302** Simpson, George Eaton. "The Rastafari Movement in Jamaica: A Study of Race and Class Conflict." SOCIAL FORCES 34, 1 (October 1955): 167-171.

Comments on the basic doctrines, meetings, themes, and the functions and dysfunctions of the Rastafari movement.

**B303** Simpson, George Eaton. "The Ras Tafari Movement in Jamaica in its Millennial Aspect." In Millennial Dreams in Action: Essays in Comparative Study, ed. Sylvia L. Thrupp, 160-165. Hague: Mouton Co., 1962.

Stresses the acephalous aspects, as well as the diversity of positions held by various groups who are members of the Rastafarian movement. See B303(a).

**B303(a)** Simpson, George Eaton. "The Ras Tafari Movement in Jamaica in Its Millennial Aspect." (B303) In Millennial Dreams in Action: Studies In Revolutionary Religious Movements, ed. Sylvia L. Thrupp, 160-165. New York: Schocken Books, 1970.

**B304**  Simpson, George Eaton.  "Religion and Justice: Some Reflections on the Rastafari Movement."  PHYLON 46, 4 (December 1985): 286-291.

Author concludes: "Rastafarianism can be seen as an individual and collective movement for the acquisition of status for blacks in colonial societies. Within Rasta communities and within individual Rastas this struggle aims to regain the sense of personal worth and dignity which society has denied."

**B305**  Simpson, George Eaton.  "Religions of the Caribbean."  In The African Diaspora: Interpretive Essays, ed. M. Kilson and R. Rotberg, 280-311. Cambridge, Massachusetts: Harvard University Press, 1976.
Brief note on the various tendencies within the Rastafarian movement and states that "they are neither an anachronism nor the wave of the future in Jamaica."

**B306**  Simpson, G. Eaton.  Religious Cults of the Caribbean: Trinidad, Jamaica and Haiti.  3rd ed. Rio Piedras, Puerto Rico: Institute of Caribbean Studies, University of Puerto Rico, 1980.  "Rastafari movement (Jamaica)," 208-228.

Elaborates on the nativistic and adjustive activities of the Rastafarian movement.

**B307**  Smith, M. G., Roy Augier, and Rex Nettleford.  The Rastafari Movement in Kingston, Jamaica.  Kingston, Jamaica: Institute of Social and Economic Research, University College of the West Indies, 1960.

The first major study on the Rastafarians which covers history, doctrines, organizations, and objectives.  See B307(a).

**B307(a)**  Smith, M. G., Roy Augier, and Rex Nettleford.  "The Ras Tafari Movement." (B307)  In The Black Experience in Religion, ed. C. Eric Lincoln, 340-354. Garden City, New York: Anchor Books, Anchor Press/Doubleday, 1974.

**B308**  Smith, Michael.  "Dread."  SAVACOU 14/15 (1979): 82-83.

Speaks of the horrendous circumstances in which the majority of the people live in Jamaica.

**B309**  Smith, Michael.  It a Come.  London: Race Today Pub., 1986.

Poems on various topics such as nursery rhymes, the Bible, Rasta talk, etc.

**B310** Smith, Michael. "Me Cyaan Believe It." <u>JAMAICA JOURNAL</u> 18 (1985): 45.

Poem which states the problems faced by persons living in poor conditions. (D147)

**B311** Smith, Michael. "Mickey Smith Dub Poet." Interview by Mervyn Morris. <u>JAMAICA JOURNAL</u> 18 (2 May-July 1985): 38-45.

Covers these perspectives: genesis of his writing, role of the poet, definition of dub poetry, and relationships with Rastafarians.

**B312** Smith, R. T. "Religion in the Formation of West Indian Society: Guyana and Jamaica." In <u>The African Diaspora: Interpretive Essays</u>, ed. M. Kilson and R. Rotberg, 312-341. Cambridge, Massachusetts: Harvard University Press, 1976.

Concludes: "Rastafarianism is the only example in the English-speaking West Indies of an attempt to fashion an aggressive social ethic based on a well-developed religious doctrine and incorporating African symbolism in a clear way."

**B313** St. Hill, Margaret V. "The Speech Patterns of the Rastafarians of Barbados." Cave Hill, Barbados: University of West Indies, [n.d.]. Typewritten.

Shows the similarities and dissimilarities of the word usages by the Rastafarians in Barbados with the kindred group in Jamaica.

**B314** Steffens, Roger. "Reggae 1984: Fragments of a Fallen Star." <u>MUSICIAN</u> 64 (February 19, 1984): 66-74.

Claims that reggae has declined since the death of Bob Marley.

**B315** Stephenson, Edward G. "A Social Psychological Analysis of a Millennium/Messianic Social Movement." Ph.D. diss., University of California, Santa Cruz, 1987.

Examines the dynamics of social change as they occur within the context of Rastafari, a social movement which emerged in Jamaica during the 1930s.

**B316** Stewart, Richard E. "A Comparison of Music Preferences of Students in Three Educational Systems: Seventh-Day Adventist, Public and Private Independent Schools." Ph.D. diss., University of Miami, 1984.

Examines student preferences from three types of educational systems concerning various musical genres, which include reggae.

**B317** Stone, Carl. Class, Race and Political Behavior in Urban Jamaica. Kingston, Jamaica: Institute of Social and Economic Research, University of West Indies, 1973. "Rastafarians," 13, 112, 121, 123, 128, 131, 133, 153-156, 158, 163-164.

Compares and contrasts the Rastafarian and Black Power movements.

**B318** Stone, Carl. Electoral Behavior and Public Opinion in Jamaica. Kingston, Jamaica: Institute of Social and Economic Research, University of West Indies, 1974. "Rastafarians," 18, 25-27, 31, 63, 79.

Explains the result of the responses to the Rastafari movement and the Rod of Correction, a symbol used by Michael Manley's political party in the 1972 general elections.

**B319** Stone, Carl. Review of Mirror, Mirror: Identity, Race and Protest in Jamaica, by Rex Nettleford. (B234) CARIBBEAN REVIEW 4, 4 (October-December 1972): 28-31.

Chides the author for doing no more "than a textual analysis which fails to locate the operative social forces that shape the direction of the [Rastafarian] movement."

**B320** Strasbaugh, Lamar Gene. "Reggae-Pop-Folklore From Jamaica." MBILDUNG 11, 9 (1979): 520-521. [German].

Traces the development of popular music in Jamaica from rhythm and blues to Rastafarian reggae music.

**B321** Tafari, I Jabulani. "The Rastafari: Successors of Marcus Garvey." CARIBBEAN QUARTERLY 26, 4 (December 1980): [1]-12.

Connects the movement to historical traditions of struggle by the people of African ancestry in the Americas in their efforts to overcome the threat of continuing denigration of Africa.

**B322** Tarte-Booth, Christine M. "400 Years: A History of Cultural Resistance in Jamaica." M.A. thesis, University of Minnesota, 1984.

Implies that the struggle being waged by the Rastafarians "will not disappear or be successfully contained as long as the racist practices of ideologies of the productive relations remain intact."

**B323** Taylor, Roy. Ras Fari. Kingston, Jamaica: Protype, 1976.

Poem which criticizes the elements in society that continuously oppress human beings based on their African heritage.

**B324** Taylor, T. B. "Soul Rebels: The Rastafarians and the Free Exercise Clause." GEORGETOWN LAW JOURNAL 72, 5 (1984): 1605-1635.

Examines Rastafarian beliefs and the first amendment.

**B325** Tesfa, Ras-J. The Living Testament of Rasta-For I. [S.I., s.n.], 1980.

Explores the genesis and development of the basic tenets in relation to the Rastafari movement. See D139.

**B326** Thelwell, Michael. The Harder They Come. New York: Grove Press, 1980.

In this novel the Rastafarian movement is a part of the landscape of an urban ghetto of Kingston, Jamaica. See V13.

**B327** Thomas, Elean. "Notes to Bob Marley." In Word Rhythms From the Life of a Woman, 56. London: Karia Press, 1986.

Describes the legacy of Bob Marley.

**B328** Thomas, Elean. "Rasta Warrior." In Word Rhythms From the Life of a Woman, 44. London: Karia Press, 1986.

Describes the association between a Rastafarian female and male.

**B329** Thomas, Michael. "The Rastas are Coming, the Rastas are Coming." ROLLING STONE (12 August 1976): 33-47.

Describes the relationships among the government of Michael Manley in Jamaica, the death of Haile Selassie, and the Rastafarians.

**B330** Thomas, Michael. "The Wild Side of Paradise: Streaming with the Rude Boys, the Rastas and Reggae." ROLLING STONE (19 July 1973): 44-46, 48, 50, 52.

Discusses the historical, social, and economic conditions which created the links between hustlers (rude boys), religion (Rasta), and music (reggae) within the Jamaican society.

**B331** Thompson, Winston A. "Reggae Music: An Affective Epistemology." UNION SEMINARY QUARTERLY REVIEW 36 (Summer 1981): 259-269.

Identifies the common ground for both Rastafarianism and reggae music.

**B332** Toch, Hans. The Social Psychology of Social Movements. New York: The Bobbs-Merrill Company, Inc. 1965. "Ras Tafari movement," 30-33, 38, 42, 43.

Suggests that "the Rasta Tafari movement illustrates that illusory beliefs originate in an intolerable situation."

**B333** Tosh, Peter. "An Exclusive Interview with Peter Tosh." Interview by Basil Wilson. (EBM March, April, May 1983). EVERYBODY'S 11, 7 (November 1987): 42-46.

Covers these topics: "performing in South Africa," "Tosh in Africa," "Peter Tosh and Musical exploitation," "Tosh and Bunny Wailer," "Tosh the Reformer," "Tosh and Rastafari," "Peter Tosh and near tragedy," and "Tosh and the Rolling Stones."

**B334** Tosh, Peter. "Peter Tosh." (press conference May 1986). Excerpts by Patricia Booth. EVERYBODY'S 11, 7 (November 1987): 4.

Fragments from Peter Tosh's answers to questions about such issues as "Nuclear War" and "South Africa."

**B335** Troyna, Barry. Rastafarianism, Reggae and Racism. England: [s.n.] 1977.

Discusses the links between Rastafarianism and African youths in Great Britain.

**B336** Troyna, Barry. "The Reggae War." NEW SOCIETY 39, 753 (10 March 1977): 491-492.

Argues that "Music is a focus for many young blacks' lives. Reggae lyrics very often express for example, hostility to the police, and may help nurture the existing alienation."

**B337** Turner, H. W. Review of The Rastafarians: The Dreadlocks of Jamaica, by Leonard Barrett. (B015) JOURNAL OF RELIGION IN AFRICA 11, 2 (1980): 154-155.

Reviewer concludes: "After reading this work one feels that the future of Jamaica depends a good deal on how the Rastas and all they represent are handled."

**B338** Valdman, Albert and Arnold Highfield, ed. Theoretical Orientations in Creole Studies. New York: Academic Press, 1980. "Rastafarian," 102, 401; "Rastafarianism," 101; "Dread Talk," 102-103, 401.

Illustrates various words and their meanings present in the Rastafarians' speech patterns.

**B339** Vincent, Theodore G. Black Power and the Garvey Movement. Berkeley, California: Ramparts Press, 1971. "Rastafari," 20, 227-228.

Elaborates on the repatriation theme of the Rastafarians.

**B340** Walcott, Derek. "O Babylon." In The Joker of Seville and O Babylon, 155-275. New York: Farrar, Straus and Giroux, 1978.

A play portraying the activities of a Rastafarian community in Kingston, Jamaica.

**B341** Walcott, Noel. "Judgement." In New Poets From Jamaica: An Anthology, ed. Edward Kamau Brathwaite, 95. Kingston, Jamaica: Savacou Publications Ltd., 1979.

Poem excoriating the activities of "Herodutus," "Christopher Columbus," "Marco Polo," "Francis Drake," "Pirate Morgan," "John Hawkins," and "Paul Pope."

**B342**  Walcott, Noel. "A Patwah Dat." In <u>New Poets From Jamaica: An Anthology</u>, ed. Edmund Kamau Brathwaite, 92. Kingston, Jamaica: Savacou Publications, Ltd., 1979.

Poem expressing the perils and plight of an African human captured and taken from his homeland involuntarily.

**B343**  Walcott, Noel. "Splash It Sploosh." In <u>New Poets From Jamaica: An Anthology</u>, ed. Edmund Kamau Brathwaite, 93-94. Kingston, Jamaica: Savacou Publications, Ltd., 1979.

Poem stating the cultural heritage of the African Jamaicans.

**B344**  Walte, Juan J. "Felix Grant's Album Sound." <u>AMERICAS</u> 35, 2 (March-April 1983): 3-7, 33.

Compares and contrasts the music of bossa nova (Brazil) and reggae (Jamaica).

**B345**  Ward, Ed. "Reggae." In <u>The Rolling Stone Illustrated History of Rock & Roll</u>, ed. Jim Miller, 445-450. New York: Rolling Stone Press, 1980.

Describes the sources of and various trends in reggae music.

**B346**  Waters, Anita M. <u>Race, Class and Political Symbols: Rastafari and Reggae in Jamaican Politics</u>. New Brunswick, New Jersey: Transaction Books, 1985.

The study suggests that as long as the injustice of "economic freedom, the influence of ethnic advantage, and the hypocrisy of symbolic democracy thrive in Jamaica, the challenge of Rastas ideology will continue." See reviews B106, B256, and item B346(a).

**B346(a)**  Waters, Anita M. "Symbols, Social Class and Politics: Rastafari and Reggae in Jamaica Elections 1967-1980." Ph.D. diss., Columbia University, 1984. (B346)

**B347**  Watson, G. Llewellyn. "Patterns of Black Protest in Jamaica: The Case of the Rastafarians." <u>JOURNAL OF BLACK STUDIES</u> 4, 3 (March 1974): 329-343.

Author argues that "As a cultural revitalization movement, the Rastas are playing the role of bearers of protest, definers of discontent and protagonists of rebellion in Jamaican society."

**B348** Watson, G. Llewellyn. "The Ras-Tafarian Movement in Jamaica: An Exploratory Analysis." M.A. thesis, University of Guelph, 1970.

Examines the metaphysical idealist outlook of the Rastafarian movement.

**B349** Watson, G. Llewellyn. "Social Structure and Social Movements: The Black Muslims in the U.S.A. and the Ras-Tafarians in Jamaica." BRITISH JOURNAL OF SOCIOLOGY 24 (June 1973): 188-204.

Contends that there are parallels between the Black Muslims of the United States and the Rastafarians in Jamaica and finds "they are only the most volatile expressions of deeper structural malignancy rooted in the sacrificial lands of racism and neo-colonialism where they appear."

**B350** Weisbrod, Robert. "British West Indian Reaction to the Italian Ethiopian War: An Episode in Pan Africanism." CARIBBEAN STUDIES 10, 1 (1970): 34-41.

Discusses the responses of various movements in the Caribbean, like the Rastafarians in Jamaica, to the invasion of Ethiopia by Italy in 1935.

**B351** Weiss, Karl-Erich. "Die Rastafari Bewegung auj Jamaika: Entwicklungsphasen und Ausdrunchsformen einer Gegenkultur." M.Phil. thesis, Westfalischen Wilhelms Universitat, 1981. [German]

Discusses the genesis, growth, and development of the Rastafarian movement.

**B352** White, Edgar. Lament for Rastafari and Other Plays. London; Boston: M. Boyars, 1983.

Focuses on the corporeal and incorporeal activities of an African West Indian family with Rastafarian ideals in its journey from Jamaica to Great Britain and New York.

**B353** White, Garth. The Development of Jamaican Popular Music with Special Reference to the Music of Bob Marley: A Bibliography. Kingston, Jamaica: African Caribbean Institute, 1982.

List of selected publications on the Rastafarians and reggae music.

**B354** White, Garth. "Reggae--A Musical Weapon." In <u>Caribe: West Indians at Home and Abroad</u>, ed. Cliff Lashley, 6-10. New York: Visual Arts Research and Resource Center Relating to the Caribbean, 1980.

Gives an account of reggae music which includes its origins, growth, development, and future. See B354(a).

**B354(a)** White, Garth. "Reggae: A Musical Weapon." (B354) <u>CARIBE</u> 6, 4 (Spring-Summer 1982): 21-25.

**B355** White, Garth. "Rudie, Oh Rudie." <u>CARIBBEAN QUARTERLY</u> 13, 3 (1965): 39-44.

Examines the "rude bwoy" culture which developed among the urban lower class youths between the ages of fourteen to twenty-five in certain areas of Kingston, Jamaica.

**B356** White, Timothy. "Bob Marley (1945-1981): The King of Reggae finds his Zion." <u>ROLLING STONE</u> 346, (25 June 1981): 25-27/86.

Biographical sketch of Marley outlining events from birth until death, with special emphasis on his Rastafarian beliefs.

**B357** White, Timothy. <u>Catch a Fire: The Life of Bob Marley</u>. New York: Holt, Rinehart and Winston, 1983.

This monograph is biographical in character and includes a broad scope of data, inclusive of Rastafarianism and the career of Marley.

**B358** White, Timothy. "Roots, Rastas and Reggae--Bob Marley's Jamaica." <u>CRAWDADDY</u> (January 1976): 35-41.

A biographical sketch of Bob Marley's life, with emphasis on his becoming a member of the Rastafarian movement.

**B359** Whitney, Malika Lee and Dermott Hussey. <u>Bob Marley: Reggae King of the World</u>. Kingston, Jamaica: Kingston Publishers, 1984.

Explores the life and times of Bob Marley, with emphasis on his commitment to his Rastafarian beliefs and practices.

**B360** Wilk, R. B. Review of <u>Peter Tosh at the Ritz</u>. (New York, 1981). <u>EVERYBODY'S</u> 11, 1 (November 1987): 40.

States that "like his immortal compatriot, Peter Tosh brought a sense of drama to the show, acting out his songs with theatrical gestures."

**B361** Williams, Chris Ahkell. <u>Rasta: Emperor Haile Selassie and the Rastafarians</u>. Trinidad: Black Starliner Inc., [1980?]

Discusses these aspects of the Rastafarian movement: life and times of Haile Selassie, characteristics (worship, women, children, food) repatriation, hair, marijuana, clothes, reggae music, meeting with Haile Selassie, and the future.

**B362** Williams, K. M. <u>The Rastafarians</u>. London: Ward Lock Educational, 1981.

Discusses the Rastafarian movement with these emphases: genesis of beliefs, language and meaning, and music.

**B363** Wilms, Anno and Lutz Khiche. <u>Rastafari</u>. Wuppertal: Jugend-dienst-Verlag, 1982. [German]

Photographs and text describing the Rastafarian way of life.

**B364** Wilson, Basil. "Introduction." In <u>The Living Testament of Rasta-For I</u>, by Ras-J Tesfa, [n.p.][S.I. s.n.], 1980.

Views the Rastafarian as the new Caribbean person. (B325)

**B365** Wilson, Basil Wilson. "So Long Tuff Gong." <u>EVERYBODY'S</u> 5, 4 (July 1981): [34]-40, 42-43.

Shows the relationship between Marley, his circumstances, and his music.

**B366** Wilson, Bryan R. <u>Magic and the Millennium: A Sociological Study of Religious Movements of protest Among Tribal and Third-World Peoples</u>. London: Heinmann Educational Books, 1973. "Ras Tafarians," 63-69, 311, 414.

Author argues: "Despite their display of tough mindedness, their deliberately disorderly behavior in the face of persecution and their frank condemnation of religion and politics, the Rastafarians are clearly a highly suggestible group not dissimiliar from other revolutionist sects in less advanced countries."

**B367** Wilson, Jackie. "Come Let Us Reason Together." In <u>Black Presence in Multi-Ethnic Canada</u>, ed. Vincent D'Oyley, 167-189. Vancouver, Canada: Center for the Study of Curriculum and Instruction, University of British Columbia, 1979.

Considers the variations in the Rastafarian movement and the effect of its concepts and practices on the African Jamaican youths residing in Canada.

**B368** Winders, James. "Reggae, Rastafarians and Revolution: Rock Music in the Third World." <u>JOURNAL OF POPULAR CULTURE</u> 17 (Summer 1983): 61-73.

Demonstrates the way in which reggae music and Rastafari simultaneously impact (active/passive) upon each other.

**B369** Witvliet, Theo. <u>A Place in the Sun: Liberation Theology in the Third World</u>. Maryknoll, New York: Orbis Books, c1985. "Rastafarians," 104-117.

Claims that "The Africa Ethiopia which the Rasta celebrates is an imaginary continent, the product of an anticipatory imagination which refuses to accept Babylon as the ultimate reality."

**B370** Wong, Ansel. "Forward." In <u>Black Youth, Rastafarianism and the Identity Crisis in Britain</u>, by Len Garrison, 6-8. London: Afro-Caribbean Education Resource Project, 1979.

Claims the author only considers "one aspect of the British black experience; an experience that is characterised not only by a process of self-discovery and journey to Zion but differential treatment meted out by the many institutions of the society, the police, education service, the judiciary, housing, etc." (B127)

**B371** Wood, William. Review of <u>The Rastafarians: Sounds of Cultural Dissonance</u>, by Leonard Barrett. (B014) <u>REVIEW OF RELIGIOUS RESEARCH</u> 21, 1 (Fall 1979): 116.

Author suggests that the flexible leadership of the Rastafarian movement may be "significiant in explaining the wealth of creative solutions which Rastafarians are proposing for personal, community, national and even international problems."

**B372** Wright, Christopher. "Cultural Continuity and the Growth of West Indian Religion in Britain." <u>RELIGION</u> 14 (October 1984): 337-356.

Discusses the factors which led certain African Caribbean migrants in Great Britain to become members of the Rastafari movement.

**B373** Wynter-Carew, Sylvia. "One Love: Rhetoric or Reality?: Apsects of Afro-Jamaicanism." Review of One Love, by Audvil King, Althea Helps, Pam Wint and Frank Hasfal. (B180) CARIBBEAN STUDIES 12, 3 (October 1972): 64-97.

Links the struggle of African Jamaicans with their African identity.

**B374** Yawney, Carole and Clemanada. "As Smoke Drive Them Out: Rastafarians and the Sacred Herb." Paper prepared for the Bucke Memorial Society Conference on Transformation of Consciousness. Montreal, October 24-26, 1973. Typewritten.

Applies the bicameral model of the brain functions (left and right) to Rastafari in Jamaican society. The authors discover that they are simultaneously competing and collaborating with the oppressors. See B374(a), B381.

**B374(a)** Yawney, Carole and Clemanada. "As Smoke Drive Them Out: Rastafarians and the Scared Herb." (B374) In Rastalogue, ed. 34-45. Ottawa, Canada: 1974.

**B375** Yawney, Carole. "Don't Vex Then Pray: The Methodology of Initiation Fifteen Years Later." Paper prepared for the Qualitative Research Conference, University of Waterloo, Ontario, May 15-17, 1985. Typewritten.

Describes the tactics and strategies used in the empirical study of Rastafarian communities in Kingston, Jamaica.

**B376** Yawney, Carole. "Dream Wasteland: Rastafarian Ritual in West Kingston, Jamaica, in Ritual Symbolism and Ceremonialism." In The Americas: Studies in Symbolic Anthropology, ed. N. Ross Crumrine, 154-178. Greeley Colorado: Museum of Anthropology, University of Colorado, 1979.

Shows the Rastafarian movement as an example of an ideology of the oppressed.

**B377** Yawney, Carole. "From Uncle Tom to Aunt Jemima: Towards a Global Perspective on Violence against Women." CANADIAN WOMAN STUDIES/LES CAHIERS DE LA FEMME 6, 1 (1985): 13-15.

Suggests that the Rastafarian movement is a product of a patriarchal system and "legitimizes among other forms of oppression, violence against women."

**B378** Yawney, Carole. "Herb and the Chalice: The Symbolic Life of the Children of Slaves in Jamaica." Paper presented at the annual meeting of the Canadian Sociology and Anthropology Association, Montreal, Canada, 1972.

Focuses on the role and impact that Haile Selassie, as well as cannabis have on the Rastafarian movement. See B378(a).

**B378(a)** Yawney, Carole. Herb and Chalice: This Symbolic Life of the Children of Slaves in Jamaica. Toronto, Canada: York University, 1972. (B378)

**B379** Yawney, Carole. "Lions in Babylon: The Rastafarians of Jamaica as a Visionary Movement." Ph.D. diss., McGill University, 1978.

Considers the effects of cannabis (ganja or marijuana) on the ideological and social dynamics of the Rastafarian movement.

**B380** Yawney, Carole. "Rastafarian Sister by the Rivers of Babylon." CANADIAN WOMAN STUDIES/LES CAHIERS DE LE FEMME 5, 2 (Winter 1983): 73-75.

Brief assessment of problems faced by women in the Rastafarian movement.

**B381** Yawney, Carole. Rastalogue. Ottawa, Canada, [s.n.], 1976.

Discusses the visionary outlook of the Rastafarian movement.

**B382** Yawney, Carole. "Remnants of All Nations: Rastafarian Attitudes to Race and Nationality." In Ethnicity in the Americas, ed. by Francis Henry, 231-266. Paris, Hague: Mouton Publishers, 1976.

Discusses Rastafarians' posture towards race and nationality. This includes examination of the conflict between Zion and Babylon as well as their position concerning population restraint.

**B383** Yawney, Carole. "To Grow a Daughter: Cultural Liberation and the Dynamics of Oppression in Jamaica." In Feminism in Canada: From Pressure To Politics, ed. Angela R. Miles and Geraldine Fine, [n.p.]. Montreal, Canada: Black Rose Books, 1983.

Examines the role of women in Jamaican society generally and in the Rastafarian movement in particular.

**B384** Yawney, Carole. "Visionary Front: The Social Basis of Dual Cognition Among the Rastafarians of Jamaica." Abstract of <u>Papers on Urban Studies at the 1974 (Mexico City) Meeting of the American Anthropological Association,</u> Prepared by Robert V. Kemper. <u>URBAN ANTHROPOLOGY</u> 4, 2 (Summer): 1975, 202.

Argues that "The Rastafarians evolved a visionary front which distinguished between meditation and reasoning as modes of cognition."

**B385** Yawney, Carole and Charmaine Montague. <u>Voice of Thunder: Dialogue with Nyah Binghi Elders.</u> Toronto, Canada: Massai Productions, 1985.

Explains the value system of Rastafarians to non-members of the Toronto community.

**B386** Zeman, Brenda Maureen Alice. "Dread Revitalization: The Rastafari of Jamaica." M.Sc. thesis, California State University, Long Beach, 1979.

Argues that the development of the Rastafari movement is a direct result of the growth of black nationalism and anti-colonialism after World War I.

**CHILLUM**

# Appendix A: Selected List of Rastafarian and Reggae Magazines

Calling Rastafari. 1979-
Kingston, Jamaica: [s.n.]
Produces entries pertaining to the structure of the Rastafarian movement and encourages both non-Rastas and Rastas to join its ranks.

Ithiopian Defender. [n.d.]
Kingston, Jamaica: Rastafarian Movement.
Features poems and essays on Rastafarian themes.

Our Own. [n.d.]
Kingston, Jamaica: Rastafarian Movement.
Contains poetry by various Rastas.

Rasta Voice. [n.d.]
Kingston, Jamaica: Rastafarian Movement.
Carries announcements of meetings and reports what occurs at them.

Rastafari Speaks. 1980-
Laventille, Trinidad and Tobago.
Conveys information concerning Rastafarian activities in Trinidad and Tobago.

Reggae. 1987-
Toronto, Ontario: Reggae Magazine.
Reggae music from Canada.

Reggae & African Beat.  1983-
Los Angeles, California: Bongo Production.
Current information on various reggae personalities including interviews.

Reggae Quarterly.  1982-1986.
Toronto, Ontario: Live Good Today.
Provides articles concerned with reggae styles, forms and performance.

Reggae Report.  1984-
Miami, Fl.: Reggae Report Inc.
Includes reggae artist profiles and regional reports.

Reggae Times.  198?-
Venice, California: CBM Reggae Time.
Covers all forms of reggae music.

# Appendix B: Selected List of Reggae Artists and Bands

Abyssinians
Aces
Adams, Glen
Aitken, Laurel
Aitkens, Bobby
Alcapone, Dennis
Alimantado, Doctor
Alphonso, Noel
Alphonso, Roland
Althea & Donna
Amazulu
Anderson, Al
Andy, Bob
Andy, Horace
Aotearoa
Asher, Bongo
Asher, Climax
Aswad
Austin, Peter
Awareness Art Ensemble
Bagga, Earl
Baley, Ras Elroy
Banton, Pato
Barrett, Aston "Family Man"
Barrett, Carlton
Batista, Martin
Beckford, Theophilius
Bennett, Deadly Headly

Bennett, Lorna
Bennett, Louise
Biggs, Barry
Black Kush
Black, Pablo
Black Slate
Black Uhuru
Blake, Paul
Blondy, Alpha
Bloodfire Posse
Blue Riddim Band
Booker, Cedella
Boom Shaka
Boothe, Ken
Bovell, Dennis
Bowen, Winston "Bo Peep"
Braithwaite, Junior
Breeze, Sister
Brevett, Tony
Brevette, Lloyd
Brimstone
Brimstone & Fire
Broggs, Peter
Brooks, Baba
Brooks, Cedric
Brown, Al
Brown, Barry
Brown, Dennis

Bunny, Bingy
Burning Band
Burning Spear
Buster, Prince
Byles, Junior
Campbell, Al
Campbell, Cornell
Campbell, Michael
Carlos, Don
Carlton & The Shoes
Carol, Sister
Chalice
Chaplin, Charlie
Charmers, Lloyd
Chin, Junior "Chico"
Chin, Tony
Chung, Geoffrey
Chung, Michael
Clarendonians
Clarke, Bunny "Rugs"
Clash
Cliff, Jimmy
Coffie, Carlton
Cole, Stranger
Collins, Ansel
Collins, Dave
Comic, Sir Lord
Congos
Cooper, Michael "Ibo"
Coore, Stephen "Cat"
Creator, Lord
Culture
Culture, Bobby
DaCosta, Glen
DaCosta, Tony
Daley, Richard
Dallol
Dambala
Davis, Carlene
Deccas
Dekker, Desmond
Delgado, Junior
Dibango, Manu
Different Stylee
Dillinger

Dominoes
Donaldson, Eric
Donovan
Douglas, Cleon
Downie, Tyrone
Dragonaires
Dread, Ranking
Drummond, Don
Drummond, Keith
Dunbar, Sly
Eastwood, Clint
Echo, General
Eek-A-Mouse
Ellis, Alton
Ellis, Bobby
Ellis, Hortense
Ellis, Tomlin
Equals
Ethiopians
Faith, George
Far I, Prince
Fitzroy, Edi
Fly, Lord
Forde, Brinsley
Foundation
Francis, Keith
Frazer, Dean
Gad, Tony
Gaylettes
Gedeon Jerubbaal
George, Sophia
Gerry, Jah
Gifford, Marlene
Gladiators
Grant, Eddy
Grant, Norman
Grey, Owen
Griffiths, Albert
Griffiths, Marcia
Hall, Pam
Hall, Sir Lancelot
Hammond, Beres
Harriot, Derek
Harvey, Bernard "Touter"
Hell & Fire

Heptones
Hibbert, Ossie
Hibberts, Frederick "Toots"
Higgs & Wilson
Higgs, Joe
High Times Players
Hill, Joseph
Hinds, David
Hinds, Justin
Hines, Rupert
Hippy Boys
Holt, Errol "Flabba"
Holt, John
House of Assembly
Hudson, Keith
Hylton, Sheila
I-Roy
I-Threes
Identity
Inner Circle
Ipso Facto
Irie, Tippa
Isaacs, Gregory
Israel Vibration
Itals
Jah Malla
Jarrett, Irvin "Carrot"
Jazzbo, Prince
Jerry, Brigadier
John, Little
Johnson, Linton Kwesi
Johnson, Michael
Johnson, Steely
Johnson, Stille
Jones, Frankie
Jones, Puma
Kamose, Ini
Kelso, Beverly
Kiddus I
Killer Bees
Kino
Kinsey, Donald
Knibbs, Lloyd
Laurel & Hardy
Lee, Byron

Lepke, Louie
Levi, I Jah Man
Light of Love
Light of Saba
Lincoln, Junior
Lindo, Earl
Lindo, Willie
Livingston, Carlton
Livingston, Danny
Llewellyn, Barry
Lloyd, Ervin
Local Hero
Locks, Fred
Lodge, June
Macaw
Machouki, Count
Madden, David
Madden, Philip
Magic Notes
Majestics
Manning, Carlton
Manning, Donald
Manning, Linford
Marley, Bob
Marley, Cedella
Marley, Rita
Marley, Ziggy
Marvin, Junior
Matos, Avi
Maytals
Maytones
McCook, Tommy
McFarlane, Wain
McGregor, Freddie
Melody Makers
Messenjah
Michael, Ras
Michigan & Smiley
Mighty Diamonds
Miller, Jacob
Minott, Echo
Minott, Sugar
Misty In Roots
Mittoo, Jackie
Mohammed, Prince

Morwells
Moses, Pablo
Mowatt, Judy
Mundell, Hugh
Murvin, Junior
Musical Youth
Mutabaruka
Mystic Revelation of Rastafari
Myton, Cedric
Nash, Johnny
Naturalites
Nicodemus
Now Generation
Oban, George
Oneness
Onuora, Oku
Opel, Jackie
Osbourne, Johnny
Ossie, Count
Pablo, Augustus
Palma, Tristan
Palmer, Michael
Paragons
Parkes, Lloyd
Patterson, Alvin "Seeco"
Paul, Frankie
Perry, Lee "Scratch"
Pinchers
Pinkney, Dwight
Pint, Half
Pioneers
Porter, Keith
Priest, Maxi
Professionals
Prophet, Michael
Ranger, Lone
Ranglin, Ernest
Ranglin, Michael
Rankin, Louie
Ras Brass
Red Cloud
Reggae Philharmonic Orchestra
Reggae Team
Revolutionaries
Rhythm Force

Richards, Michael "Boo"
Riley, Jimmy
Riley, Mykaell S.
Rivals
Robinson, Nambo
Robinson, Tony
Rodney, Winston
Rodriquez, Rico
Romeo, Max
Roots Radics
Rose, Michael
Roy, Congo Ashanti
Royal Rasses
Ruina De Moda
Sandii & The Sunsetz
Saw, Tenor
Scorcher
Scully & Bunny
Sensations
Shaka Man
Shakespeare, Robbie
Sheiks
Shelley, Count
Shinehead
Sibbles, Leroy
Simpson, Derek "Duckie"
Sinclair, Charles "Tower"
Ska Kings
Skatalites
Skin, Flesh, & Bone
Sky Juice
Slim & The Uniques
Sly & Robbie
Smart, Ansel
Smart, Leroy
Smith, Earl "Chinna"
Smith, Malachi
Smith, Michael
Smith, Slim
Solar System Band
Sons of Jah
Sons of Negus
Soul Brothers
Soul Mates
Soul Syndicate

Soul Vendors
Soulettes
Spence, Cecil
Sporty, King
Steel Pulse
Stewart, Willie
Sticky & Skully
Stirling, Lester
Stitch, Jah
Stitt, King
Supersonics
Sutherland, Nadine
Sweet, Roslyn
Swelele
Swinging Cats
Tanamo, Lord
Taylor, Tyrone
Taxi, Ranking
Tea, Coco
Techniques
Teenagers
Tesfa, Ras-J
Third World
Thomas, Jah
Thompson, Lincoln
Thompson, Linval
Tiger
Tomlin, Ellis
Tosh, Peter
Tradition
Trinity
Tuff, Tony
Twinkle Brothers
U-Brown
U-Roy
UB40
Uniques
Upsetters
Viceroys
Wailer, Bunny
Wailers
Wailing Rude Boys
Wailing Souls
Wailing Wailers
Wales, Jose

Walker, Albert
Walker, Bagga
Walker, Constantine
Wallace, Mickey
Washington, Delroy
Watson, Winston
We The People
Wilmington, Delroy
Wilson, Delroy
Wilson, Jackie
Wilson, Roy
Word, Sound, & Power
Wright, Winston
Yates, Haile
Yellowman
You, Yabby
Youth, Big
Youth Professionals
Zap Pow
Zephaniah, Benjamin
Zohn, Bob
Zukie, Tapper

**CUTCHIE**

# Index

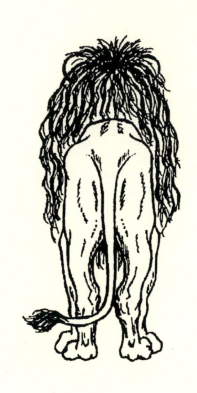

## About the Author

REBEKAH MICHELE MULVANEY is an Assistant Professor in the Department of Communications at Florida Atlantic University. Her article "Popular Art as Rhetorical Artifact: The Case of Reggae Music" appeared in the book *Culture and Communication: Language, Performance, Technology, and Media, Volume IV.*

## About the Bibliographer

CARLOS I.H. NELSON is Associate University Librarian at Florida Atlantic University. A citizen of Jamaica, he has compiled several in-house bibliographies for the Florida Atlantic library and has written articles for *The Hampton University Journal of Ethnic Studies* and the *International Review of History and Political Science.*

ISBN 0-313-26071-0

90000>

EAN

9 780313 260711

HARDCOVER BAR CODE